Parenting apart

Parenting apart

How Separated and Divorced Parents Can Raise Happy and Secure Children

Christina McGhee

LONDON

1 3 5 7 9 10 8 6 4 2

Published in 2011 by Vermilion, an imprint of Ebury Publishing

Ebury Publishing is a Random House Group Company

The Random House Group Limited Reg. No. 954009

Addresses for companies within the Random House Group can be found at
www.randomhouse.co.uk

A CIP catalogue record for this book is available from the British Library

The Random House Group Limited supports The Forest Stewardship
Council (FSC), the leading international forest certification organisation.
All our titles that are printed on Greenpeace-approved-FSC certified paper
carry the FSC logo. Our paper procurement policy can be found at
www.randomhouse.co.uk/environment

Mixed Sources
Product group from well-managed
forests and other controlled sources
www.fsc.org Cert no. TT-COC-2139
© 1996 Forest Stewardship Council

Designed and set by seagulls.net

Printed and bound in Great Britain by Mackays, Chatham, ME5 8TD

ISBN 9780091939830

Copies are available at special rates for bulk orders. Contact the sales
development team on 020 7840 8487 for more information.

To buy books by your favourite authors and register for offers visit
www.randomhouse.co.uk

CONTENTS

WHAT YOU NEED TO KNOW ABOUT THIS BOOK

I won't tell you that it's going to be easy. Divorce is complicated and confusing. Right now there's probably nothing you want more than to help your children through this difficult time. The good news is you don't have to put your crisis on hold while you search for answers. *Parenting Apart* offers parents, like you, quick access to the information you most need at the time when you need it most.

Use this go-to resource in whatever way feels most comfortable. Unlike other books you don't have to read chapters in any specific order. Instead you can pick and choose the sections that address issues you are dealing with right now. Rather than just survive the experience, this book provides you with the tools to stabilise situations, take action and successfully parent your kids through family change, one chapter at a time.

FOREWORD

This book is aimed squarely at parents rather than their lawyers. Its origins are in America and are borne from the enormous experience of Christina McGhee, who has immersed herself in working with mothers and fathers who are coming to terms with discharging their role as parents to their children in the alien landscape that flows from parental separation.

Whilst there is undoubtedly much wisdom, humanity and plain common-sense in these pages, you may wonder why a family judge is taking the unusual step of penning the foreword to such a book. The answer to that question is, to my eyes, very simple. The law courts should be the place of last, rather than first, resort for separating parents. Rearranging family relationships following a split is not a matter of law. The courts will, if they have to, provide a resolution to any stated issue, but the imposition by a judge of a solution against the wishes of one or more of the family members is a very blunt instrument indeed and the very process of achieving a court order is highly likely to inflict further emotional damage on each of the family members involved.

Many, if not all, professionals who encounter separated families now believe in the importance of 'early intervention' to ensure that each parent has a realistic approach to the task of planning for the future arrangements for their child. The recommendations of the recent Family Justice Review in England and Wales aim to enhance the potential for each parent to address the issues, respect the role of the other parent and jointly exercise the parental responsibility that they share for their child in agreeing a 'parenting plan' at an early stage, before matters become unduly embittered and entrenched. The aim of *Parenting Apart* is bang on target in making an easy to read, yet detailed, self-help manual available for parents, who, if they read it and take on board its guidance, will be empowered with insight into the situation that now faces them and the means that may be available to resolve disagreements at an early opportunity and without going to court.

This longer work builds on the success of the Parenting After Parting programme, an initiative that is promoted by the family law organisation, Resolution. Provision of the Parenting After Parting message is already a commonplace in many solicitors' firms and is on the way to becoming a natural component within the separation process. The timely publication of this much fuller manual is therefore most welcome.

It is my earnest hope that separating parents will appreciate the true value of this book and use it, and any other early intervention that is available to them, as a guide and support when exercising their joint responsibility to plan for their child's future care.

Andrew McFarlane
The Hon. Mr Justice McFarlane
High Court, Family Division

INTRODUCTION

Sarah, who had been separated for several months, was the mum to two young boys, Dillon and Thomas. Although she thought of herself as a good parent and an educated person, there were so many things she didn't feel prepared to deal with. She regularly struggled with a mixture of guilt and self-doubt, especially where her kids were concerned. The boys were having such a hard time, and when their dad didn't show up for his scheduled time with them the children were absolutely devastated. Talking to her ex about the situation didn't do any good. They usually just ended up getting into another fight. More than anything, Sarah wanted to know if she was making the right choices for her boys, and if she wasn't, she wanted to know what she should be doing differently. She simply didn't know where to turn.

The information she had been able to find surfing the net was somewhat helpful but most of it ended up being too vague. The bookstore had a few resources; however, finding the time to read a book cover to cover seemed virtually impossible. Thank goodness Sarah was fortunate enough to have the support of her family and a few good friends. However, they weren't much help when it came to figuring things out for her children. While well intentioned, everyone seemed to have his or her own opinion, and usually the advice wasn't what she needed. She considered going to therapy, but waiting for an appointment and then taking time off from work when finances were tight didn't seem realistic. And even if she did see a counsellor, would a professional really be able to help?

Toby felt shattered on every level. His battle with his children's mother over support and custody had financially devastated him. While he felt very bitter towards his ex-partner, Toby remained determined to be actively involved in Emily's and Luke's lives in a positive way. He knew he needed to keep the children out of the middle, but sometimes it was *so hard. Shouldn't the children know the truth, or at least hear his side of the story? What should he say when his children talked about their mum's new boyfriend, Greg? He especially had a difficult time listening to the kids talk about all the things they got to do with their mum and Greg – how Greg would take them to fun places, and out to eat, and buy them expensive toys, all things Toby couldn't afford to do.*

Although it was tough, Toby was really concerned about not making it any harder for Emily and Luke. Last night Emily wanted to know why her parents had never married. She was worried that if her mum ended up marrying Greg Toby wouldn't be her real father any more. Luke had stopped talking altogether. Toby didn't know if it was because he had been told not to say anything or if Luke was worried about making him angry. Toby knew he needed help, but he just didn't know what to do.

If you are reading this book it's probably because, like Sarah and Toby, one of your biggest concerns right now is, 'How do I help my children get through this?' Like Sarah and Toby, you probably have lots of questions weighing heavily on your mind and worries about how this change will affect your children. Maybe you're wondering if your divorce is the reason two-year-old Zack cries uncontrollably when you take him to nursery. Perhaps you're agonising over whether you should force your 12-year-old daughter to go to her mum's house for the weekend, even though she is insisting she doesn't want to go. Is it OK to introduce the kids to your new partner, or is it too soon? Maybe you haven't even told your children about your decision to separate, and you are concerned with what to say. Like many parents, you may not know where to turn for help or how to get your questions answered. Finding what you need when you need it isn't easy, especially when your life is changing in almost every conceivable way. And that's exactly why I wrote this book.

As a divorce coach and parent educator, I have been working with parents, children and families for well over a decade. Throughout my career I have had the benefit of not only teaching parents but also learning from them. Whether a parent has been a coaching client or a participant in one of my seminars, whether they worked with me individually or chose to work jointly with an ex-partner, and whether they have been dealing with a high- or low-conflict situation, each one has taught me something about how children and families are affected by separation and divorce. The most important lesson I have learned is that the defining difference in how a family copes with separation and divorce is actually quite simple: **Parents who are able to get support and information sooner rather than later have a distinct advantage**. Mums and dads who seek guidance and education about the separation process early on are more likely to:

- Place their children at the centre of their parenting decisions
- Be more successful at managing the separation process
- Continue parenting their children effectively
- Experience less transitional stress
- Balance their personal needs with the needs of their children
- Help their children gain important life skills amid family change
- Have an increased level of awareness and insight
- Be solution-focused rather than overwhelmed by challenges

Overall, these parents experience better outcomes more quickly. It's just that simple.

You probably have a very specific reason for picking up this book. Maybe you are struggling with an issue, worried about how to handle a situation with your children, and you are seeking answers. Should you and your soon-to-be ex tell your children about your decision to separate as a team or individually? What should you do if your child won't talk about it? When your 16-year-old doesn't want to spend the weekend with you, should you make him? What if your ex is telling the children terrible things about you? How do you handle it?

While you probably have good instincts when it comes to your children, it's normal to doubt those instincts as you navigate through this process. How many times have you found yourself wondering if you were making the right choice or doubting how you handled a situation? Ever wished you had someone who could answer your questions, find some way to get sound advice, or at least discover an idea of what you can do? If you have, you're not alone. Regrettably, one comment I have consistently heard from parents over the years is, 'I wish I had known this sooner.' Your life is happening now, and putting your crisis on hold while you search for answers is probably the last thing you want to do. Having access to good information is important; having access to good information when you are in the middle of dealing with a massive number of changes in your life is even more important.

> **Parenting through divorce is a lot like playing poker. Being a good poker player isn't about being dealt a good hand; it's about playing your best with the cards you've been dealt.**

Four key components of helping your children successfully deal with family change involve:

1. **Knowledge:** Getting the information you need when you need it
2. **Planning:** Taking the initiative to deal with issues before they become critical
3. **Preparation:** Knowing what to expect.
4. **Action:** Putting supports into place that improve the quality of life for you and your children

The goal of this book is to address all four of these components.

WHAT YOU WILL GET FROM THIS BOOK

As a parent, you are one of the most important and valuable resources your children have right now. You know your children better than anyone else. Without a doubt, you have the ability to make some incredibly meaningful changes for your children during this time. However, even the most loving mum or dad can feel unprepared for the task of parenting children while ending a relationship.

In my coaching practice I work with parents to identify obstacles and create solutions. A significant part of that work involves helping my clients:

- Get the information and support they need
- Learn how to use their strengths and create solutions
- Find ways to take positive steps forward

While numerous how-to books have been written about the topics of separation, divorce and parenting, few actually provide practical, straightforward, easy-to-read information focused on the needs of children when parents live apart. It's been said, 'When all you have is a hammer, every problem begins to look like a nail.' I would also argue, 'When all you have is a hammer, *every problem gets treated like a nail.*'

Consider this book an additional tool, a comprehensive guide designed to address your most basic and fundamental questions about post-separation parenting. While it may not address every issue, it will offer you new ideas and strategies regarding some of the most common issues that arise when parents live in different homes. It will also give you insight regarding how to make life better for your kids.

From years of teaching I have learnt it's not just what you say that matters, it's also how you say it. Therefore I wrote *Parenting Apart* in a conversational tone and used simple, everyday language. It is a book for parents, not professionals. You won't find lots of overly complicated psychological theories or professional jargon. Instead, I provide simple, direct and easily digestible bits of information. Each chapter is intended to be short and concise, yet thorough. Most chapters can be read in 10 to 15 minutes.

Parenting Apart will:
- Teach you how to manage your reaction to separation and divorce while supporting your children's feelings about divorce
- Assist you in maintaining a healthy, supportive relationship with your children
- Enhance your understanding of your children's needs and help you guide them toward a positive, healthy adjustment
- Help you focus on how to make a positive difference in your children's lives, even in less-than-ideal situations
- Provide you with information on restructuring life for yourself and your children
- Offer you tools to minimise conflict between the two households
- Offer practical help for dealing with the challenges of parenting from two separate homes

HOW TO USE THIS BOOK

While there are common and expected stages most families go through, how each family, parent and child experiences separation is uniquely different. There is no one-size-fits-all. I realise everything offered in this book may not necessarily apply to your situation right now. For this reason, the material offered has been structured so that you can pick and choose various topics that apply to your individual situation. Certainly reading the book cover to cover can be really helpful, especially when you are starting the process. However, when you are in a crisis, finding the focus or time to read an entire book, no matter how well intentioned you might be, is tough.

When appropriate, feel free to pick sections that have the most meaning or relevance to you right now. If you have a child who is misbehaving or upset, then it would probably help to start with Chapter 25: 'How to handle things when your child is angry'. If you are agonising over how to break the news that you're separating, Chapter 14: 'How to tell your children you are getting a divorce', offers tips regarding what to say and when. On the other hand, if you're feeling unsure about how to manage your own feelings, you may choose to start with Chapter 3: 'Understanding the emotional divorce'. Again, this information has been put together for you to use in whatever way feels most helpful. It's okay to skip around and read the chapters that seem most relevant to you.

Given the number of changes you may be dealing with at one time, bear in mind there may be sections you are not ready to read yet. There's an old saying that asks, 'What's the best way to eat an elephant?' The answer? 'One bite at a time.' Taking on a major life transition such as restructuring a family warrants the same response. Looking at the whole picture all at once can be incredibly overwhelming. When you are in the middle of a crisis like divorce, the idea of taking in lots of information can be just as intimidating as the event itself. However, breaking life into smaller parts and getting through it bit by bit, step by step, allows you to move forward at your own pace.

Since divorce is a lifelong process, you will probably find, as your children grow and situations change, that new issues will surface. At times it may be helpful to revisit certain sections of this book for additional information. It's possible that issues that weren't relevant six months ago now are. Much like a guidebook, you can repeatedly return to various chapters as and when particular concerns arise for you or your children.

I also understand there are certain situations in which some of what is offered may not apply. Circumstances involving alcoholism, drug abuse, incarceration, alienation, domestic violence or the abuse of a child – physical or sexual – are specialised issues. Those situations often require a more direct or specialised response, and how you interact with the other parent will need to be adjusted. While these issues are not the focus of this book, they are nevertheless extremely important. For that reason I have included a chapter that provides a brief overview explaining how to manage such issues. You will also find a resource section at the back of the book.

Keep in mind that *Parenting Apart* is also not a cure-all. It is definitely not a replacement or substitute for therapy, counselling or coaching. However, it is meant to be a guide and a resource to help you take positive steps towards helping your children.

WHO IS THIS BOOK FOR?

The goal of this book is to offer guidance to parents who have made the choice to part and raise their children in two separate homes. I realise that not all relationships involve the institution of marriage. Clearly the number of parents who have chosen to live together as a family rather than marry has grown substantially. When a partnership breaks down, parents who have lived together usually don't consider themselves divorced. Whether you were legally married or not, the process of loss is the same for your children. It has also been my experience that, regardless of marital status, parents deal with similar issues. To avoid redundancy and to keep ideas from becoming unclear, I have used the words *separation* and *divorce* interchangeably in many ways.

LANGUAGE USED AND EXAMPLES

I believe words tremendously shape perceptions and beliefs. This could not be more true when it comes to separation and divorce. The way you speak to your children about how family life is changing will affect how they view it. For that reason I do not support, and I work very hard not to use, terms that minimise the importance of the parent–child relationship. Examples of words that diminish the value of family relationships are: *parent with care, custody, contact, residence, parental responsibility, custodial parent, non-custodial parent, access, former matrimonial home* and *non-resident parent*. Throughout this book you will notice that I use different terms. My words encourage and support parents who are striving for an active, healthy relationship with children regardless of how time is spent between households.

Some of these terms are:

- Two-home concept
- Parenting time
- Parenting schedule
- On-duty parent (the parent who is with the child)
- Off-duty parent (the parent who is not physically with the child)
- Time with a parent
- Mum's house
- Dad's house
- Time with Mum
- Time with Dad
- Bonus parent (instead of step-parent)
- Bonus children (instead of step-children)

While there have been some changes regarding post-separation parenting, in reality many children of divorce grow up spending more time with mothers than with fathers. Although there are many fathers who fill the role of primary parent for children, today the family courts still tend to view mothers as the primary parent responsible for the daily care of children. Fortunately there are a growing number of parenting situations in which that primary care-taking role is shared in a more equal way between parents. Throughout the book you will find that I have used numerous examples to help illustrate concepts and ideas. From my perspective, any of the scenarios or examples given could apply to either mothers or fathers and parenting roles can be interchangeable. These illustrations were not designed to make gender-specific assumptions. Many of the examples were randomly assigned or based on past work with clients.

ULTIMATE GOAL

You may feel that many of the suggestions in this book are easier said than done. I understand staying committed requires a great deal of patience, persistence and dedication. Some days will be much harder than others. Plan on making mistakes – lots of them. Being a good parent isn't about always doing everything right. It's about recognising your mistakes and learning from them. When it comes right down to it, the bottom line for any of us is making sure the love we have for our children always outweighs the feelings we may have about the situation we are in.

More than anything, my goal is to offer you a sense of hope and validation. As a parent and a professional, I believe children are resilient. Family separation does not doom children to negative outcomes, poor self-esteem, academic failure or a lifetime of dysfunction. However, ongoing exposure to fighting between Mum and Dad, a lack of structure and inconsistent parenting can put your children at a significant disadvantage. The choices you are making right now matter.

Children deserve nothing less than the very best we have to offer. I encourage you to strive for more than merely helping your children survive this experience. Michelangelo once said, 'The greater danger for most of us lies not in setting our aim too high and falling short, but in setting our aim too low, and achieving our mark.' Set your sights high; you can aspire for more. Even though you no longer live under one roof, you can still create opportunities for your children to thrive. I personally believe families can redefine themselves in meaningful ways when parents part. It's not just a philosophy that I teach; it is one I live by daily as a child from a divorced family and as a bonus parent. I hope this book will provide you the support you need to make that difference in your children's lives.

Best wishes to you and your children,

Christina

PART ONE

How Am I Going to Get Through This?

Dealing with Separation from a Parent's Perspective

1.
THE DEFINING DIFFERENCE

Be faithful in small things because it is in them that your strength lies. – Mother Teresa

Parenting children takes an enormous amount of energy and patience under the best of circumstances. When your life has been turned upside down by divorce, clearly you are not dealing with the best of circumstances. Right now you and your children are going through lots of changes on many different levels. Some of those changes you may be prepared for, while there will be others you hadn't planned on. Some changes you may be looking forward to and others you may dread. Regardless of the circumstances, with change – any kind of change – comes stress. Stress is a normal part of life and it's an issue every parent, married or unmarried, on the face of the planet deals with daily. As you begin this transition you may find the intensity of those everyday stress factors has increased considerably. And like lots of other separated parents, you've probably gained some new sources of stress too. When your plate feels more than full, how you cope with everyday stress may also change.

While you are dealing with life on a day-to-day basis it's not always easy to see the connection between how you are managing life and how your children are functioning. Remember the saying, 'Children do as you do'? Children are like mirrors. They will reflect what they see in you. If you are overwhelmed, children may respond by becoming overly anxious themselves. When you are feeling negative or depressed, your children will soak it up like a sponge. You may find your children pick more fights with each other, become more challenging to discipline or may just be generally agitated. In short, expect that when you're not coping well, your children will show it.

THE RELATIONSHIP BETWEEN STRESS AND PARENTING

Over the years I have worked with literally thousands of separating and divorcing parents. What I have learnt is that most parents are doing the very best that they can for their children. In fact, my guess is you are probably doing a lot of things right when it comes to supporting your children.

> When it comes to divorce, there's good news and bad news. The bad news is things are going to change. The good news is things are going to change.
> – Anonymous

As a coach, I also know that most parents are often unaware of the direct impact stress has on their ability to parent effectively. When issues come up involving children's adjustment to divorce, parents tend to put a lot of energy into examining external factors. Think about it. When your kids are fussy, throwing a fit, not getting ready for school, having daily emotional meltdowns or just generally not coping well, what's the first thing you do? If you are like most parents you deal with what's in front of you and save mulling over the reasons why for later. If you do reflect on why, your first thought might be it's your ex's fault for making things so difficult. Or perhaps it's because your children aren't spending enough time in your home. Maybe the going back and forth is too much for them, or possibly there's a problem at school.

Don't get me wrong – children will have reactions to how life changes. When parents separate, there are lots of different factors that affect how children deal with the transition. Yet one of the most significant factors in how well children adjust to divorce relates directly to how *you* are adjusting to divorce. In turn, your ability to manage life is greatly affected by how well you are able to balance your stress level. **Rarely do parents consider their own reactions or feelings as a factor in how their children are coping.**

Imagine you had a day that went something like this: You got up late and were extra tired. All week you haven't been able to sleep at night because you have been worried about your upcoming court date. As a result of getting up late, you skip taking a shower and begin rushing around the house to get yourself and the kids ready. Freddie couldn't find his homework again and Zara didn't want to get up. Both of them seem grumpy because they went to bed late too. After an hour of listening to complaining and arguing, you finally get the kids to school. On the way to work you spill coffee on your lap, get caught in traffic and arrive at work late – again. To make up for lost time, you decide to skip lunch and eat something out of the vending machine. While at work your ex calls to ask about trading weekends, which immediately leads to another argument, and you spend the next hour replaying the conversation in your head. When you get home you realise you're starving, only to discover there's nothing for supper because you haven't had time to go to the shops. Freddie and Zara are back to fighting; neither one seems to be listening, so you send them both to their rooms. As you stand in the kitchen you curse your ex under your breath and wonder if life will ever feel normal again.

Now imagine things happened differently

Freddie and Zara seem to be having a difficult time getting ready in the morning, so you decide to set your alarm and get up 15 minutes earlier than normal. Since you've not been sleeping well, you choose to take a hot shower and read a good book to take your mind off the upcoming court hearing. While you still feel a little tired, you wake up on time and get the children started on their morning routine. Because you have been consistent with their schedule, Freddie and Zara know what's expected of them and get ready fairly easily. Getting up a little earlier also proves to be a good choice, as it gives you extra time to focus on them. Knowing that you have extra work to catch up on, you decide to pack yourself lunch and steer clear of the vending machine. On the way to school you remind the kids that they will be staying at the neighbour's for a couple of hours so you can do the shopping after work. While driving to work you listen to your favourite CD. Although you still have to deal with traffic, you manage to stay in a good mood and arrive at work on time. That afternoon your ex calls to talk about changing the weekend schedule. Instead of launching into an argument, you take a deep breath and ask to call them back later. After work you swing by the shops and pick up something quick for supper. Over dinner you talk to Freddie and Zara about their day and remind them of what they need to do that evening. You help them stay focused on the evening routine and find you even have enough time before bed to read them a story.

What's different about these two scenarios? Did you notice that the same stress factors were present in both examples? The kids had to go to school, you had to go to work, the ex still called and asked about the schedule, food had to be bought, and you still had to be a parent. The second scenario, however, illustrated a different response to those stress factors. Now let me be clear: I am not saying if you listen to your favourite CD on the way to work and read a book every night you and your children will sail through this experience with flying colours. Divorce is hard, and at times it will be very stressful. No matter how skilled you are as a parent, everyone has good and bad days. The point I am making is this: when you are experiencing high levels of stress, it is imperative that you find some way to balance that stress. When you don't make appropriate adjustments to counterbalance your stress, your ability to be available to your children on any level becomes diminished. **As stress levels increase, your ability to parent your children effectively decreases.**

HOW YOUR STRESS AFFECTS YOUR CHILDREN

In Texas they have an old saying that goes, 'If Mama ain't happy, ain't nobody happy.' When it comes to children coping with divorce I would say, 'If Mama and Papa ain't making it, ain't nobody gonna make it.' Your children will naturally react to your stress. When their stress levels are high, you will see your children's behaviour and functioning begin to falter. This is when you will find yourself dealing with more fighting, playing up, temper tantrums and strong emotional reactions. They simply won't be able to cope. While it is impossible for you to completely remove stress from your children's lives, it is possible for you to keep it in check. As you balance your own stress level, you will be better equipped to provide the structure your children need to function. As a result, when your children see you handling life in a balanced way they will feel more secure and less anxious. Although keeping your stress under control won't guarantee you will never have to deal with another tantrum or emotional meltdown, in the long run it's much more likely you will have healthy, well-adjusted children.

What can you do?
Over the past decade the idea of taking good care of yourself has become a lucrative industry. We're bombarded daily by marketing promising we can look better, feel better and become instantly wealthy beyond our wildest dreams if only we learn the secret to focusing on our needs and desires. But all this marketing often has the opposite effect: instead of helping us to feel inspired to lead a balanced life, we've become more apt to tune out the hype.

For some parents, the idea of taking good care of themselves seems impractical or something they don't have time for, especially now. They envisage 'taking care' would involve chucking the kids with a baby-sitter for an afternoon to engage in a power yoga class, followed by a massage and a Starbucks latte. While any or all of this might sound enticing, it's probably not where you're at right now. It's possible that making time to think about your needs may be the last thing on your mind at the moment.

When I talk about taking care of yourself, essentially I am suggesting that you find some way to balance your life. Just as you can only go so far on a tank of petrol before you need to fill up your car again, as a parent you can only go so far before you hit empty. If you don't find some way to refuel, you are no good to your children. The goal of balancing your life and your level of stress has to do with finding ways to put energy back into you. It could be as simple as taking time to go to the cinema with friends, having an hour to yourself one evening a week or taking 20 minutes a day to do something just for you.

In Chapter 2 I talk about the importance of prioritising your needs. If the idea of putting energy into yourself seems over-whelming, take the time to read through the next chapter. It offers suggestions regarding simple ways you can refuel and counterbalance the stress in your life. You will also find a 'Taking Care of You' inventory to help you assess the various areas of your life that might need attention. I realise making time for yourself may feel completely impossible or unrealistic at the moment. Do your best to keep an open mind.

SOMETHING TO THINK ABOUT

How well are you balancing your life right now?

- What's the last film you saw that you wanted to see? If it's been more than six months, what would it take to see a film you wanted to see in the next month?
- When's the last time you went out with friends? If you were to plan time with friends, what would that look like and how can you make it happen?
- What hobby or activity do you enjoy doing (for example gardening, reading, dancing, fantasy football, painting or camping)? Is this activity a regular part of your life? If not, how can you fit it in? Is this hobby or activity something you can share with your children?

2.
BALANCING YOUR LIFE

*It's not only children who grow. Parents do too.
As much as we watch to see what our children do
with their lives, they are watching us to see what
we do with ours. I can't tell my children to reach
for the sun. All I can do is reach for it myself.*
– Joyce Maynard

Suppose I asked you, 'What's the single most important thing you can do for your children right now?' What would be your first thoughts? If you are like most parents, you might be thinking:

- Not arguing with the other parent in front of the children
- Letting your children know you still love them
- Telling your children it's not their fault
- Not exposing children to the adult details of divorce
- Making sure children know it is okay to talk about their feelings
- Not saying bad things about the other parent

You may be surprised to learn that one of the best ways you can help your children is to take care of yourself.

Taking good care of yourself is a difficult concept for most parents, and we almost always underestimate the importance of it, especially when we are in crisis. From the time our children are born, our natural tendency is to place our children's needs above and before our own. This is particularly true when separation or divorce happens in a family.

Divorce is a crisis in the life of a family. When you are in crisis it is normal to react by throwing yourself into survival mode. For most, this means taking life day by day or sometimes even moment by moment, doing whatever you can to make sure you and your children survive the experience. When this happens, your own personal needs often take a back seat to a laundry list of responsibilities and issues, such as:

- Managing day-to-day life for your children
- Dealing with changing schedules and two different households
- Trying to balance the needs of work and family
- Navigating the legal divorce process and the stress of litigation
- Dealing with significant financial changes
- Parenting on your own
- Dealing with children's reactions and feelings
- Parenting with your ex-spouse or soon-to-be ex-spouse

While managing life is important, when you place your needs last you ultimately end up compromising your ability to care for your children. Think of it this way: Ever notice when you are on a plane, the flight attendant always says: 'In the event of an emergency, an oxygen mask will drop down in front of you. If you are travelling with children, place the oxygen mask on yourself first before offering assistance to your child.'

Clearly if you, as a parent, pass out from a lack of oxygen your children will have little hope of surviving a crisis. The same is true when it comes to divorce. If you pass out emotionally, physically, mentally and spiritually, how will you take care of your children?

The simple truth is you cannot give your children what you don't have. I know that as a parent when I am worn out, tired, emotionally overwhelmed or stressed I behave differently with my children than when I have had a good night's sleep, am taking care of my needs and am feeling balanced. My guess is you do too.

Divorce is a time when children will naturally feel uncertain, anxious and worried about how life is changing. During this time children look to their parents for cues about how to handle this life-changing transition. How can they feel confident about their future if you are falling apart? While healing will take time, children need you to reassure them that life is going to be okay and that they can and will make it through this experience.

> How you manage life from this point forward will be the lens through which your children view and experience divorce.

Taking good care of yourself is also extremely important when you consider the emotional dynamics of separation. Because separation and divorce stir up so many strong emotions for both parents and children, it is essential that you have emotional clarity. This means that you, as a parent, are able to separate your feelings about divorce from the feelings your children have about divorce.

While parents and children will experience similar stages during the transition, each group has very different feelings and perspectives about the separation. When parents are not dealing with their feelings, the emotional boundaries between parents and children often become blurred. Children are then put in the adult role of caring for their parents and can easily fall into the trap of feeling emotionally responsible for their mum or dad.

Allow children to be children by taking responsibility for your own feelings and perspectives.

One of the key factors in successfully managing divorce is self-awareness. This means that you are paying attention to your own feelings, thoughts and reactions about divorce. Make time to identify what is working for you and what is not.

- What about day-to-day life is most challenging?
- What would help you manage those challenges in a more constructive way?

- Where in your life do you need support? Who could help provide that for you (for example, baby-sitting or childcare, somebody to talk to, a friend to do things with or help with household chores and managing finances)?

WHAT DO YOU WANT FOR YOUR CHILDREN?

WHEN YOU TAKE GOOD CARE OF YOURSELF, YOU ARE ABLE TO	WHEN YOU IGNORE YOUR NEEDS YOU MAY
Be available for your children physically and emotionally	Feel overwhelmed, frustrated and stressed, leaving you less available for your children
React to situations in a more constructive way	Let decision making be influenced by strong emotions
Manage conflict between households	Expose your children to conflict (often unintentionally)
Deal with strong emotions and keep your feelings about divorce separate from your children's feelings	Struggle with separating your feelings from your children's feelings
Provide your children with a relatively stable, consistent environment	Have difficulty providing children with consistency and stability (for example, living from moment to moment
Help yourself and your children make a successful adjustment after the divorce	Experience negative adjustment issues for yourself and your children
Focus energy on creating solutions	Spend your energy focusing on problems

HOW TO SUPPORT YOURSELF THROUGH THE EARLY STAGES OF SEPARATION AND DIVORCE

In the very early stages of separation, implementing basic strategies for taking care of yourself can feel incredibly overwhelming if not damn near impossible. I have yet to meet a parent – divorced, separated or married – who does not find leading a balanced life daunting at one time or another. Like many things in life, taking good care of yourself is a process that ebbs and flows. The following guide will help you take steps towards acknowledging and prioritising your needs in a positive and healthy way.

▶ Change the way you think about divorce

Given the nature of divorce, it is understandable why you might have a less than optimistic outlook. Almost all of us struggle with negative thoughts or carry around a critic inside our heads who tells us how and what we are doing wrong. Negative thoughts block your ability to take in information and be creative and can reduce your energy levels; they also affect your mental and physical health. Quite simply, how you think shapes how you feel, which guides how you respond to situations in life.

Understand there is a difference between responding and reacting. *Responding* means giving a situation or issue thought before taking action. *Reacting,* however, involves taking action based on impulse and emotion.

When faced with a challenge or problem, pay attention to your first thoughts. For example, when you see your ex's phone number on your caller ID, do you think 'Now what?' and prepare yourself for a fight? Are you spending your days beating yourself up about how the divorce is hurting the children? Or feeling guilty for the pain it has caused them?

When you catch yourself slipping into a negative mode of thinking, avoid acting on your first thought or reaction. Reshape how you think. For example, when your ex calls, instead of mentally preparing yourself for a row, consider reminding yourself that while you cannot control what happens, you can focus your effort on a positive outcome for your children.

One of the first things I do in my work with parents is help them identify their strengths and focus on what it is they are doing well and how they can do more of it. Write down your top five strengths. If you are having trouble identifying what you do well, ask a friend for help. Post your strengths somewhere you will see them daily. When a challenge comes up, think about how you can use your strengths to help you deal with the situation.

▶ Pay attention to your needs

One of the key factors in successfully managing divorce is self-awareness. This means that you are paying attention to your own feelings, thoughts, reactions/responses and needs. When you are able to recognise how you are managing things, it puts you in a better position to recognise and respond to your children's needs.

Take time to identify what is working for you and what is not. What about day-to-day life is most challenging? What would help you manage those challenges in a more constructive way?

▶ Give yourself permission to feel your feelings in a healthy way

You have every right to feel the way you do about what is happening in your life. However, what you do with those feelings can make a world of difference to you and your children. Avoid expressing you feelings in a destructive manner, such as drinking alcohol to excess, rebounding into a new relationship, playing mind games, overworking yourself, seeking revenge or trying to control your ex-spouse. Instead, generate ideas about healthy, appropriate ways to manage your feelings, such as

- Making time to write down why you feel angry or upset
- Giving yourself time to grieve and acknowledge your loss

- Talking with family and friends who can support your feelings
- Using exercise as a way to manage stress
- Walking away from an argument with your ex-spouse

▶ Be gentle with yourself

Bear in mind some days will be harder than others. It is very normal in the early stages to experience a wide range of emotions that fluctuate from one extreme to the other. For example, one day you may feel very confident and prepared to handle anything that comes your way but the next you may feel overwhelmed, out of control or hopeless. When you are having a tough day, give yourself a break. Take things slow, use your supports and remind yourself tomorrow is another day.

▶ Find support

Consider making a list of your top five stress factors. Spend some time brainstorming what you can do to help yourself deal with these issues constructively. Don't make the mistake of thinking you need to handle them all on your own. Ask for help when you need it. Help can come in many different forms, from seeing a professional counsellor or life coach to talking with a trusted friend, joining a community group or perhaps having a reliable baby-sitter who can pitch in when you are short-handed. Most important: make sure you have people or activities outside of yourself and your children for support.

▶ Find ways to validate yourself daily

Be sure to monitor your level of stress and strive to maintain balance. Although it may be difficult at times, do something every day that contributes to the quality of your life or helps you move forward in this process. Make time to do something you enjoy. Take a long soak in a hot bath, read a good book, have a cup of tea or dinner with a friend, walk in the park or develop a new hobby. Put energy into activities that promote your confidence and self-worth, even if it's only for 20 minutes a day.

▶ Take small bites (remember the elephant)

Divorce changes your life on almost every level. During this time dealing with the loss and multiple changes can be overwhelming. Just like the analogy of eating the elephant, when you're facing a problem or issue break it down into small, manageable steps. Focus on your most immediate needs first. Instead of worrying about how you will get through the year, think about what you need to get through the next week or day. Remember: every journey begins with a single step.

> Studies indicate that when you are focused on the positive parts of your life, your happiness and general outlook on life improve. To avoid being overwhelmed by what's not working, consider keeping a daily gratitude diary. Pick a specific time each day when you can spend 15 minutes writing down three or four things you are thankful for that day. Items can be as simple as hearing your children laugh, recognising that it's a beautiful day or getting a good night's sleep.

TAKING CARE OF YOU

The purpose of the following inventory is not to identify all the things you should or shouldn't be doing. Rather it is a tool to inspire you to think about how you are currently caring for yourself. It may also help you generate new ideas.

Review the questions under each of the four areas listed. Using the rating scale provided, indicate how often you do the following activities. Circle the score (in columns A–C) that best describes your answer. Place a tick in column D for items you would like to consider incorporating into your life.

PHYSICAL FACTORS

How often do you?	Often	Sometimes	Seldom	Willing to try
	(A)	(B)	(C)	(D)
Eat breakfast, lunch and dinner regularly	5	3	1	
Enjoy meals and eat foods that are good for you	5	3	1	
Exercise at least twice a week	5	3	1	
Get at least 7 hours of sleep a night	5	3	1	
Give yourself a break when you feel tired or overwhelmed	5	3	1	
Leave your desk for lunch	5	3	1	
Follow up with routine medical care (e.g. annual dentist and doctor appointments)	5	3	1	
Plan physical activities you enjoy (e.g. riding a bike, hiking, working outdoors, fishing)	5	3	1	
Turn off your mobile phone or ignore calls when you're relaxing	5	3	1	
Take a day off from work when feeling ill	5	3	1	
Make time to care for your body (e.g. get a massage, schedule a haircut, work out at the gym)	5	3	1	
Buy clothes that you like and feel comfortable in	5	3	1	
Go on day trips or vacations	5	3	1	
Schedule fun activities for yourself when children are with the other parent	5	3	1	
Give yourself enough time to complete tasks or arrive for scheduled events on time	5	3	1	
Total score for each column	☐	☐	☐	☐
Add scores for each column:				
A+B+C = Total Score for Physical Factors	☐			

EMOTIONAL FACTORS

How often do you?	Often (A)	Sometimes (B)	Seldom (C)	Willing to try (D)
Allow yourself to talk with a trusted friend	5	3	1	
Let yourself cry	5	3	1	
Give yourself the space you need to feel angry or sad and vent in a healthy way	5	3	1	
Feel proud of yourself	5	3	1	
Celebrate an accomplishment and feel good about what you have achieved	5	3	1	
Seek out support instead of going it alone	5	3	1	
Spend time with friends or family members you enjoy	5	3	1	
Take time to think about situations in your life and how you feel about them	5	3	1	
Give yourself time to grieve losses or disappointments	5	3	1	
Accept help from others without feeling guilty	5	3	1	
Say no to things you don't want to do without worrying about what others think	5	3	1	
Graciously accept compliments without dismissing them	5	3	1	
Pay attention to your own needs and make them a priority	5	3	1	
Take a break when you are feeling overwhelmed versus pushing through	5	3	1	
Set boundaries with others that support your needs even when family and friends disagree	5	3	1	
Total score for each column	☐	☐	☐	☐
Add scores for each column:				
A+B+C = Total Score for Emotional Factors ☐				

INTELLECTUAL FACTORS

How often do you?	Often	Sometimes	Seldom	Willing to try
	(A)	(B)	(C)	(D)
Take time to read books/magazines you enjoy	5	3	1	
Engage in activities that stimulate your mind	5	3	1	
Make time to explore ways to balance and enrich your life	5	3	1	
Take steps to reduce your day-to-day level of stress	5	3	1	
Seek out projects either in the community or at work that are challenging and rewarding	5	3	1	
Make time to learn new things or enjoy a hobby	5	3	1	
Think about your goals for the future	5	3	1	
Seek out support to help you deal with your separation or divorce	5	3	1	
Feel focused and undistracted	5	3	1	
Regularly remember things you need to do or simple everyday tasks	5	3	1	
Mentally 'let go' of situations that upset versus mulling them over	5	3	1	
Feel organised and prepared for the day	5	3	1	
Get up from work and take a break	5	3	1	
Seek out new experiences	5	3	1	
Have meaningful conversations with others about issues that are important or engaging to you	5	3	1	
Total score for each column	☐	☐	☐	☐

Add scores for each column:

A+B+C = Total Score for Intellectual Factors ☐

SPIRITUAL FACTORS

How often do you?

	Often (A)	Sometimes (B)	Seldom (C)	Willing to try (D)
Journal or take time to reflect on your life	5	3	1	
Make time to acknowledge what you are grateful for	5	3	1	
Give time to a cause or organisation that you care about	5	3	1	
Spend time in prayer or meditation	5	3	1	
Listen to music that is meaningful to you	5	3	1	
Play with your children	5	3	1	
Get so engaged in an activity that you lose track of time	5	3	1	
Feel connected to something greater than yourself	5	3	1	
Say thank you to people who make a difference in your life	5	3	1	
Participate in activities that nourish your soul or help you feel connected to others	5	3	1	
Surrender control of a problem or situation	5	3	1	
Read books or literature that inspires you	5	3	1	
Feel fulfilled and connected to others	5	3	1	
Enjoy time outside or in nature	5	3	1	
Embrace challenge as an opportunity for growth	5	3	1	
Total score for each column	☐	☐	☐	☐

Add scores for each column:

A+B+C = Total Score for Spiritual Factors ☐

Scoring instructions

Compare your individual scores for each of the four sections (Physical, Emotional, Intellectual and Spiritual) to the scoring chart below to evaluate how well you are looking after your needs in each of the listed areas.

Overall Score
75–60 = Great Job
59–45 = Good
44–30 = Fair
29–15 = Poor

After reviewing your scores for each of the four areas, consider the following:

- In which areas are you doing well?
- In which areas could you do a better job?

Now take a look at the items you ticked in column D for each group of factors, and ask yourself:

- Are there any strategies for managing or reducing stress that I have forgotten and would like to reintroduce to my life?
- Are there new strategies for balancing my life that I am willing to try?
- How would I do that?

Keep in mind the goal is not to beat yourself up about what you aren't doing. Instead use this inventory as a tool for recognising small ways you can improve how you take good care of yourself. When incorporating a new strategy, remember change takes time. Start with small steps such as doing one thing different each week. Consider using the action steps on the following pages to help you get started.

TAKE ACTION: MAKE TAKING CARE OF YOURSELF A PRIORITY

▶ Make a date with yourself

Over the next week mark a date in your diary and schedule at least 30 minutes to think about how you are currently taking care of yourself. Choose a time when you can be alone and minimise distractions (for example, turn off your mobile phone, step away from your computer and avoid background noises like TV or radio).

▶ Evaluate your needs

Look over your answers from the 'Taking Care of You' inventory. Notice where you are doing a good job and where you are falling short of the mark. Based on your answers, compose a list of ways you could do a better job of addressing your needs on a daily basis. If you have other ideas about any of the listed categories add them to your list.

▶ Make a plan

Review your ideas and make a commitment to do something for yourself for 20 minutes every day over the next week. Refer to your list each morning and choose one item for that day. You can also choose one item to work on for the week if that is a better fit for your situation. Examples of activities that positively contribute to your life are:

- Eating a healthy lunch
- Getting to bed at a reasonable time
- Scheduling time to do something you really enjoy
- Exercising twice a week
- Reading a good book for 20 minutes a day
- Booking a massage
- Ringing up a friend

▶ Be accountable

One of the most significant parts of taking good care of yourself is consistency and follow-through. If you need support to stay accountable, tell a friend or family member what you are doing. Ask if they would be willing to follow up with you in a week. Or you can mark the date in your diary and call them. When you share your goals with another person, you increase your chances of being successful.

▶ Review your progress

Make sure to schedule time in your diary to review your progress. Again, if needed, ask a friend or family member for support in helping you stay accountable. If you have problems following through with your daily goals, don't give up. Instead, think through what you need to do differently to be successful and try again. Remember, even small steps can make a big difference in your energy level.

3.
UNDERSTANDING THE EMOTIONAL DIVORCE

Remember it's a marathon, not a sprint.
– Anonymous

In the early 1970s anthropologist Paul Bohannon in his book *Divorce and After* proposed the idea that divorce was not a single-moment event but rather a multi-level process that involved a series of stages and transitions for families. Truth be told, when you have children, separation and divorce become more than an experience you go through and move on from: this is actually a lifelong process. One of the biggest hurdles for many parents is learning how to manage their own emotional needs without compromising the needs and feelings of their children. Again, this is where emotional clarity – keeping your feelings separate from your children's feelings – becomes essential.

DYNAMICS OF THE EMOTIONAL DIVORCE
Divorce involves multiple changes

Separation and divorce involve change in nearly every area of family life. During this time you and your children are dealing with not only one major change but also many changes at the same time. With each new change there will be a mixture of emotions and feelings of loss. When possible, minimise the number of changes and adjustments you and your children have to make for the first year. For example, keep children in the same school or neighbourhood, maintain their contact with extended family members and friends and keep them involved in extracurricular activities.

Understand some changes are necessary and important. For example, think about:

- **How children spend time with their parents**
  Make sure your children are having consistent, regular contact with both parents. Don't limit a parent's time with a child or avoid overnights and weekends because the child isn't used to the other parent's home.
- **How children cope with having two homes**
  Children function best when they have a positive emotional and physical connection to a home with Mum and a home with Dad. Support the idea that your children have two homes. Don't create a situation in which one home is considered your child's real home or stable home, making the other parent's household just a place to visit.
- **How time is scheduled between households**
  Children can manage transitions between households when they are supported by parents and know what to expect. Don't avoid creating a parenting schedule between households because your child isn't used to being away from the family home.

Children will need time with both parents, especially in the early stages of separation. While having two homes is a change for children, it is a necessary and expected change they need to deal with in a supported way. Do what you can to provide consistency in the schedule and help create predictability for your children. For more information about how to establish consistency and structure for children living in two homes see Chapter 17.

Grieving is not time specific

While it is estimated that it takes families anywhere from one to three years to adjust to a divorce, there are a number of factors that may speed up or slow down that adjustment. Some of the factors affecting this process for you or the other parent are:

- Circumstances surrounding the breakdown of the relationship
- Suddenness of the divorce
- Lifestyle changes
- Financial pressures
- New adult relationships
- Support outside the family
- Your personality
- Your ability to manage stress
- Intensity of conflict between you and your ex-spouse
- Influence of significant others (that is, extended family and friends)

Children have different feelings and perspectives

Even though the family goes through the act of separation and divorce at the same time, expect that as life unfolds each member of the family will have different feelings. It is also important to understand that everyone will need to grieve individual losses in his or her own way and time. This is especially true for children.

It is not uncommon for children in the same family to have very different reactions and feelings about divorce. You may have one child who seems as if he couldn't care less, whereas another seems constantly on the verge of tears. Pay attention to your children's individual needs. Offer one-on-one time to discuss how they are handling things and make sure you are spending quality time with your children on a regular basis.

It is estimated that it takes families one to three years to adjust after parents separate. Keep in mind that the time frame for adjusting may be different for every person in the family. Just because you feel ready to move on doesn't necessarily mean your children will be ready to move on.

When parents are in different stages

Not only will your children's experiences be different but also you and your ex may be managing the divorce in very different ways. Often when a marriage or relationship begins to break down, one parent will begin to emotionally distance him- or herself before initiating a separation. This places one parent further along in the process and closer to accepting the reality of divorce, while the other parent may be in the beginning stages, feeling a sense of shock or disbelief. This dynamic usually adds to the existing tension in the parenting relationship and prevents each from seeing the other's perspective.

Take, for example, the story of Monica and Paul.

Monica's husband told her he was in love with another woman and wanted a divorce. According to Monica, her husband had abandoned his family, disregarded his responsibilities and ruined the lives of their two teenage children. Since the separation, the children were having limited contact with their father and would often refuse to talk with him. From Monica's perspective, she completely supported the idea that the children have a relationship with their father, but only if he were willing to end his affair with the other woman. She described him as someone who had literally changed overnight, lost his mind and was probably going through some crazy midlife crisis.

Paul saw things much differently. He described his relationship with Monica as being estranged, distant and unfulfilling for many years. He had decided to stay in the marriage despite his unhappiness because he felt it would be better for the children. Paul was angry with Monica for using the children as a way to control and punish him for falling in love with someone else. He just wanted her to get over it and let him go.

While both children wanted to spend time with their father, they could not bring themselves to betray or hurt their mother any further. Monica viewed her children's resistance as confirmation that they shared her feelings and perspectives about their father. Out of anger, Paul reacted by withdrawing from the children because he felt they had chosen their mother over him.

Unfortunately, both Monica and Paul allowed the intensity of their own emotions to override their judgement about the needs of their children. Paul was unable to understand that Monica was still in a state of shock over his decision and Monica could not accept that, emotionally, Paul had left the marriage years ago. Paul and Monica were both so focused on their own anger that neither had the insight to manage their own feelings in a healthy way. Sadly, their children ended up paying the price.

Regardless of which position you are in, it is imperative that you increase your level of emotional awareness and clarity. Understanding how you, your children and the other parent are managing the stages associated with loss is an important part of the process.

EMOTIONAL STAGES OF LOSS

While there are a number of variations on how parents and children experience loss, the following five stages represent the core process. These stages are largely based on work done by Elisabeth Kübler-Ross, a well-known and respected psychiatrist who pioneered the study of death and dying. Her work is regarded as the foundation for understanding grief and loss. Again, keep in mind while reviewing these stages that even though there is some universality to this process there are many different ways children and parents can react.

Denial

Joe was devastated when his wife said she wanted to end their 17-year marriage. To him, she was not only his wife but also his best friend. While the couple had separated and initiated divorce proceedings, he was adamant that he would not help his wife destroy their family. He tried to slow the process down at every step by refusing to sign papers and delaying court dates. Joe couldn't let go of the idea that maybe if he waited long enough she would snap out of it and change her mind.

After finding out about her husband's affair, Susan asked Bob to move out. Shortly after they separated she began filling up her days with activities, special projects, and managing events for their two children. Her household quickly became chaotic and messy. As a result of her busy schedule and disorganisation, she would frequently put off making appointments with her lawyer or her counsellor, paying bills or taking care of herself. When asked how she was doing, Susan would focus conversations around how much she enjoyed her volunteer activities. If asked about her divorce she would often reply, 'I'm doing great, it's really not that big of a deal.'

Susan and Joe's experiences are just two examples of how parents may manage the early stages of divorce. Denial is a way many of us get through the initial stages of a painful or incredibly overwhelming experience. You may even feel a sense of shock or disbelief. While logically you acknowledge that things are changing, a part of you resists the change. This can occur either by hanging on to the hope that things will somehow go back to the way they were before or by minimising the impact it will have on your life. You may also find yourself tempted at times to engage in self-destructive behaviours, such as eating when you are not hungry or missing meals, drinking alcohol more frequently, vegging out in front of the television every night and increasing the use of medications to help you get through the day or sleep at night.

RECOGNISING DENIAL IN YOURSELF OR IN THE OTHER PARENT

Have you or your partner:

- Said or thought, 'This can't be happening to me (us)'?
- Avoided taking steps to begin divorce proceedings or seek legal advice?
- Refused to leave the family home or justified not moving out (thinking, for example, it would be too hard for the kids)?
- Tried to change your partner's mind or prevent him or her from moving out?
- Chosen not to tell family, friends or co-workers about the situation?
- Hoped that maybe your partner will realise leaving was a mistake and change his or her mind?
- Put off talking to your children about what is happening?
- Started working more hours or found ways to stay away from the family home?
- Told yourself it's too early to tell the children, it will only upset them?

What can you do?

In the early stages, give yourself the time and space you need to think through your situation. As much as possible, maintain regular routines for you and your children. Creating structure at home will give you and your children stability while the family is in a state of change. You may also need to give yourself permission to take life at a slower pace for now. While it may be hard to think about talking to others, accessing support early in the process can make a tremendous difference. If you don't want to talk with family or friends, consider seeking out a local support group, counsellor or life coach.

Anger

Anger is a healthy and understandable reaction to divorce, and yet it is also often misunderstood. I am always amazed at the number of people who view anger as a negative emotion. In actuality, when managed in a healthy way, anger can be a powerful motivator. When a situation in life becomes unacceptable, anger can be the force that moves us from staying with what is comfortable to embracing change. Anger can also be a catalyst for stretching our personal boundaries or standing up for what we believe in. Anger may also help provide the emotional distance we need to end an unhealthy relationship or situation in our lives.

However, when it comes to divorce, anger is often a stage most of us don't manage well. For some parents, anger becomes a way of avoiding responsibility for the relationship not being successful. Take Andy, for example:

Andy had been divorced for five years and was still incredibly angry with his ex-wife for breaking up their family. He absolutely refused to accept that he had done anything that contributed to her decision. Truth be told, being married to Andy was not exactly a walk in the park. He was frequently verbally abusive, demanding and inflexible. However, because his hurt and pain were so great, he couldn't bring himself to accept the fact that he had some responsibility for the marriage not being successful. By staying connected to his anger at his wife, Andy avoided dealing with his own hurt. Andy's anger also made a really hard situation even worse for Julie, his eight-year-old daughter. Julie was frequently subjected to horrible rows between her parents and often put in the middle of adult issues and situations, such as relaying messages from one parent to the other, being asked to make decisions about the schedule, or being told that some day she would have to tell the judge whom she wanted to live with.

RECOGNISING ANGER IN YOURSELF OR IN THE OTHER PARENT

When angry, you or your ex may:

- Feel or act more irritable and short tempered with children or others
- Make irrational parenting decisions (for example, suddenly change rules without reason, use overly harsh punishment because you feel out of control)
- Become overly reactive to situations (such as blowing up over small issues or problems, telling the other parent she can't see children because she was 15 minutes late)
- Shut down emotionally
- Feel extremely tense and stressed
- Continually bring up past issues from the marriage
- Fantasise about ways to get even with the other parent
- Become less emotionally available or affectionate with your children
- Engage in behaviours that undermine the other parent's relationship with your children
- Openly criticise or say bad things about the other parent
- Find yourself stewing over a row or situation involving the other parent
- Choose to keep anger to yourself by withdrawing or cutting yourself off from others

When anger and upset are not dealt with appropriately the results can be incredibly damaging to both you and your children. Staying connected to your anger and upset leaves you:

- Unable to move forward and find peace in your life
- Likely to experience physical symptoms such as headaches, digestion problems, fatigue or depression

- Unable to take responsibility for what went wrong in the relationship
- Unavailable for your children
- In a constant state of stress and upheaval
- Connected to your relationship with your ex in an unhealthy way
- Likely to compromise the emotional needs of your children

Key factors in successfully dealing with this stage involve recognising the feeling and then finding healthy, appropriate ways to deal with it.

What can you do?

When you are feeling angry, don't operate in extremes by either staying silent or exploding. Both have repercussions that will affect your health and ultimately your children. Instead use some of the tips listed below.

▶ Be proactive, not reactive, when you are angry

Anger is an emotion that often catches us off guard. Know that you will feel angry and honour the fact that you have a right to feel that way. Give some thought to how you will manage the anger when it comes up and how you will keep your children from getting caught in the line of fire. Healthy options for dealing with anger can be:

- Exercising
- Taking a deep breath
- Walking away from an argument or a situation that might lead to conflict
- Venting to a friend or family member
- Writing things out in a letter or journal (NB: avoid sending anything to your ex when you are feeling angry)
- Engaging in prayer, meditation or reflection

▶ Distance yourself from your immediate reaction

Aside from emergencies, very few situations require an immediate response. If you find yourself reacting to something, find a way to distance yourself from the situation. Walk away and give yourself some time to cool off or perhaps call a friend to talk things over and gain some perspective.

▶ Identify the reason you are angry

In the beginning stages, when emotions are at their strongest, it's easy to misdirect your anger. Give yourself some time to figure out what is going on before taking action. Suppose your children come home and tell you your ex has a new boyfriend or girlfriend. You instantly feel angry and compelled to call your ex to say how incredibly irresponsible they are to have a new fling around the kids. It may help to spend some time thinking about what is fuelling the anger. Is the issue not exposing children to new adults before they've had time to adjust? Are you feeling angry that your ex seems to have moved on so quickly? Whatever the reason, giving yourself time to think things through can give you an opportunity to handle the situation in a better way.

▶ Take action and reapproach the situation

Once you have sorted through your reaction to a problem, take a look at the situation again with fresh eyes. Make sure you stay focused on the issue at hand. Sometimes it can be tempting to think about issues in the moment instead of viewing the problem using a big-picture perspective. Consider how this issue will affect you or your children in six months, a year or five years. Ask yourself, when your children look back, what they will remember about how you handled the situation.

▶ Think about what you do when you get angry

- Do you shout? Scream? Withdraw? Leave the situation?
- How does your current response help or hurt the situation?

- How do you think your current response is helping or hurting your children?
- Is there something else you could do that might be more helpful to you and your children?

Also, while it is helpful to seek support and advice, use some discretion when you're angry. Anger can often leave you feeling very vulnerable.

Although family, friends or co-workers may have good intentions, remember that their perspective might be biased or based on their own experiences. There will be times when the advice you receive from others is not right for you or your children. Therefore, choose your support people wisely. Seek out those who are able to listen and support you in a helpful way, rather than those who want to help you fuel the fire. If you are having problems finding good support, it may be the right time to seek out the professional help of a counsellor or life coach.

Bargaining

The decision to divorce or separate is a very personal and often challenging choice to make, particularly when you have children. As you move forward, you may question your decision and consider reconciling or giving the relationship a second chance. If you have done this, you're not alone; about 50 per cent of separating couples opt to patch up their differences and try again. This desire to save the relationship or reconsider the decision to separate is known as bargaining. Bargaining may or may not be a significant stage for you. The degree to which most parents experience it tends to vary, and depends on the dynamics of the relationship. Some may not feel drawn into the bargaining stage until the divorce is in its final stages.

RECOGNISING BARGAINING IN YOURSELF OR IN THE OTHER PARENT

During bargaining, you or your ex may:
- Ask for a second chance or consider trying again
- Request or offer to attend relationship therapy or counselling
- Wonder if you are making the right decision
- Feel guilty about ending the marriage or hurting your children
- Waver in your decision regarding the divorce or separation
- Be willing to do whatever your spouse wants in hopes of getting back together
- Move back into the family home
- Talk with children about changing the other parent's mind

What can you do?

Making the decision to separate or divorce is never easy. Give yourself time to think through your decisions before acting on them. Almost all parents, at one time or another, feel some guilt about ending their marriage or relationship and wonder if they should reconsider. If you are having second thoughts, find someone (for example, a friend, family member, co-worker, professional counsellor or life coach) you can talk to who will help you weigh up your options.

Depression

Expect that at some point you will feel a sense of sadness over the loss of your relationship and your family. The degree to which we feel that sadness is different for each one of us. You may find that you have a greater sense of sadness about certain aspects of your separation. For most, these feelings eventually diminish over time. However, in some circumstances feelings of sadness can become persistent or intensify and lead to depression. Depression is one of the most dangerous stages for you to get stuck in. If depression is affecting your day-to-day life, you should seek professional help. Consider making an appointment with your GP to discuss your situation and explore options. Do what you can to help yourself move through this stage in a healthy way.

In general, professional intervention is recommended if you are experiencing multiple symptoms on a regular or frequent basis, such as most of the day or nearly every day for a period of several weeks.

RECOGNISING DEPRESSION IN YOURSELF OR IN THE OTHER PARENT

- Changes in your eating habits that cause either considerable weight gain or a lack of interest in eating
- Significant changes in sleeping habits such as an inability to sleep or wanting to sleep all the time
- Persistent or overwhelming feelings of sadness
- Not caring about anything or feeling empty
- Lack of motivation to do normal activities, such as cleaning the house, managing financial matters or caring for yourself
- Feeling empty or alone
- Inability to concentrate or focus
- Often becoming upset, tearful or crying
- Physical symptoms, such as frequent headaches, stomach aches or a constant state of fatigue
- Being irritable and short tempered
- Inability to find pleasure in activities you used to enjoy
- In more serious cases, frequent thoughts of hurting yourself, wishing you could just go away or even die

What can you do?

▶ Get professional support

If you are having difficulty managing your sadness on a daily basis, seek out professional support. Professional support can happen in many different ways, from finding a counsellor who can help you move through the grief and loss to joining a local divorce support group for parents. In some cases it may be helpful to seek out a psychiatrist to evaluate the need for medication. Keep in mind that medication is not a cure-all and is most effective when paired with therapeutic support.

▶ Identify major stress factors or triggers and find solutions

Pay attention to what triggers the depression or sadness for you. Consider using the self-awareness tracking questions at the end of this chapter to help you gain some insight about your feelings on a daily basis. Is there a certain time of the day or perhaps a situation that is more difficult for you to deal with? Do you have a harder time when you are by yourself or with others? Does the idea of even mentioning the word 'divorce' to your children bring you to tears?

Once you have identified your triggers for the sadness, think through what you can do to support yourself during those times. For example, if you are having a difficult time in the evenings after the children go to bed, consider changing your routine or doing something different. If you are having a tough time coming up with ideas, try talking with a friend.

▶ Get help managing day-to-day activities

During this stage, even simple daily tasks may feel overwhelming. Think about what is most challenging or draining for you right now and what would help. If your house is a mess, hire someone to clean once a week or every other week. If finances are a problem consider swapping services with a friend or trusted neighbour, like trading baby-sitting or sharing the school run to give yourself a break when you are feeling spread thin.

▶ **Find ways to take positive action every day**

When dealing with depression, getting motivated to take action is hard. Work towards finding small ways to support yourself throughout each week such as the following:

- Going to bed half an hour earlier
- Keeping a diary for 15 minutes every day
- When feeling overwhelmed, writing down three things you are thankful for
- Going outside for a 10-minute walk
- Doing something nice for someone else
- Asking someone you find interesting out to lunch
- Limiting yourself to talking with others about your separation to no more than 20 minutes a day

Remember even small things can make a big difference in helping you find the energy you need to get through the day.

Acceptance

Most parents find that, after some time has passed, life eventually begins to feel more 'normal' and settled. The transitions between homes become smoother and you will find the initial intensity of your feelings has started to subside as you and your children begin moving into regular daily routines. You may also notice that you and the other parent are more flexible with one another and better able to share information between households.

As your life moves forward there will be new life events and challenges for you and your children. It is quite common for some of these feelings or stages to resurface as life unfolds. Don't view it as a setback but rather a normal part of the process. After going through the initial grieving process, when issues come up for you they will probably be much less intense. You may also find you feel more in control and confident in how you approach future situations or challenges.

RECOGNISING ACCEPTANCE IN YOURSELF OR IN THE OTHER PARENT

Once you've reached acceptance you may:

- Feel confident and hopeful about your future
- Become interested in re-establishing goals for yourself
- Be able to disengage from strong emotions
- Feel emotionally balanced
- Be objective about the divorce
- Have a balanced perspective about the other parent
- Be able to manage the transition between homes for yourself and your children
- Re-engage in activities or develop new interests
- Be able to communicate with the other parent more easily
- Make peace with the past and be able to acknowledge your part in things not being successful

RAISING YOUR LEVEL OF EMOTIONAL AWARENESS

As mentioned earlier, divorce is a crisis, and the vast majority of us respond to it in that way. While you are in the early crisis stage don't make the mistake of ignoring or discounting how you feel. While these techniques may get you through the moment, none of these methods will be helpful to you or your children longterm.

In the beginning stages you may find paying attention to how you feel really challenging, inconvenient and difficult. When stress levels are high, most of us just go through the day reacting without giving any real thought to how we feel. We think we know how we feel, but usually we don't. Often we just focus on what is happening from one moment to the next. However, paying attention to how you feel is a lot like dieting. Have you ever gone on a diet and tried to keep track of what you eat every day? Were you surprised at how many calories you ate without even realising it?

The same is true about paying attention to how you feel on a daily basis. Consider using the questions on page 29 to gauge how you are managing your emotional process. For at least a two-week period, make a habit of doing a quick check-in with yourself several times a week. If writing your thoughts in a diary works for you, that's great. If writing is not your thing, then set aside a few minutes during your day when you can reflect on what happened. To help you keep track of past events think about jotting down one word, feeling or symbol in your diary or daily calendar. As you review significant or memorable events, consider the emotional connection you had to each of them. Think about not only what you were feeling in the moment but also how you felt after. Keep in mind that events can be either positive or negative. For example, one day you may have a row with your ex over the weekend schedule that leaves you feeling really angry and resentful. On another day you may feel optimistic and thankful when you come home and find your teen cooked you dinner to help out.

After a couple of weeks, take time to look at what you wrote in your diary or jotted down on your calendar. Were there any patterns or distinct changes in how you felt throughout a week? If certain feelings seem to be challenging to deal with or occurring more frequently, use some of the suggestions in this chapter to support yourself.

Self-awareness tracking questions

- What was the event?
- What was the feeling? Did your feelings change after the event?
- Is there anything you would do differently?

EMOTIONS YOU MAY EXPERIENCE

Afraid	Content	Guilty	Optimistic	Sad
Alone	Control	Happy	Out of control	Satisfied
Ambivalent	Depressed	Hesitant	Overwhelmed	Tearful
Angry	Empty	Hopeful	Powerful	Thankful
Anxious	Encouraged	Hopeless	Powerless	Unsure
Bitter	Energetic	Irritated	Regretful	Upset
Calm	Excited	Jealous	Relaxed	Vengeful
Certain	Fearful	Liberated	Relieved	Vulnerable
Concerned	Frustrated	Lost	Resentful	Wronged
Confident	Glad	Numb	Restless	

4.
TILL DEATH DO YOU PART

Honey, your father is a good man, he's just not good for me. – Mother from a parenting class

One afternoon while running a court-ordered workshop for parents, a dad in the back of the room challenged me. I had just finished going through my usual speech, chapter and verse, about the importance of having a good co-parenting relationship with your ex. 'Christina,' he said, 'if I could get along with my ex, I wouldn't be sitting in this class.' Another parent quickly added, 'Yeah, what you're saying about getting along sounds great, but what if your ex doesn't want to get along?'

It wasn't the first time I had heard this. As a matter of fact, you may be wondering the very same thing as you read this chapter. The truth is, two good people don't always make a good couple together; however, it doesn't mean two good people can't be good parents apart. No matter who else comes into your children's lives, you will be your children's mother and father for ever. While your relationship as husband and wife has ended, your role as parents is a lifetime commitment.

Just like the father who challenged me, lots of parents want to know, 'How do I parent my children with someone I don't want to be married to?'

The first step in answering this question involves thinking about your relationship with the other parent in a different way.

CHANGING HOW YOU THINK

One of the biggest challenges you will face as you go through this process will be changing your relationship with your ex. While relationships and divorce situations come in all different shapes and sizes, you and your ex have a history together, ways of acting with each other and reacting to each other. You probably have a very good idea of which buttons to push if you want to really aggravate your ex. He or she can probably rattle off a rather lengthy list of your not-so-desirable qualities as a partner. Even if you are fortunate enough to get along with your ex, you will still have to work at not falling back into those old patterns. Setting all of that history aside and finding a new way to work together for the benefit of your children can feel about as easy as nailing jelly to the wall.

After working with parents for over a decade, I have found the single most influential factor in how parents manage divorce, regardless of circumstance or situation, is **attitude**. Charles R. Swindoll, noted author and Evangelical pastor, once said, 'The longer I live, the more I realise the impact of attitude on life.... I am convinced that life is 10 per cent what happens to me and 90 per cent how I react to it ... And so it is with you.'

> You will never be able to change or control your ex but you always have control over your attitude, your perceptions and your actions.

If you gain one thing from this reading this book, I hope it is an understanding of this one universal truth. Your attitude about your relationship with your children's other parent has the ability to make or break you. More important, it has the ability to make or break your children's future.

Most people underestimate the power of attitude, hope and optimistic thinking. Yet how you think about your separation and the other parent can alter your life substantially. Consider the following examples:

Nick was in an awful divorce situation. Since he had moved out, his ex, Mary, had become more hostile, more difficult, and seemed devoted to turning their eight-year-old son, Sam, against him. He often showed up to see his son only to find that his ex had scheduled another activity for Sam during his time with him, such as a friend's birthday party. If Nick told Sam no, he instantly became the bad guy. If he said yes, Sam could go to the party, then Nick didn't see his son.

Despite the increasing difficulties with his ex, Nick never abandoned his positive attitude. He worked hard to disengage from the drama Mary created and made a conscious choice to focus on taking steps forward to maintain a positive connection with his child. While there were lots of opportunities to increase the conflict, Nick channelled his energy into more positive things like finding a job he enjoyed and going back to university to pursue a degree. Nick made a conscious choice to acknowledge that Mary was an important part of their son's life. He remained hopeful that some day things would improve. Also, by not feeding into his ex-wife's anger and bitterness when issues came up, he was able to approach them in a more controlled way.

Although Nick eventually had to use legal intervention, he was able to successfully re-establish his relationship with Sam and be the loving, positive father his son needed.

Barbara described her ex, Stewart, as impossible to deal with and incredibly stubborn. They had weekly – sometimes daily – arguments over parenting their three children. Barbara often spent her days consumed by the latest problem and talking to all her friends about her horrible ex. It usually took just one phone call, email or text from him to completely stress her out. Instead of backing off from the arguments or the situation, Barbara would spend her time thinking about how to get back at Stewart or prove that he was wrong and she was right. As a result, her outlook on life was pretty grim. She felt the fighting would never end and her ex would always ruin her life no matter what. She frequently felt angry, overwhelmed, hopeless and out of control.

Although she and Stewart were no longer married, Barbara had dedicated her life to maintaining a negative connection to their relationship. Barbara had given Stewart the ability to control not only her feelings but also the quality of her life.

Regardless of what the other parent does or doesn't do, **you always have the ability to choose how you view the situation,** how much energy you give to it and how you respond to it. Again, while the logical part of you may realise this, the emotional part may not buy it. Try the exercise below to help you get a handle on your perceptions.

When working with the other parent becomes challenging, you may find it helpful to have a visual reminder. Find a favourite picture of your children and keep it with you, in your wallet or purse. Write an inspirational quote, phrase or perhaps a commitment statement to your children on the back of the photo. For example:

- 'The love I have for my children is greater than the upset, anger or frustration I am feeling at this moment.'
- I am committed to not putting Tommy, Becky and Mark in the middle of my problems with my ex.'

Cost–benefit analysis

Answer the following questions.

- How does it benefit me to have a negative view of my ex?
- How does it help my children if I maintain a negative view of my ex?

- What does it cost me to maintain a negative view of my ex?
- What does it cost my children?
- Regardless of the choices my ex makes, what can I do to improve the situation between myself and the other parent?

Review your answers, and think about how you would like things to change. What can you do to create that change?

CHANGING YOUR RELATIONSHIP

In the early stages of separation or divorce, you may find it easier to think about managing your parenting relationship with a businesslike attitude. Think back to a time when you worked with someone you didn't get along with very well or had a colleague who drove you up the wall. Imagine yourself in that situation again. Suppose quitting your job or transferring to another office wasn't an option and that you both had a substantial investment in the company's success. How would you make that work? How could you have a successful business without liking each other?

Think of your relationship with your ex as changing from that of husband or wife to a lifetime business partner. The business at hand, from here on out, is raising happy, successful children. Remember, even though your feelings for each other have changed, your children's needs have not. Children still need the same level of love, nurturing, support and guidance as they did when you were together. Everything your children needed before the divorce they continue to need after you have separated.

The feelings you are having right now will eventually pass. However, how you manage those feelings and thoughts has the potential to affect your children for the rest of their lives.

Much like a business relationship, a successful co-parenting relationship involves:

- Setting aside personal feelings and opinions
- Detaching yourself from strong emotions
- Staying focused on the task at hand
- Treating each other with respect
- Learning to compromise when possible
- Minimising opportunities for conflict

Guidelines for communicating with the other parent

▶ Treat the other parent with respect

Don't forget the quality of your marriage relationship does not determine the quality of your child's relationship with the other parent. Just because your ex may have been a lousy spouse doesn't mean he or she can't be a great parent. While you may not respect your ex-partner as a person, you can respect him or her as the other parent of your children. Challenge your negative thoughts about your ex and work on balancing your perception.

▶ Don't make it personal

When making arrangements with your ex, it may help to ask yourself how you would handle the issue with a colleague or business partner. In particularly difficult situations, you may want to ask yourself how you would want the other parent to manage the problem with you if the situation were reversed.

▶ Use restraint

Avoid knee-jerk reactions to situations or issues involving the other parent. Try to listen to each other's opinions and ideas before responding or giving your perspective. If the other parent says something that stirs up strong feelings, do not act on your immediate reaction. If necessary, ask to continue the discussion later. Give yourself time to calm down, think things over, and then respond.

▶ Practise neutral communication

Statements such as *you always* and *you never* usually leave people feeling defensive and increase tension. Instead use more neutral statements, such as:

- I understand your point, but I have a different perspective.
- When this happens, I feel …
- This situation is frustrating to me because …

If dealing with the other parent is challenging, make sure you are managing your feelings and opinions in a healthy, supportive way. This will leave you less inclined to vent your opinions or personal feelings with your ex. When possible, think through situations ahead of time and decide how you will handle it if things get personal. Remember: stay focused on the issue, not the person.

▶ Avoid bringing up past issues

Don't use past issues as a way of making a point or to reinforce your perspective. If the other parent tries to rehash past issues, don't retaliate or get sidetracked. Instead, remind your ex that you want to focus on the children, not each other. If he or she persists, calmly end the conversation and ask to continue once you have both cooled off. For example:

BILL: Pam, here we go again. Why do things always have to be your way? You are so selfish, just like your mother. Can't you think of anyone but yourself? This is exactly what you were like when we were married. You'll never change.

PAM: Bill, I understand you are frustrated. However, insulting each other isn't going to change things. I don't want to argue, but I would like to talk about how we can work things out for the kids next Saturday. If we can't do that without fighting then maybe we need to stop now and talk to each other later once we've both had time to calm down.

▶ Give notice

Instead of springing an issue or discussion on the other parent, it may be more helpful to let your ex know beforehand that you want to discuss something (leave a short voicemail, text or email). If you're face to face, before launching into a discussion ask if this is a good time to talk. If not, ask to schedule a time.

▶ Meet in a neutral location

If you need to meet face to face and tensions are running high, consider holding discussions in a local coffee shop or restaurant. Meeting in a public place can sometimes be more helpful and less emotional than sitting at the kitchen table. A neutral place also tends to keep both people calmer and can reduce the chances of things getting heated or out of hand.

▶ Don't use child drop-offs and pick-ups to discuss issues

Pick-ups and drop-offs are usually times when emotions run especially high for children and parents. If you have something you need to share or discuss, it is best to phone, write a short note or ask to schedule a convenient time to talk when the children are not around.

▶ Follow up agreements in writing

If you and the other parent have made a change to the schedule or an agreement involving the children, follow it up in writing. It is not uncommon for parents to walk away with completely different understandings or impressions of what was said or agreed. Written follow-up helps minimise misunderstandings.

> Love your children more than you hate your ex.

Tips for emails and letters

▶ **Don't contact or email the other parent when you are angry**

Educator Laurence J. Peter once said, 'Speak when you are angry and you will make the best speech you will ever regret.' It is very difficult to have a constructive discussion when you're feeling angry. Before approaching the situation, consider sleeping on it. Give yourself some time to cool off and gain perspective. Calming down before taking action will give you the opportunity to respond instead of react.

▶ **When you receive an angry email, delay your response**

If you receive an angry email, letter, voicemail or text message from your ex, avoid the temptation to reply immediately. If you have to get it out, write your response but don't send it. Unless the matter is time sensitive, wait 24 hours and then reread your response.

▶ **Edit before you send**

Here's a way to ensure you stay focused on the children: When editing your letter, take a red marker and cross out everything that doesn't have to do with the children. Ask yourself the following before taking action:

- Do I need to respond to this email or letter?
- What is the issue? Is it an issue I need to resolve?
- How does this affect the children now?
- How will it affect the children in six months? In a year?

▶ **Think of your children**

Imagine that your children will read what you wrote when they are adults. What will they think about what you have said?

5.
MANAGING THE LEGAL SYSTEM

When it comes to divorce there are no winners;
everybody loses something. – Anonymous

How you navigate through the legal system is another factor that can substantially change how you and your children handle other parts of the divorcing process. Unfortunately, when you are in the middle of litigation you don't always think about the long-term impact court-related drama can have on the quality of your life.

Historically, lawyers have been accused of being the primary reason that divorce has become a battlefield for separating parents. More often than not we view lawyers as professionals who are simply looking to line their pockets at your expense. Right now, even as you read this, you may be thinking of lawyers as a necessary evil. However, consider the role of a family lawyer from a different angle.

Imagine you were sick and needed medical treatment. Would you blame your doctor for making you sick? Of course not, yet you would expect your doctor to help you responsibly manage your illness. Still, the decision-making power about your overall health and well-being would belong to you. Your doctor's responsibility would be to guide your treatment and help you arrive at the best possible outcome; the same is true for your lawyer. Family lawyers have the ability either to responsibly manage or to mismanage how you experience the divorce process. But it is important to remember you are the one in the driver's seat, you are the one calling the shots and you have to live with the consequences of your decisions – not your lawyer. Your lawyer did not create the conflict between you and your ex. Certainly there are some lawyers who can fan the flames and make things worse. But there are also lawyers who can help you work on putting the fire out. My advice is to choose wisely.

A good divorce lawyer helps you:

- Identify your priorities
- Understand your choices and the consequences of those choices
- Decide which option will most likely lead to the best end point for you and your children

In almost all cases, children benefit most when parents can engage in a series of open discussions and make mutual decisions about matters. In short: **court should be a last resort, not a first option**.

Be mindful that the paperwork associated with the legal process is often highly technical. While there may be parts of this process you are capable of handling, a competent lawyer who can assist you in understanding the different components, weigh the long-term implications of various decisions and help you prioritise matters accordingly can be a real asset.

FINDING THE LAWYER WHO IS RIGHT FOR YOU

While seeking a lawyer with the lowest hourly rate might seem like a good idea, often it backfires. Keep in mind that a *less expensive* alternative may also mean *less experience*. In the long run, what started out as a great deal might end up costing you more. In some situations lawyers who charge higher rates not only bring more experience but they usually do the work needed in a fraction of the time.

Most importantly, you should seek a lawyer who is:

▶ A specialist in the area of family law

While all lawyers have been through the same basic training, after qualification most focus on developing expertise in specific areas. Make sure the lawyer you work with is both experienced and knowledgeable about the law and the court system regarding family issues.

▶ Familiar with your set of circumstances

When considering the particular aspects of your case, make sure that your lawyer has matching strengths. Many family lawyers have specialised skills in particular areas of family law, such as finance, children's issues, international cases, never married separations, domestic violence or matters related to the Child Support Agency. Even within the area of finance, there are those who handle 'high net worth' cases and those that are skilled at dealing with cases involving welfare benefits. It may also be helpful to ask a prospective lawyer if he or she has accreditation or other additional training, which may be a mark of advanced skills and experience.

▶ Settlement orientated

Lawyers who are trained mediators or experienced collaborative lawyers (or ideally both) are more likely to have the skill-set and determination to help you stay out of the courts. While in some circumstances you may need someone who is able to take robust action, you don't want litigation where there is a chance of settlement.

▶ Ethical

Ethical in this context refers to those who are committed to clients before profits, who are upfront and transparent about charges and whose agenda is definitely that of the client rather than their own. Lawyers committed to ethical standards often affiliate themselves with organisations, which hold to a higher standard of practice.

In England and Wales, the family law organisation Resolution (resolution.org.uk) requires all members to adhere to a code aimed at promoting constructive and child-focused solutions. In

Scotland, the Family Law Association (familylawassociation.org) has a similar code of conduct that its members must adhere to.

A lawyer who is active with a national or local organisation that supports high standards of practice may be well worth considering.

> Once you have identified a couple of potential candidates, consider requesting a brief meeting (20 minutes or so) with each, either by phone or in person. This will help you have a better sense of whether they are the right lawyer for you. Be sure to ask if there is a fee for an introductory meeting; some lawyers are willing to have such meetings without charge.

GETTING THE BEST FROM YOUR LAWYER

Most lawyers charge according to the time that they spend working on your case. The lesson here is obvious. The better organised you are, the less time your lawyer will need to spend completing things for you. Saving your lawyer time means saving money.

Before meeting with your lawyer consider the following points:

▶ Prepare information
Sending information through to your lawyer in advance of the first meeting can be a good first step. Create a concise summary that highlights significant events instead of a lengthy document filled with intimate details.

Key information that the lawyer is likely to need:

- **Clarity about the issues**
  What are the particular problems or issues that you know you face?
- **What matters to you**
  Do your best to be clear about your aspirations.

This offers your lawyer a guide against which to assess your options.

- **What you think your partner wants**
  This information will help to define potential conflicts and common ground. Knowing this in advance allows your solicitor to start generating third options which could help to provide solutions.
- **Who is involved**
  Prepare a family tree of important people who are either involved or play a significant role in your family.
- **Financial summary**
  Where financial issues are involved, aim to bring a balance sheet showing
  - Assets and debts (including pensions) you or your partner have
  - Household income

The information does not have to be perfect, but providing an outline of your estimation offers a starting point and means your lawyer can give you a broad outline of your position and your options.

▶ Clarify fees and costs

Lawyers' rates can vary widely. Be sure you are very clear about your lawyer's rates and fees prior to engaging their services. Establish when the meter starts running, which is often from your first meeting.

Keep in mind very few lawyers are willing to guarantee their initial estimates. Be wary of simply selecting the lawyer who seems to offer the lowest estimated overall cost. It could indicate either inexperience or a sign of a lawyer who is unrealistic about the needs of your case.

When it comes to funding legal services, lawyers will typically ask for payment at the time of the first meeting. From that point forward billing is generated on a monthly basis and your lawyer will expect settlement of each bill as your case advances.

Some lawyers have schemes that may enable you to borrow the money that you will need to fund the costs of the process. It may be possible to ask for your partner to help with your costs (if she or he has the means to do this).

When you receive each bill there will usually be a breakdown of the time spent (if there isn't, then ask for one). Immediately raise any queries you have.

THE LAW RELATING TO CHILDREN IN ENGLAND AND WALES, AND IN SCOTLAND

Although the legal rules are different between England/Wales and Scotland, many of the underlying principles are very similar. One strong similarity between the two jurisdictions is the belief that mutual agreements arrived at through negotiation between parents produce much better outcomes than those achieved by litigation. In short, legal principles are rarely an exact match for the realities of family life. While courts try to do what is best for children, their ability to do so is limited.

What is best for children usually involves:

- Focusing on what children need rather than what parents want
- Good communication and cooperation between parents
- Arrangements with flexibility

Court-based outcomes usually involve:

- Arriving at an agreement that addresses generalities instead of the specific needs of children
- Creating strain on an already strained parenting relationship
- Arrangements with clearly defined, rigid structures rather than the flexible agreements most families need

UNDERSTANDING THE COURT PROCESS

Because litigation is often the most tangible part of divorce it is very easy to become overinvested in the outcome. In the grand scheme of things, the legal process is only one small part of a much bigger picture. Essentially the court only becomes involved in parenting arrangements within the family when:

- An application is made by one parent or the other; or
- The family comes to the attention of the local authority because of concerns for the safety or well-being of the child

If an application is made then different courts will have different ways of having the parents prepare their cases for a final hearing. In England and Wales the judge will often bring the parents in together at an early stage to see if an agreement can be reached. Where this is not possible, then statements are filed. The parents and children will then meet with a court-appointed expert for independent information about the child's wishes and feelings to be put before the court.

Once these matters have been completed, the court will have the information that it needs to be able to make a decision in the child's best interests.

In Scotland parents are automatically asked to attend a Child Welfare Hearing where the sheriff will normally have a discussion

Most courts seek to promote flexibility, cooperation and understanding between parents. However, judges and family courts don't know your children. Therefore decisions are made based on the information that is presented to them and within the limits of the powers that they have. These standard approaches may or may not be helpful or workable for your children.

with parents and their solicitors about the issues between them. Very often, the Child Welfare Hearing is continued for further investigation of the matter. Many cases are settled due to the early intervention of sheriffs at the Child Welfare Hearing.

WHEN IS COURT AN APPROPRIATE OPTION?

When no agreement is possible due to an impasse, drastic differences in opinion, high levels of conflict or specialised circumstances regarding safety issues (which includes substance abuse and domestic violence), court involvement may be necessary. The one thing that the court does that no other process can offer is provide an imposed outcome.

While there are some issues or situations that must be dealt with in court, the vast majority can be resolved in a less adversarial way. Make every effort to think through your motivation before pursuing matters in court.

WHAT ORDERS CAN THE COURT MAKE?

Courts have the ability to make decisions about:

▶ Where a child will live
This is called 'residence', which may be 'shared residence' between two adults. Keep in mind that *shared residence* does not mean that children spend equal time in each home. The parent responsible for day-to-day care of children is often referred to as the *parent with care* whereas the parent who has scheduled time with children is considered the *non-resident parent*.

▶ How a child will spend time with the other parent
Contact orders outline how time is structured between the children and the parent who has scheduled time. Often contact

orders also cover things like telephone/videophone time, sharing of holidays and distribution of time between parents. Often the distance between each parent's home along with their respective work schedules plays an important role in how time is scheduled with children.

▶ Supplementary orders

The court has the ability to require steps that encourage parent compliance; some measures are broadly educational, while others may penalise non-compliance.

▶ Specific issues, or prohibition of certain actions

When parents can't agree, the court may also be asked to make parenting decisions about religious upbringing, education or medical treatment. They may also forbid actions such as removing a child from school or bringing a child into contact with family members where there are safety concerns.

OTHER OPTIONS WORTH CONSIDERING

Over the past decade there have been many significant steps taken by family court systems to make divorce a more humane process for children and families. As a result there has been a growing movement to use professionals within both the legal and the mental health professions to help parents make child-centred decisions and minimise conflict. The following resources are some of the options you can consider.

Workshops for separated and divorced parents

In various parts of the UK there are organisations that provide educational workshops for separating and divorcing parents. These courses often help parents gain perspective, generate new ideas, develop an enhanced understanding of their children's needs and learn better problem-solving skills. While classes can vary in presentation and format, most are between three and four hours in length and provide informational support on topics such as:

- How children are affected by divorce
- What to expect, depending on your child's age and developmental stage
- How to establish a workable parenting relationship with your ex
- How to talk with children about divorce

Although you may have mixed feelings about attending a workshop, it might help to know that most parents find the information and experience quite valuable. Not only does it give you an opportunity to meet others dealing with similar situations or circumstance; courses also offer a sense of validation for the things you are doing well. For more information about workshops see the appendix.

> Divorce doesn't make you a bad parent; it makes you a parent going through a bad time.

Mediation

A mediator is an independent neutral professional, often a lawyer or someone from a background in social work. These professionals usually have a range of expertise from the law to child development or family systems.

Whatever their background, a mediator's role is to:

- Facilitate discussion
- Structure the dialogue between parents
- Explore options for solving issues raised by parents

- Record the principles or structure that parents conclude should underpin the agreement going forwards. Keep in mind that a mediator's records are not, of themselves, legally binding. A binding agreement would only emerge once you have taken the additional step of conversion. This usually occurs after taking legal advice.

Mediation, particularly with the right mediator, can be enormously effective. Along with gaining new insight and perspective, it can also be very cost efficient. Instead of parents paying two separate professionals throughout the entire process, they can work with one professional to help them navigate discussions and initial agreements. See the resources section for further information.

Collaborative practice

Collaborative practice is a different sort of process but it also aims to maximise the chance of reaching an agreement through face-to-face discussion. While mediation has a neutral mediator who cannot offer advice, in the collaborative process each parent has their own lawyer who *can* offer advice during negotiations and the lawyers are on hand to finalise any agreement reached.

At the centre of the collaborative law process is a contract where the parties promise to do their best to resolve the case without taking it to court. Parents also make a variety of commitments regarding how they will behave during discussions and each lawyer commits to helping both parties reach an agreement. If at any point parents decide they want to go to court, both collaborative lawyers must withdraw themselves from the case. Each parent will then be required to seek new representation. Additional information about collaborative law can be found in the appendix.

Arbitration

'Arbitration' or 'private judging' aims to offer parents the option of an externally imposed outcome without all of the demands, delays and costs of court process. The arbiter or private judge should have more time to meet with parents and get to know the family better.

6.
WALKING THE WALK: PITFALLS TO AVOID

It's not hard to talk a good game; in fact, it is easier than easy. But actually getting out there and backing up your words with full-fledged effort is anything but easy. In fact, it's one of the most challenging aspects you'll ever encounter in day-to-day living. – Anonymous

In all honesty, I have to admit that a great deal of what I teach sometimes seems a little idealistic to parents. Yes, it is very easy to say don't badmouth the other parent and don't fight in front of the kids. The logical part of you understands conflict is damaging to your children. However, when your ex is standing in front of you and calling you every name under the sun or blaming you because Robbie got a B– on his homework last week, biting your tongue takes on a whole new meaning.

As a bonus parent, I have had lots of opportunities to dig deep and practise what I preach. I understand it is much harder to live those ideals day in and day out than it is to talk about them. Yet if you are genuinely committed to making sure your children grow up to be healthy, successful people, it is essential you understand putting those concepts into action is where the real work begins.

It is also worth mentioning that talking the talk and walking the walk is an area where even the most well-intentioned parent can falter. Take Brian, for example:

By all accounts, Brian was a devoted father who very much wanted to do whatever he could to help his children. His divorce had been nasty, unfair and financially devastating. While he had every reason to feel resentful and angry with his ex, he also realised his bitterness was hurting his kids. On the surface he knew he shouldn't talk badly about his ex in front of his children. However, when he was feeling overwhelmed or irritated by her he would inadvertently let his guard down and say things to his children he later regretted. Although he made sure to apologise to his children after he said something offensive, his behaviour continued. Eventually his apologies became meaningless to the children because he didn't walk the walk.

Over the years I have worked with a wide range of parents from high-powered executives of large firms to shop assistants in the local store. Some of the parents I've coached have been highly educated, whereas others never completed sixth form. The one characteristic they nearly all shared, regardless of educational background, social standing or how much money they had in the bank, is that most were really good parents who were trying to do the best they could for their kids. But even really good parents struggle and make mistakes.

> How you manage separation and divorce plays a big part in how well your children are able to manage life from this point forward.

In my coaching practice I offer practical information that helps parents identify potential pitfalls. I have found that knowing what to look for, paired with an idea of what you can do, not only helps you sidestep the pitfalls but helps you be a better parent.

So what helps you steer clear of temptation and stay committed to walking the walk? The information in this chapter will help you pinpoint the pitfalls to avoid and then recognise what you can do.

DOS AND DON'TS
Don't ignore or mismanage your feelings

As mentioned earlier, divorce is a crisis in the life of a family. When you are in crisis you may be tempted to:

- Ignore how you feel
- Overindulge certain feelings such as anger or depression
- Put your emotional needs second to everything else
- Find ways to disengage or numb your feelings

While these ways of coping may get you through the moment, none of them will be helpful to you or your children long term.

Do pay attention to your feelings

One of the most important first steps you can take for yourself and your children is to pay attention to how you feel. When you are paying attention to your feelings you are more able to:

- Deal with your feelings in a constructive way
- Recognise and support your children's feelings
- Respond rationally to situations
- Be available to your children
- Manage stress
- Be objective and avoid unnecessary conflict

Consider writing in a diary or tracking how you feel daily as a way to increase your level of emotional awareness. Although it may feel awkward at first, if you stick with it you will find the results surprisingly valuable. You can also revisit the Self-Awareness Tracking Questions in Chapter 2 as a guide. Think about helping your children find some way to track their feelings, too. For younger children, you can make a chart and give them either stickers or markers to show how they feel. Working on this exercise as a family will not only provide a good example for your kids but can also be an excellent way to start conversations with children about how they are doing.

Don't assume you know how your children are feeling

Have you ever caught yourself telling your children to put on a jacket because *you* feel cold or started to prepare them a snack because *you* are feeling hungry? Often we apply the same kind of thinking to feelings. Don't make the mistake of thinking you know how your children feel about divorce.

> What you think your children are feeling and thinking is usually different from what they are actually thinking and feeling.

A related problem many parents run into is thinking that their children have the same feelings they do about the divorce. I have frequently heard parents say things like, 'We feel really angry about what happened,' or 'She left us.' If you are using *us* or *we* language it may be an indication that you are having trouble separating your divorce experience from your children's experience.

Your children will probably have very different feelings and perceptions about how the family is changing. It is much more helpful to children if you avoid assuming you know how they feel or that they feel the same way you do.

Do practise listening to your children

Truly listening to children is perhaps one of the most difficult and challenging parenting skills to learn. While the concept seems simple, putting it into action is tough.

Listening does not involve:
- Fixing the problem for your child

- Having all the answers
- Changing your child's mind
- Telling your children how they should feel
- Telling your children how you feel

Good listening does involve:
- Giving your child your full attention
- Hearing what your child has to say
- Suspending judgement, criticism or advice
- Asking questions to make sure you understand what your child said
- Supporting your child's feelings by repeating back what you heard your child say

To get more information on how to become a better listener, please see Chapter 24.

Don't allow your children to become emotionally responsible for you

Divorce, much like a death, can leave families feeling lost and isolated. When families experience bereavement, others usually gather around to offer their support and help to manage the loss. However, when a divorce happens it often feels as if former friends and family have taken sides or disappeared, leaving you feeling as if you were on your own. Avoid falling into the trap of allowing children to fill the void by becoming your confidantes or new best friends. Your children still need you to be their parent.

Children will often worry about how parents are managing the break-up. When they see a parent having a difficult time adjusting and in need of help they naturally fall into wanting to care for Mum or Dad. It may feel comforting to have the support of your children. However, when you allow children to take on that role it puts them in the position of feeling emotionally responsible for you. To get through this you need to develop supports for yourself outside the family. For more information on how to support yourself see the tips listed in Chapter 2 and review the list of resources at the back of the book.

Likewise, at times your children may need someone to talk with besides Mum or Dad. Even when you are doing a great job of parenting, kids often worry about how their feelings will affect a parent. Having a supportive network outside the family offers children:

- Another perspective about the divorce
- The ability to separate themselves from parental feelings in a healthy way
- An opportunity to connect with others

Do create a supportive network for both yourself and your children

Spend time brainstorming where and how you are accessing support for yourself and your kids. Also, think about in which areas you are falling short of the mark. To help you get a better idea of which areas you need to work on improving, refer to the Taking Care of Yourself Inventory in Chapter 2. You also can create support for yourself and your children by:

- Minimising the number of changes your children experience after your separation
- Maintaining positive connections to extended family members on both sides
- Keeping children involved in extracurricular activities
- Developing a hobby or adult activities outside the house for yourself
- Creating structured routines and rituals in your home

Don't let your divorce take over your life

During one of my seminars a parent commented on how easy it was to tell which people took care of themselves during their divorce and which ones didn't. She said, 'The ones who don't, you can spot a mile away because all they can talk about is the divorce, how awful everything is and what is going on with their soon-to-be ex. It's almost as if they'd been infected. Pretty soon their lives start to sound like a never-ending soap opera. After a

GETTING UNSTUCK

In the early stages of separation, when your emotions are running at an all-time high, you may find it incredibly difficult to step away from divorce-related drama. In the coaching profession a technique called clearing is used for clients who become so emotionally and mentally cluttered that they can't move forward.

Imagine you are having a really bad day, everything that could possibly go wrong has, and to top it off you got another angry call from your ex. Suppose you had the chance to acknowledge your frustration and anger in a way that cleared it off your plate. Clearing allows you to get in touch with what's draining you so you can focus your energy in a more positive direction. To use this technique, follow these steps:

1. Find a friend or family member who is willing to let you vent.
2. Before you start, agree on a specified time for venting (for example, two to five minutes).
3. Make sure your support person understands he or she is only supposed to keep time and not offer comments or advice.
4. During your specified time, talk, rant or complain about anything you need to get out of your system – no holds barred.
5. Have your support person give you a one-minute and then a 30-second warning.
6. When your time is up, stop talking. Make a commitment not to talk about the issue or the divorce for the rest of the day.

If you don't have a support person available, you can also use a timer and write your thoughts down. When the time is up, put the paper away, tear it up or throw it out, and move on with your day.

while, you see everybody avoiding them like the plague because they just don't want to hear it any more. When I went through my divorce I knew I did not want to be that person.'

My guess is none of us wants to be that person. However, when you are smack bang in the middle of it, even the most level-headed person may have a tough time not getting sucked into the drama of divorce.

Do make good choices about how you spend your energy

While sharing your feelings and getting support is healthy, draining the life out of everything around you is not. Avoid self-created stress whenever possible and try to keep your life drama free by using some of the following techniques.

- **Limit the amount of time and energy you give to divorce drama**
  If you find that you are obsessing over something your ex said or thinking an issue to death, it's time to change how you are spending your energy. Make a commitment to yourself to limit the amount of time you spend talking and thinking about divorce-related issues. If you find yourself overindulging, get out a piece of paper and write down a few sentences or words, fold it up and put it in your desk drawer to deal with later.
- **Think about what you want to share with others**
  There are times when friends and family can be a great resource, and many have the best of intentions when they ask how you are doing. Think through how you want to handle questions about the divorce and what information you want to share. Remember, less is usually best. You can always decide to say more later, but you can't take back what you have already said. Try to be discreet with the information you share. You will be glad you did later.

- **Realise some days will be tougher than others**
  If something happens that stirs up strong feelings, try
  not to get caught up in the moment. Take a brief break
  and regroup. You might consider going for a walk
  around the block, getting a cup of coffee or going to
  the bathroom to take a couple of deep breaths. During
  this time, remind yourself that you have every right to
  be angry or upset. However, make a conscious effort
  not to let it take control of your day.
- **Stay connected to the positive**
  Help yourself stay focused on what's going right in
  your life. Find ways to keep your energy up at home
  and work by surrounding yourself with things that help
  you feel good. Think about posting quotes that inspire,
  putting up favourite pictures of your children where
  you will see them often, or playing music you really like
  when you need a pick-me-up. You'll be surprised at
  what a difference it can make!

> Some days will be tougher than others. Instead of waiting until it floods
> to build a boat, plan how you want to sail the sea.

Don't expect to get what you never got

Sandy was at her wits' end with her ex, John. 'If he would just
listen to me when I try to tell him what's going on with the kids
or just talk to me, things would be so much easier.'

I asked Sandy how much she and John talked before the
divorce, and she quickly replied, 'John has never talked to me
about the kids. I always handled things on my own, even when
we were married.'

'So,' I asked, 'what's changed?'

Sandy quickly realised nothing had changed except that she
and John were no longer married. She had fallen into the trap of

trying to get something from her ex that she never got in the marriage. Life coach Cheryl Richardson refers to this kind of thinking as 'going to the DIY store for milk'. No matter how many trips you make, you still won't get what you need. Unfortunately, when couples split up they make the mistake of trying to resolve past issues or get what they never got. This usually spawns a series of attempts to control or change the other parent, which is not only frustrating but almost always impossible.

CALL TO ACTION

Write down one thing you will do differently this week that will have a positive effect on your children. Complete the following statements to put your commitment into action:

- This week I will make a difference for my children by ...
- Three things I can do to make this happen are ...

The key to managing divorce with integrity starts with you. Make a commitment to honour your children's needs above all else, not just with words but also with action.

Do change your expectations

Instead of focusing on trying to change or control your ex, put energy into changing your expectations. While you have little to no control over what your ex says or the choices he or she makes, you can control how you choose to handle situations or issues.

For example, if your ex isn't interested in talking about how the kids are handling the divorce, stop trying to force the issue. Just because one parent isn't willing to understand how the children feel doesn't mean you can't. Rather than continue to feel frustrated, focus on what you can do to make things better for your children. When issues come up, ask yourself how you would handle the situation if the outcome didn't depend on the other parent.

PART TWO

How Children Are Affected by Divorce

7.
FACTORS THAT AFFECT HOW CHILDREN HANDLE DIVORCE

*Live so that when your children think of fairness
and integrity, they think of you.*
– H. Jackson Brown Jr

*Mike said he just didn't understand what to do. His 11-year-old
daughter, Kelly, was a roll-with-the-punches kind of kid. She rarely
talked about her feelings and often commented that she didn't understand what all the fuss was about. On the surface Kelly seemed fine
with her parents' decision to divorce. While she wished they had made
a different choice, she told her father sometimes you just have to deal
with things and move on. Her 14-year-old sister, Brenda, however,
was another matter entirely. Brenda was devastated by the divorce.
She was frequently moody and cried often. She talked about her feelings in detail with her father on a regular basis. While Mike was
concerned that Brenda was taking the divorce so hard, he felt reassured that at least she was talking about it. 'I don't know which one
to be more worried about, Brenda, the one who is sad and talks to
me, or Kelly, the one who seems okay, but never talks about it.'*

Much like Mike, you too may be wondering what's normal and
what you should be worried about. The truth is no two children
will go through divorce in exactly the same way. What seems okay
for one child may be a warning sign for another. While there are
similar stages that every child will experience, how each one goes
through them and to what degree they are affected will vary. As
in Mike's case, it is also quite common for children in the same

family to have very different divorce experiences. If you have more than one child, you may have your work cut out for you. To recognise where your children are in the process and how they are handling it, you need to have an understanding of the various factors that influence adjustment.

FACTORS THAT AFFECT HOW CHILDREN MANAGE AND ADJUST TO DIVORCE

In general, your children's reactions can be influenced by a number of factors. Some of those factors you can shape and some you cannot.

Factors you may have some influence or control over:
- How you are managing the divorce
- Amount of tension and conflict between yourself and the other parent
- How and what your children are told about the separation or divorce
- The number of changes your children experience while the divorce is happening
- The level of support your children receive from outside the family

Factors you can't control but need to be aware of:
- Age and level of development of your child
- Personality of your child
- Gender of your child
- How the other parent is handling the divorce

All of these factors have some bearing on your child's overall adjustment. Yet time and time again professionals and researchers have identified the two most influential factors as:

- How parents handle the divorce process for themselves
- How Mum and Dad interact with each other after the break-up

More about these factors can be found in Chapters 1 and 16.

EMOTIONAL STAGES OF LOSS FOR CHILDREN

Has this ever happened to you? Your child comes home from school, and you innocently ask, 'How was your day?' Your child responds with the typical one-word answer: 'Fine.' Yet the look on his face and the tone of his voice suggest that his day was anything but fine. Curious, you decide to dig a little deeper. 'Is something bothering you?' To which your child quickly responds in a rather put-out tone, 'No, nothing's bothering me. Why do you have to ask so many questions?' If your house is anything like mine, these kinds of conversations usually take a quick nosedive. The downward spiral typically results in either a stern reminder about the need to be respectful or, in more serious cases, somebody getting sent to his room. However, if you remain patient and persistent, with a certain amount of luck the walls usually crumble, and your child ends up confessing that he has had the worst day ever.

Children don't always use words to tell you how they feel. Often kids *show* us how they feel. Sometimes the slam of the door, the way they roll their eyes when you ask them a question or the expression on their face tells you more than what they have said. When divorce and separation enter the scene, you may find that when your children do tell you with words the words sometimes don't always match up with their behaviour. To make things more complicated, you can't necessarily tell what is related to divorce and what is just normal developmental kid stuff. While it is important to hear what children are saying with their words, it is also important to know what kinds of behaviour to look for. Thus this chapter reviews the process of grief and loss, looking at both what kids might say and what kids might do when they are struggling with these stages. How these stages affect you as a parent are addressed in Chapter 3.

Denial

Denial is one way children try to protect themselves from events in life they cannot change or control. When faced with the possibility of separation or divorce your children might choose to deal with the issue by not acknowledging it as real. You may find that your children will either flatly refuse to talk about divorce or simply change the subject every time you bring it up. They may give the outward appearance that Mum and Dad's splitting up is really no big deal and casually talk about how other kids in their school have divorced parents too. Older children might use physical distance as a way to disengage or separate themselves from the reality of divorce. When this happens, children spend more time hanging out with friends or may keep themselves busier than usual with activities. This helps them avoid the reality of what is going on at home between Mum and Dad.

In some situations when parents choose to separate, one parent remains in the family home while the other parent sets up a new place to live. For some children, spending time in the other household may be a painful reminder that things have changed permanently. If your children are not ready to accept that reality, they may avoid or minimise time in their other parent's home. When this happens, you can easily make the mistake of thinking your child is refusing time in the other home because the other parent did something wrong. For example, let's say Johnny doesn't want to see Mum in her new apartment. Dad might assume it is because Johnny is angry with Mum or perhaps because Mum's apartment isn't Johnny's real home. Mum, in turn, may think that Johnny's reluctance is Dad's fault because he is not supporting her relationship. From her point of view she may believe Dad is deliberately sabotaging her time with Johnny to get even with her for leaving. While there are lots of reasons children might resist spending time with their other parent, be careful not to jump to conclusions.

RECOGNISING DENIAL IN YOUR CHILDREN

When children are in denial they may:
- Refuse to talk about the divorce
- Hang on to the hope that Mum and Dad will work things out
- Change the subject when you talk about separation or divorce
- Choose not to tell others (friends, teachers, other family members)
- Make up excuses to explain changes in the family
- Talk about the family as if nothing had changed
- Act as if everything is okay or say it's no big deal
- Arrange or plan events that involve both parents being together
- Resist spending time in the other parent's home because it makes the situation more real for them
- Create distractions or keep themselves busy so they don't have to deal with what has happened (getting involved in activities, spending more time with friends, spending more time away from the family, spending time alone watching TV or playing video games)

What can you do?

Understand your children will need time to accept that the family has changed. **In the early stages, do your best to keep life in your home predictable by maintaining regular routines and normal activities.** This means making sure your children go to bed at a reasonable hour, having regular meals as a family, providing children with opportunities to be active, and maintaining their ongoing access to supportive people outside of the family. Consistency in their day-to-day lives will also help your children feel more secure while they adjust to the separation. If possible, avoid making significant changes such as moving, changing schools or withdrawing your children from extracurricular activities that they enjoy. Divorce is a tremendous loss for a child and involves lots of changes. Don't give them more to deal with than necessary.

Also, make sure your children are having consistent and regular contact with their other parent. Even though you may have strong feelings about the situation, it is very important to encourage your child's relationship with your ex. Children need the security of knowing that while you may be divorcing each other, neither of you is divorcing them. Keep in mind that even though you may tell your children with words that you will always love them, it is imperative that you back it up with action. This means that you offer children reassurance by doing things like giving them hugs, spending quality time with them or making a point to check in regularly to see how they're doing.

Anger

No doubt about it, anger is probably one of the most challenging and difficult stages to cope with for parents. While dealing with angry children is certainly no fun, keep in mind it is an expected and normal part of their grieving process. Most important, when your children are expressing their anger and frustration make sure you do not:

- React to your child's anger by becoming angry yourself
  (Try not to fight fire with fire and respond by shouting, arguing, or threatening.)
- Allow the situation to become a power struggle
  (Try not to become focused on enforcing a rule instead of acknowledging the feeling by saying something like, 'I don't care what you do at your Mum's house. You will go to bed now because I said so!')

- Inappropriately use humour by belittling or putting down your child's feelings (Try not to say something like, 'Only babies whine and throw temper tantrums when they don't get their way. Are you a little baby?')
- Ignore or dismiss how your child feels (Try not to say something like, 'Stop carrying on and do what I say.')
- Punish your child for feeling angry (Try not to become focused on punishing the behaviour without addressing the feeling by saying something like, 'You will not speak to me that way,' 'I don't want to hear another word from you,' or 'Go to your room, you're grounded.')

RECOGNISING ANGER IN YOUR CHILDREN

When children are feeling angry they may:
- Break rules or test limits
- Say 'I hate you' or 'I want to live with my other parent.'
- Blame one or both parents for the divorce
- Throw temper tantrums or start biting, hitting, kicking or breaking things (especially toddlers and primary-school-age children)
- Fight with siblings
- Become physically aggressive at home or in school (pushing, shoving or threatening to hit)
- Overreact to situations (become intensely angry over minor issues)
- Have frequent emotional outbursts (shouting, screaming or being openly rude to others)
- Withdraw or emotionally shut down (go to their room to be alone, become silent or refuse to talk)
- Engage in risky or dangerous behaviours, such as drinking and driving, using drugs or engaging in sexual activity (especially teens and pre-adolescents)

The upset that children feel is often increased by the uncertainty divorce brings to their lives. Often they may not understand or even be able to identify how they are feeling. Instead they are reacting to their feelings of frustration. After all, life as your children have known it is over. Virtually everything has changed and they can't do anything about it.

It's also important for you to realise that when children are feeling angry they typically direct their anger towards the parent they feel safest with. When your children get angry with you, rest assured you are doing a marvellous job as a parent. Children need to know that, no matter how upset, frustrated or angry they get, you will always love them. It's when children know they can trust you that they feel safe enough to express their feelings.

This issue of trust and anger can create additional complications for parents, especially if one parent is getting stuck dealing with most of the anger and upset from the children. More information about what you can do when your children are playing up at one house but not the other is offered in Chapter 25.

What can you do?

Even though your children will have to make lots of adjustments, they still need to know that life will be okay. One way you can reassure your children is by continuing to be a family. An important part of being a family is not just providing children with love and understanding but also having respect, guidelines, structure and discipline. Unfortunately, this is when the *divorce guilt syndrome* kicks in for most of us. It goes something like this: Imagine you feel incredibly guilty about the hurt and pain your children are feeling because of the divorce. Evie is having emotional meltdowns and temper tantrums around the clock. Harry decides to take advantage of Evie's meltdown and won't turn off the TV to do his homework. Next thing you know, it's nine o'clock, supper's not ready yet and it's already past their bedtime. When this happens, you find yourself threatening the children within an inch of their lives: 'If you two don't knock it off, I am going to ground you for a month.' Of course, this is about the 20th time today you have told the children this.

During this time you might be tempted to back off from disciplining or staying consistent with your children. After all, aren't they hurting enough already? Do you really need to send Evie to bed because she lay in the middle of the floor and screamed for 20 minutes? Should you take away Harry's mobile phone because he failed his maths exam? In a word, yes. While you may be tempted to go easy on the kids during this time, children need both love and limits. Especially when they are feeling angry. Yes, they need you to give them love and support. ('I can understand why you would feel angry about this,' 'I am sorry this is so hard for you.') However, they also need to know you will continue to be a family, and that means providing discipline and structure. ('While I understand you are angry, it is not okay to hit your sister. If you hit your sister you will be grounded.')

Bargaining

Bargaining is a time when children put their energy and effort into trying to save the family. While parents experience bargaining as having second thoughts, children usually wish for things to go back to the way they were. It is important to know that even when life improves for children after parents separate, the wish that things could have been different between Mum and Dad does not go away easily.

Almost all children feel some level of responsibility for things not working out between Mum and Dad. While you may tell them with words they are not to blame, your children may not believe you. Actually, if you think about the situation from your child's perspective it's easy to see why they feel responsible. When you and your ex have a row, what are you usually arguing about? If you are like most parents, your answer is the kids, from what time they are picked up on Sunday to who gets to open presents with them on Christmas morning. Regardless of the reason, from your children's point of view, if all the rows are about them or have to do with them, then it must be their fault. This is another reason parent conflict is so incredibly damaging to children. When parents engage in open warfare with one another, children naturally feel they are to blame.

RECOGNISING BARGAINING IN YOUR CHILDREN

When children are bargaining, they may:

- Promise to be good, behave better or follow all the rules
- Invent or even create health problems (stomach ache, headache) so parents will have to care for them
- Create a crisis or an emergency situation so parents will have to work together
- Ask or expect parents to hug or kiss at an exchange (especially young children)
- Plan special events or reasons for parents to have contact with one another
- Focus on becoming the perfect child so parents don't have anything to fight about
- Become a discipline problem at school or home so that parents have a common cause (get parents to focus on the child rather than each other)
- Feel responsible or blame themselves for the separation or divorce

What can you do?

One of the most effective ways to help your children is to minimise conflict with the other parent. Again, this is one of those areas where it is much easier to say it than to do it. However, for your children to resolve their feelings of guilt and responsibility you need to find some other way to manage your differences.

Consistently reinforce for your children that your decision to divorce had nothing to do with them. Your children will also need to hear that no matter how much they wish or hope they cannot fix or change what has happened in the family. The bottom line is that divorce is never a child's fault.

Depression

When children realise that they can't change or fix what has happened in the family, the loss and sadness they feel can become very strong. As with the other stages, the degree and intensity of children's sadness will depend on a number of factors. For more detailed information about helping children successfully cope with depression, be sure to read Chapter 26.

Much like anger, depression is often a hard stage for parents to deal with. While it is incredibly painful to see your child being upset or hurt, the sadness they feel over the loss of the family needs to be recognised and given value. Although it is natural to want to fix or shield your children from hurtful situations, don't avoid your children's sadness by:

- Dismissing the feeling (Try not to say something like: 'Oh, you're just tired. Why don't you get some sleep, that'll make you feel better.')
- Making it better (Try not to say something like: 'Hey, we don't need to sit around the house and be sad. How about we go out to eat and see a film?')
- Removing the problem (Try not to say something like: 'If Dad's phone calls make you feel sad then maybe he should stop calling you every night.')
- Explaining the feeling away (Try not to say something like: 'Oh, you know, sometimes things just happen.')
- Ignoring it (Try not to say something like: 'Everything will be better tomorrow.')
- Denying or shaming the feeling (Try not to say something like: 'Come on, you're too big to cry about this.')
- Changing the subject (Try not to say something like: 'Yes, I know that was upsetting for you. But wouldn't you rather talk about something happy like what we're going to do this weekend?')

RECOGNISING DEPRESSION IN YOUR CHILDREN

When children are feeling intensely sad they may:

- Start having problems in school (lower grades, easily distracted, lack of motivation or interest)
- Become withdrawn (ask to be left alone, or choose to do things separately from others)
- Pull back from important relationships with family and friends
- Be unable to stay focused or concentrate
- Seem tense, on edge or irritable
- Not have an interest in activities they used to really enjoy
- Appear to be consistently sad day after day
- Have trouble sleeping at night
- Feel tired, lack energy or want to sleep all the time
- Become easily upset or frequently tearful
- Be disinterested in food (skipping meals, no appetite, noticeable weight loss)
- Use food as a way to deal with feelings (eating comfort foods when upset, noticeable weight gain)
- Say things like 'I wish I had never been born' or 'Maybe life would be better without me around.'

Let your children know they have a right to feel sad. Make sure that you are also dealing with your own sadness in a healthy and responsible way. If not, you run the risk of confusing your emotional needs with the needs of your children. Of course, this does not mean you should hide your feelings from your children. Sharing your upset or sadness can be an opportunity to help kids understand that it's okay to be sad. Children learn by example. Even though divorce is difficult, use it as a way to teach your children how to cope with tough situations.

WHEN CHILDREN SAY THINGS LIKE 'I WISH I HAD NEVER BEEN BORN'

Any statement made by a child that indicates a wish to die, disappear or no longer exist needs to be taken very seriously. Don't wait for your child to act on these feelings. Seek help immediately. While your child may not have the intention of permanently hurting himself or herself, children are often impulsive and lack good decision-making skills, especially when they are depressed. When children make statements about taking themselves out of the picture, they are sending you a clear message: They need your help. Further information about seeking professional intervention can be found in Chapter 27.

What can you do?

In addition to telling children it is okay to be sad, help them find appropriate ways to deal with the sadness. Most children and parents find that as time passes the sadness related to divorce begins to decrease. However, if feelings or symptoms related to depression seem to be getting worse for either you or your children, seek out professional help. In most circumstances a good first step would be making an appointment with your GP and gaining some advice about how to proceed.

Typically professional intervention is recommended if you or your children are:

- Experiencing multiple symptoms for extended periods of time (having two or more symptoms for most of the day, nearly every day for several weeks)
- Finding symptoms interfere with day-to-day functioning (can't get out of bed in the morning, are unable to focus or concentrate, can't accomplish simple daily tasks, have significant change in grades or school performance)

- Feeling an overwhelming sense of hopelessness (don't care about anything; view everything as bad, negative or never getting better)
- Having thoughts of suicide, self-harming or just going away (making statements like 'Life would be so much better if I would just disappear')

Acceptance

For the vast majority of families, after the dust settles and some time has passed life begins to feel normal again. Children begin adjusting to their schedules between homes, and transitions become smoother. You may also notice that you now have some emotional distance from issues that used to set you on edge. Often parents are able to talk things through more easily and can be more flexible with one another regarding arrangements. Essentially, life settles down for you and your children.

RECOGNISING ACCEPTANCE IN YOUR CHILDREN

When your children have reached acceptance they may:
- Feel more comfortable with transitions between homes
- Be able to see benefits to Mum and Dad being happier
- Do a better job of managing their feelings
- Have the ability to separate themselves from their parent's problems
- Feel more emotionally balanced
- Have less intense feelings about the divorce
- Be able to acknowledge both the positive and negative aspects of divorce
- Re-engage in activities or develop new interests. Feel a sense of hope and have a more positive view of their future

Don't forget that separation and divorce are lifelong processes that do not end once you receive your final orders from the family court. As life changes for you and your children, expect that old feelings or new issues will come up. Usually when feelings resurface, they will be less intense, and you as well as your children will be better at managing them.

8.
INFANTS (NEWBORN TO 18 MONTHS)

Children are like wet cement. Whatever falls on them makes an impression. – Haim Ginott

If you have very young children you may be wondering how your decision to divorce will affect your little one. After all, it seems as if it would be easier for her to adjust to growing up without memories of what life was like before and knowing only a mum's house and a dad's house. Instead of thinking of your child's adjustment as easier, think of it as different. While your baby will not adapt the same way an older child might, there will be issues regarding how life changes that you will need to consider.

DEVELOPMENTAL ISSUES FOR INFANTS
Bonding

One of the most important developmental milestones for infants is developing a secure attachment to Mum and Dad. This important connection takes place through simple daily activities, such as feeding your baby, playing with him, changing nappies and comforting him when he is upset. Meeting those needs consistently also helps your baby develop a sense of security and trust in the world. Of course, meeting this developmental need becomes much more challenging when parents live in different homes.

Historically, there has been a considerable amount of debate among professionals about how to structure parenting time between households for infants. Across the board, however, most professionals agree that infants need two things from Mum and Dad.

▶ Frequent and consistent contact with both parents

Unlike older children, infants don't have the ability to remember experiences or retain memories. Therefore ongoing consistent contact with both Mum and Dad is essential. Be creative in how you arrange time for your child between households. Since children do not benefit from long periods of time away from either parent, consider developing a plan that allows for shorter, more frequent periods of time with each parent. Most important, remember that the schedule needs to be focused on your child's needs. While seeing your ex may not be at the top of your Things-I-Like-to-Do list, it is important for your baby to have regular contact with each parent. Additional information on developing a child-focused parenting schedule can be found in Chapter 18.

▶ Quality time with parents

Although spending time with your little one is important, remember *how* you are spending that time with your baby matters too. Babies build trust in the world by having their needs met and by parents responding to those needs in a consistent, loving way. Although you may feel overwhelmed or short-handed at times, make sure when your child is with you the time is well spent. This may mean restructuring your priorities. Time with your baby will be more beneficial and meaningful when you give him blocks of one-on-one time. Consider putting off doing the laundry, avoiding phone calls and forgetting your daily chores for at least a couple of hours each day. During this time give your child your undivided attention and engage him in positive activities, such as reading a book, playing a simple game, rocking or singing or talking to him in a calm, soothing way.

Quality time and quantity time

How to schedule time between homes for infants can create a considerable amount of tension between parents. During your separation you most likely have experienced a decrease in either the quality or the quantity of time you once had with your baby. If you are usually the on-duty parent (the parent who is the primary caretaker) for your baby, then you may often feel frustrated about not having enough time to enjoy him. In the early stages of divorce it is normal to feel very overwhelmed by the care of your little one. Breaks from parenting responsibilities and time for yourself are usually hard to come by when you are the only parent in your home. Realise stress can be a significant influencer in how you respond to your baby, and stress significantly influences how your baby responds to you.

If you are the parent who has less time with your baby, your challenge is different. Because you have more time to yourself you may find giving your baby all of your attention when he is with you much easier. However, you may struggle with not having the day-to-day contact with your infant. Because the amount of time you have is now limited, you may need to focus on being creative about arranging a consistent schedule. Regardless of which role you are in, be aware that both quality and quantity are important factors in how your baby develops.

MANAGING YOUR BABY'S STRESS

Unlike older children, your baby will not be able to use words to let you know how she feels. When she is feeling stressed or anxious, it will show through her behaviour. Your baby may go through periods where she is especially cranky or perhaps fusses every time you put her down. Sometimes it may be difficult to know the exact cause of your child's discomfort. Just because your baby is not sleeping well doesn't mean she automatically has divorce distress. However, keep in mind that infants are extremely sensitive to parental stress. So if your baby is having a tough day, remember to do a quick check with yourself and take note of what is going on around you. Ask yourself, 'How am I feeling?' or perhaps notice the level of unrest in your baby's current environment. Once you have identified what needs to change, make an effort to help your baby calm down by engaging with her in a more soothing way. This may mean taking a deep breath and slowing things down or it could be as simple as taking 10 minutes to sit quietly with your child.

Your infant's needs

▶ Regular and frequent contact with both parents

Make every effort to provide your little one with frequent and consistent contact between her two homes. This does not mean that every family should attempt a 50–50 split in time between homes. Schedules need to be based around the needs of your child. It does mean, however, that regardless of how you feel about one another your child deserves time with both of you.

Striking a good balance between quality and quantity is much easier when parents work together.

▶ Opportunity to establish a trusting relationship with each parent

Children need to feel emotionally, psychologically and physically connected to both parents. As mentioned earlier, this connection occurs through children having consistent contact and positive interactions with Mum and Dad. While you may not be able to control how time is spent between the two homes, you can control how you spend the time you have. Be responsive to your child's needs and make time to give her your full attention when she is with you.

▶ A stable and predictable environment

Ideally it is best for your baby if you and the other parent can agree on a similar structure and routine between your two homes. This means having the same daily routines, such as consistent bedtimes and feeding and napping schedules. Also it is helpful if both homes have the ability to meet your child's physical needs (toys, favourite blankets, clothes, nappies, foods she likes, and so on). If possible, consider having two sets of everyday items used to care for your baby, such as car seats, buggies, high chairs and extra clothes.

▶ Minimise drastic changes in your baby's world

Young children usually respond to significant changes in their environment with anxiety. While there will be obvious differences in the physical environments between the two homes, you can set a similar tone. Do what you can to make your home a calm, nurturing environment.

- Plan handovers from one home to the other
- Keep routines for your baby consistent
- Avoid rushing around or packing too much into your day

▶ Shield your baby from parental stress and tension

Be aware that even though your little one does not understand what is going on she will respond to your feelings of upset and frustration. Although it can be difficult to detach yourself from the stress of your separation, make sure you are paying attention to how you are handling your feelings. Your baby also needs to be shielded from arguments and fighting between you and the other parent. Although she cannot process the words you say, she can and will respond to your tone, volume and pattern of speech.

IDEAS FOR PARENTING YOUR INFANT

When you are frustrated, stressed out, upset and emotionally over-whelmed it is very easy to lose sight of how you are interacting with your children. During this time make sure you are finding ways to positively connect with your baby and strengthen your relationship with him.

- Schedule time to play with your child throughout the day when they are with you
- Be sure to offer lots of eye contact and smiles
- Hug and cuddle your child frequently
- Read, sing or talk with your little one often

WHAT TO LOOK FOR	HOW TO HELP
Problems sleeping (e.g. restless, waking frequently throughout the night, doesn't go to sleep easily)	Give children regular and consistent contact with both parents.
Overly fussy or cranky	Maintain routines and schedules.
Changes in appetite or digestion problems (upset stomach)	Manage transitions in a positive way. (e.g. avoid rushing around, keep household calm before other parent arrives, don't argue or fight).
Crying frequently, difficult to settle down	Minimise exposure to parent tension.
Clingy (doesn't want to be put down)	Help child develop trust in their environment.

9.
TODDLERS (18 MONTHS TO TWO YEARS)

The problem with being a parent is that by the time you are experienced you are usually unemployed.
– Anonymous

As your baby grows into toddlerhood, the world begins to change. Not just for her but for you too. Gone are those days when you could set her down somewhere and she would stay where you left her. During this stage everything is about action, and your child is on the move. Her insatiable curiosity takes her places you never thought she could go and helps her find things you never thought she could reach. Now that your child is no longer completely dependent on you, she starts seeing herself as separate. Along with this, your toddler also begins to assert some of her newfound independence by expressing likes and dislikes and by using wonderful words like *no* and *mine*.

Of course, for your child to confidently explore the world she needs to feel safe. Understand that when you and your partner separate, life changes. The world may not seem as safe to your budding two-year-old. To ensure that your child's development is not compromised, you will need to focus your energy on providing her with consistency on a number of different levels.

DEVELOPMENTAL ISSUES FOR TODDLERS
Feelings of security

Even though your toddler has moved out of infancy, feeling secure is still a major issue. Much like babies, this sense of security is reinforced through day-to-day structure and routines. Across the board, young children function best when they know what to expect. However, divorce creates lots of changes for children. Life may no longer be predictable or consistent. You might not even know yourself how life will be from one day to the next. Now add to the mix two separate households with possibly different rules, different schedules and different surroundings. It's not hard to understand why your small explorer might feel a little insecure, uncertain and anxious.

What can you do?
Ideally it is best for toddlers if parents can work cooperatively to establish a similar structure between their two homes. However, for some parents, especially in the early stages of separation, agreeing on rules and structure is about as easy as herding cats. If maintaining the same structure is not possible, focus on making your home as predictable, safe and nurturing as you can. Children can still make a successful transition between homes if they know what to expect when they are with you. Make rules, schedules and routines consistent and simple. Also, avoid over-stimulating your toddler by packing too many activities into the day. Work towards providing your child with a calm, predictable home environment.

Anxiety over new experiences

It is normal for a child in this age range to feel anxious when facing a new experience, like having a different baby-sitter, meeting an unfamiliar adult or changing childcare centres. When parents separate, it is easy to forget that the transition between homes is a new experience too. Let's say, for example, two-year-old Mia doesn't go to Daddy when he comes to Mum's house to pick her up. Maybe Mia becomes fussy and starts crying for Mum. Instead of Mia's reaction being viewed as a normal developmental issue, Mum may think Mia doesn't want to see Dad. Maybe Mum even thinks Dad is doing something wrong or that Mia just needs the stability of one 'real' home. Dad, on the other hand, may see Mia's reluctance as Mum's fault. He may view Mum as too clingy or overprotective. Once Mia is with him she seems just fine. In his eyes Mum is the one making the transition difficult for Mia.

Be careful not to jump to conclusions. Young children need security and stability, therefore they need help adjusting to big changes. While in this scenario dad is a familiar person whom Mia loves, the circumstances around her seeing Dad are different. He is no longer someone she gets to hug every day or the person who tucks her in every night. Now he picks her up, and they leave without Mummy. Everything is different to this two-year-old. It is also quite possible that if there is tension between Mum and Dad Mia's anxiety level may well be off the chart.

What can you do?

It is not uncommon for a two-year-old to cry about leaving one parent and 10 minutes later act like nothing ever happened. As a parent you feel gutted when your child cries for you, but by feeding into it you may be making the situation worse for your child. On the other hand, it's equally difficult to be understanding when your child doesn't want to go with you. Each situation is a potential hotbed for some serious finger pointing between parents. Before assuming there is a problem with the other parent, think about paying attention to what is going on for your child.

If your child is having difficulty transitioning from one parent to the other, pay attention to:

- Your child's environment (What is different or perhaps adding to the difficulty?)
- Your feelings about the other parent (Do you feel angry, pressured, upset or sad?)

- Your feelings about the transition (Are you worried, feeling sad about your child leaving, or already missing him?)
- The tone in the room (Is there unspoken tension in the room that is affecting your child? How are you and the other parent behaving towards each other?). What happened right before the other parent showed up?)

Once you have assessed what is going on around your child, consider how you could make the transition easier for him. For example, if handovers seem more difficult at one home than the other, think about choosing a more neutral location, such as a park, local playground or relative's home. If you are having a difficult time saying goodbye to your child, then think about managing your feelings differently. Your toddler needs you to positively support his time with the other parent.

EXPRESSING FEELINGS

Although toddlers are beginning to learn how to talk, they still communicate their feelings through actions. This is the stage during which you will see your toddler use hitting, kicking, biting, spitting and temper tantrums to express her anger, upset or stress. It usually takes every ounce of patience you have not to come completely unglued when your two-year-old is having a major meltdown in the middle of the supermarket. Remember, however, developmentally she doesn't have the ability to understand or manage her feelings. It is just the way toddlers are wired. They feel, and then they act.

What can you do?
When young children are acting out their feelings, take the following steps.

1. Stay calm and don't react to the behaviour. ('Throwing a temper tantrum in a shop is not okay. You need to use your words to tell me what's wrong.')
2. Address the problem and identify the feeling. ('You look like you are really angry that you can't have a biscuit right now.')
3. Set limits. ('If you don't get up, we will leave the shop.')
4. Enforce the limit. ('Since you are still behaving this way, we will have to go to the car.')
5. Be consistent. (Make sure you leave the shop.)

LETTING YOUR CHILD SLEEP WITH YOU

It's late, you're exhausted, and your little one is restless. Even though you have tucked him in for the millionth time, he just won't settle in. Desperate for sleep, you finally give up and put him in bed with you. Sounds familiar? It is understandable why parents put their children in bed with them from time to time, but be careful not to make it a habit, especially during your separation. Even though this is a difficult time for your child, he still needs to work on being independent.

Letting children sleep with you on a regular basis:

- Sends the subtle message that things are not okay
- Keeps children from developing skills that lead to self-competency
- Makes transitioning from one house to the other more difficult
- Can keep parents from dealing with their own sense of loneliness

Although it may seem like you are soothing your child's anxiety by allowing him to sleep in your bed, it is only putting a bandage on the situation. Yes, it's normal to want to comfort your child when he is upset, and sometimes it may be the most sensible thing to do. However, avoid using it as the only way to deal with nighttime problems. Your child will gain more long-term benefits if you work towards helping him sleep in his own bed.

Consistency is especially important. In the scenario just presented you can choose to return to the shop another day or, once your toddler calms down, you can choose to go back in. Even though it may be inconvenient, stay consistent. If you stand your ground, your toddler will quickly learn this tactic doesn't work.

Don't forget this is a time when children need you not only to love them but also to set appropriate limits and provide discipline.

IDEAS FOR PARENTING YOUR TODDLER

▶ Give lots of cuddles and physical affection

Young children need lots of physical affection, especially when they are feeling overwhelmed and anxious. Remind your child how special he is by making sure you are giving him plenty of hugs throughout the day.

▶ Encourage curiosity but avoid overstimulation

Toddlers are naturally very curious and want to explore their surroundings. Set up each household as a child-friendly, safe place. Consider having two sets of toys and belongings to help your child feel connected to both homes. When you are not able to see your child every day it can be tempting to pack lots of activities into your time with him. Be careful not to overdo it. Remember that young children do best when they have a structured and pre-dictable environment. Make sure you balance your child's day with naps and quiet time to play.

▶ Help children maintain positive connections

You have probably already discovered that your child has a pref-erence for certain objects over others, like stuffed animals, special toys or books. Often those objects can be a source of security and comfort for your child, especially when things are changing. Be creative about how you help your toddler feel connected to the important people in his life. Consider creating a soft child-friendly photo book that has pictures of important people (both parents, grandparents, extended family members, friends, and so on). This gives your child visual images to connect with when he can't see the people he loves. It also provides an opportunity to reinforce a two-home concept.

WHAT TO LOOK FOR	HOW TO HELP
Acting out frustration and stress through behaviour (e.g. hitting, kicking, biting, temper tantrums)	Set appropriate limits and provide discipline when necessary.
Becoming clingy and anxious	Make life predictable (e.g. regular bedtime and daily routines).
Sleeping problems (doesn't want to go to bed or wants to sleep with parent)	Create a child-safe home with both parents.
Difficulty leaving one or both parents	Maintain regular contact with both parents.
Problems transitioning between homes	Offer reassurance of love through physical affection and giving children your undivided time and attention.

10.
PRESCHOOLERS
(THREE TO FIVE YEARS)

The real menace about dealing with a five-year-old is that in no time at all you begin to sound like a five-year-old. – Jean Kerr

During the preschool years your child starts developing ideas about who she is. Of course, the most important influences on your child's identity are clearly Mum and Dad. In fact, children view themselves as half Mum and half Dad. It is in this age group that this kind of thinking becomes most obvious.

In addition, preschoolers have a very narrow perception of the world. They think that everything happening around them is in some way related to something they thought, felt, said or did. Basically, children at this age are under the impression that they are the centre of the universe and everything revolves around Planet Me. This concept is often referred to as *magical thinking*. During the process of divorce, magical thinking may contribute to your preschooler's perception that she is somehow responsible for problems between you and the other parent. While you probably won't be able to reason your way around her I-am-master-of-the-universe theory, you can begin to introduce the concept that divorce is not something she can control or fix.

To help your child develop a positive self-image, let's take a look at some of the key developmental issues that may influence your preschooler's self-esteem.

DEVELOPMENTAL ISSUES FOR PRESCHOOLERS
Image of self

The biggest question on your preschooler's rapidly growing mind is: what does it mean to be me? To answer this question, children start paying close attention to Mum and Dad. They begin to notice what parents like and dislike, what parents do and don't do. Most important, your child wants to figure out how he is like Mum and what about him is like Dad. Essentially, your child begins identifying individual characteristics of his parents as a way of defining who he is and who he wants to be. You may have already heard your child say things like, 'Mummy and I both have blue eyes,' or 'When I grow up, I want to build things like Daddy.'

Identifying with parents in a positive way is a really important developmental need for kids. When Mum and Dad are in a loving, happy relationship, kids usually get loads of positive feedback about how they are like their parents. Think about it. Haven't you ever lovingly told your child, 'Oh you have your mother's smile,' or 'You wrinkle your nose just like Dad when you laugh.' Unfortunately, when parents are not happy with each other the tone of those comparisons can change considerably.

Imagine five-year-old Charlotte is playing in her room and has made quite a mess. Toys and clothes are scattered everywhere. Enter Mum. When she sees Charlotte's mess she immediately becomes annoyed. She cleaned Charlotte's room just yesterday. Suppose Mum responds by saying, 'Charlotte, look at what you've done to your room. Why do you have to be so messy? Honestly, you are just like your father. He never cleaned up after himself either.' What do you think that means to Charlotte? Or suppose Dad and Thomas are sitting down to eat dinner. Thomas begins talking about what a great cook Mum is and how much he likes to eat her chicken casserole. Dad ignores Thomas's nice comments about Mum and says, 'I never liked Mum's chicken casserole.' While neither of these parents has directly attacked their children's self-esteem, over time those subtle negative messages begin to take their toll.

Further, your child's relationship with each parent forms the building blocks of future social skills and gender identity. That means that your child's image of you and the other parent has the ability to shape how he interacts with other people. Your preschooler is also in the process of figuring out what it means to be a boy and what it means to be a girl. If you have ever talked to a five-year-old about the subject of boyness or girlness, no doubt you have discovered he already has some pretty strong opinions on the matter. Understand that your child's need to positively identify with a parent isn't just about boys needing to relate to Dad or girls needing to relate to Mum. Developmentally your child needs to positively identify with both parents. This is one of the many reasons it is important to remain positive about your ex in front of your children.

What can you do?

While you may feel less than enthusiastic about each other, **your children have every right to feel good about both of their parents**. Whenever possible, support your children's self-image by saying positive things about the other parent. Of course, I would not recommend being insincere and saying something you truly don't believe or feel about the other parent. If you can't think of anything positive to say, best to follow the old rule: 'If you can't say something nice, then don't say anything at all.'

Let's go back to our example of Mum and the messy room. Probably it would have been best for Mum to drop the negative comparison with Dad and simply tell Charlotte to clean up her mess. Dad, on the other hand, could have responded to Thomas by saying something like, 'You must be really proud of Mum. I can tell you really like the way she cooks.' Now you might be asking yourself, 'Okay, but isn't that being insincere? What if Dad doesn't think Mum is a good cook, and he really doesn't like her chicken casserole?' Notice, however, that Dad didn't share his opinion about the chicken casserole, he only reinforced Thomas's positive image of Mum.

Also, keep in mind that children are extremely sensitive to comments made by parents. What you think about who they are and what they do is very important to them. However, don't forget it's not just your words that your children are paying attention to. At a very early age kids become acutely aware of your body language, the tone of your voice and inconsistencies between what you say and what you do. Pay attention to what kind of non-verbal signals you are giving your child about their other parent.

Regression

Children in the three- to five-year-old group have already tackled lots of developmental milestones. Perhaps you have just got them off to sleep in their bed all night without wetting the sheets, maybe your four-year-old stopped sucking her thumb, or possibly your five-year-old finally decided he no longer needs the hallway light on at night when he goes to bed. When parents separate, children may react by going through a period of regression. Simply put, regression is all about children trying to get back to an earlier, safer time. For example, from your child's point of view, if life felt okay when he was sucking his thumb, then maybe if he starts sucking his thumb things will be okay again. Please understand, your children are probably not consciously thinking this

When you find yourself running low in 'the positive comments about your ex' department, you may find it helpful to view the other parent through the eyes of your children. Consider asking your preschooler to name five things she loves, likes or really appreciates about her other parent. Write down her answers and post them in a place where both you and your child can see them daily. Although at times it may be tough, remember, even if your ex was a lousy partner he or she can still be a great parent to your child.

one through. Regression is their way of coping and managing the stress they are currently feeling.

WAYS CHILDREN MAY REGRESS

BEFORE	REGRESSIVE BEHAVIOUR
Potty trained	Wetting again or refusing to use toilet
Independently plays in another room without parent	Becomes clingy Follows parent from room to room May panic when left alone or suddenly realises parent is not visible
Consoles self without sucking thumb or pacifier	Returns to sucking thumb or wanting pacifier, especially when upset or anxious
Able to sleep through the night without wetting sheets	Recurrence of bedwetting
Curious and independent	Clingy and anxious, especially when facing new situations May ask parent to rock them or care for them like they did when they were younger

What can you do?

If your preschoolers are taking some steps backwards developmentally, keep the following in mind.

▶ Provide your children with a structured environment

When children are feeling insecure or stressed, creating a more predictable and calming home environment can really help. As mentioned previously, kids function best when they know what to expect. Predictability and sameness offer them the structure they need to feel safe and more in control of their world.

▶ **Minimise changes**

As much as possible minimise the number of changes your children are experiencing right now. Give them time to adjust to the idea of Mum and Dad being in two separate homes before introducing new situations or different circumstances.

▶ **Avoid punishing or shaming your children for the behaviour**

Although it can be frustrating when your children return to a behaviour you thought they had outgrown, remember to be patient. Lots of children experience regression when they are feeling stressed or overwhelmed. Recognise this as a sign that your children are having a tough time. Right now they need your understanding.

▶ **Talk to your children about the problem**

Let your children know you realise they are having a difficult time. Reinforce that you believe when they are ready they will be able to handle things in a different way.

▶ **Go back to square one**

Whatever you did the first time to help your children become potty-trained or to stop sucking their thumb, go back to the beginning steps and start all over again. Avoid over-focusing on the behaviour, which could lead to your little ones' feeling pressured or more anxious.

Feelings of responsibility

Developmentally, preschool-age children can understand and experience the world only as it relates to them. For this reason they just can't grasp that what is happening with Mum and Dad doesn't have anything to do with them. Their me-centred perceptions also affect their ability to process situations and feelings. It's not uncommon for a young child to say things like, 'I'm sorry I was bad. I promise to be good if Mummy comes back home.' In this instance the child has assumed that his bad behaviour caused the problem between his parents. Along with this may come a strong sense of guilt and responsibility. Pay close attention to what your child says and how he interprets his role in things not working out.

What can you do?

While you probably won't be able to talk your children out of their feelings, giving them the consistent message that they are not to blame is essential. Consider using other resources, such as children's books, DVDs or perhaps television programmes as a way to talk with your children about the divorce. Often using different media can be a non-threatening way to introduce concepts about separation and divorce to preschoolers. Not only do these materials give you the ability to reinforce to your children that divorce is not their fault, it can also help you learn how to talk to your preschoolers in a meaningful and age-appropriate way. See the resources section at the end of the book for recommended materials.

Expressing feelings

Remember the days when you wished your toddler could tell you what she was thinking and feeling? Now she can. Along with sharing how and what she thinks, at this stage your child also probably has a million and one questions for you. 'Mum, how does that work?' 'Dad, why did they do that?' Sometimes you may feel as if you are going to go into information overload. However, don't forget, even though your child can express ideas with words your preschooler still has a tendency to play up how she feels, especially when she is upset or angry. When children in the three- to five-year-old range become upset they will often react without really understanding how they feel. The two things they need the most during this time are love and limits. During this time you can help your preschoolers substantially by:

- Helping them identify their feelings with words
- Giving them acceptable ways to manage their feelings
- Providing consistent discipline when they choose to play up

WHAT TO LOOK FOR	HOW TO HELP
Regressed behaviour (toilet trained yet wetting again)	Routines and predictability
Showing anger through temper tantrums or physical aggression	Reinforce acceptable ways to express feelings and set appropriate limits when behaving badly
Blaming themselves or feeling guilty	Reassurance that divorce is not their fault
Missing the parent they are not with, especially at bedtime or mealtimes	Be sure contact with each parent is consistent, even if unequal
Anxious or worried; sensitive to parents' perceptions	Provide them with the opportunity to love and feel positive about both parents

IDEAS FOR PARENTING YOUR PRESCHOOLER

▶ Create a predictable environment

You have probably already worked out that your child responds well to things he can see, feel or touch. This age group really loves to use lists and charts. You may have also noticed that your child's concept of time is either right now or for ever. For this reason you may want to consider creating tangible, concrete ways to help your child manage life in two homes.

Think about using visual aids, such as colour-coded calendars, to help your preschooler keep track of time. Assign one colour to show time with Mum and another for time with Dad. It is helpful if your child can have a calendar at both homes. This gives him a visual way to process transitions and can also relieve some of his anxiety about future events.

▶ Prepare your child for transitions

Transitioning from one home to the other can be really stressful for young children. Often a little planning can go a long way. Between 15 and 20 minutes before a pick-up or drop-off, consider giving your child a reminder that things are getting ready to change. Sometimes it can help to have a countdown in 15-, 10- and 5-minute intervals. For example, you may want to say to your child, 'In 10 minutes Mum will be here to pick you up.' Wait five minutes and then give your child another reminder. 'In five more minutes you will see Mum.' While developmentally your child does not grasp the concept of time, it will give her a way to prepare for the coming change.

Another way to help children manage transitions is to use a 'first and then' schedule. For example, you might say to your child, '*First,* we will brush our teeth, *then* we will read a bedtime story.' For more examples of how to help your children transition between households, see Chapter 17.

▶ Provide support at bedtime and mealtimes

Bedtimes and mealtimes may be emotionally unsettling for your little one. These are times that your child relates to being a family. As a result, her feelings of loss may be at an all-time high when evening rolls around. It is also a time when your child may feel homesick or really miss the parent she is not with. Don't take her feelings personally. Instead offer her comfort and support. Also keep in mind that maintaining a consistent structure or developing evening rituals (for example, having a specific bedtime routine) may help them manage these times in a better way.

▶ Promote a positive self-image

To a preschooler Mum and Dad are everything. Be mindful that your words have a lot of influence on your child's self-esteem. When you are feeling overwhelmed or stressed it can be easy to lose sight of how important your words are to your children. Parents may fall into the trap of seeing only the negative and what needs to change instead of acknowledging the things that are positive. Be sure to recognise when your children are being good and give them positive feedback for the things they are doing right. Remember, it's not only about saying the right words but also about paying attention to your tone and volume. As I frequently tell my children, it's not just what you say that matters, it's how you say it.

> It's been estimated that children need to receive between three and five positive statements to offset the impact of one negative comment.

11.
PRIMARY SCHOOLERS
(SIX TO NINE YEARS)

*Your children will see what you're all about by what
you live rather than what you say.* – Wayne Dyer

Imagine you are meeting someone for the very first time. Suppose
this person said, 'So tell me about yourself.' What would you say?
My guess is you would probably start by describing yourself as a
mum or a dad, maybe you would talk about your job or possibly
even your hobbies. Most of us think about ourselves in terms of who
we are in relation to our family and what we do, or, more important,
what we do well. Your seven-year-old isn't any different.

Now that your child has developed an idea of who he is, he
has a new mission. At this stage your children's attention shifts
from working out who they are to feeling good about who they
are and building self-esteem. While relationships with Mum and
Dad are still a key factor regarding your children's self-image,
there are also other issues at work. Your children have started
paying attention to what they are good at and what they are not.
They are also busy sizing themselves up to see how they compare
to others. Nicole may become really involved in sports and take
pride in being the fastest runner in Year 2. Max might discover he
has a real ear for music and wonders if he is better at playing the
piano than his friend Rosie. Realise that these developing skills are
the building blocks of children feeling good about who they are
in the world.

It is also important to note that, developmentally, school-
age children view divorce differently from younger children.

Understand that your child now has the ability to consider the feelings and thoughts of others, not just her own. Although she is now better able to identify and talk about her feelings, she may be reluctant to do so. For this reason your child may give the outward appearance that everything is okay when actually she may be feeling confused and upset.

Of course, all of these factors have the potential to affect your child's developing self-image and self-esteem. To keep children moving in a positive direction, we need to be aware of how these various developmental issues are influenced by separation and divorce.

DEVELOPMENTAL ISSUES FOR PRIMARY SCHOOL CHILDREN
Self-esteem

While it is really important for kids to feel good about themselves at every age, it is perhaps most critical at this stage of their development. First, when parents choose to divorce, school-age children are more likely to personalise the break-up. In Chapter 10 we talked about younger children being under the impression that everything happening around them in some way relates to their actions, thoughts or feelings. This is what leads preschoolers to the conclusion that they have some responsibility for things not working out between Mum and Dad. As children get older this kind of magical thinking transforms into the idea that they can somehow save the family. It goes something like this: 'If I am really clever I can figure out a way to make things okay between Mum and Dad,' or perhaps, 'If I am good enough and follow all the rules then we can be a family again.' When kids aren't able to change what has happened between Mum and Dad, they may take the divorce very personally and feel as if they have failed. The burning question some children may ask themselves is, 'Why couldn't they stay together for me? Wasn't I worth it?'

What can you do?

Stay mindful of your child's perception about himself, especially in relation to the divorce. If you hear your child making critical statements, such as 'I can't do anything right,' 'I mess up everything' or 'I am such a loser,' pay attention. Instead of trying to change his mind or talk him out of his feelings, let him know that when a divorce happens sometimes kids feel as if they had done something wrong.

So what does your child need to hear?

- 'No matter how much you wish or hope, things between Mum and Dad are not going to change.'
- 'We both love you very much and think you are wonderful. We want you to understand this decision had nothing to do with you or anything you did.'
- 'You cannot fix what has happened in the family. You did not cause this. Divorce is a problem between a husband and a wife.'

In short, reinforce the ideas that kids don't cause divorce and kids can't fix divorce. Also remember that self-confidence starts at home. Make sure during this time you find ways to build your child's positive image of himself.

Here are some ideas for helping your children build self-esteem.

▶ Provide them with opportunities to be successful

Get children involved in positive activities such as sports, community clubs, local organisations or extracurricular events. Plan for success by choosing activities that will help your child feel a sense of accomplishment.

▶ Let your child know they are special and important

When parents separate, school-age children often worry about losing the special relationship they have with a parent. Remind your children often how very special they are to you, and that they will always be an important part of your life.

▶ Give children choices

During this time your children may feel very overwhelmed by change. When possible talk with children about how things will be different and give them a chance to share their feelings, opinions and ideas. When possible offer your children the opportunity to make reasonable age-appropriate choices. Learning how to make choices helps children learn to trust their judgement, develop critical thinking skills, learn problem solving and feel confident in their ability to handle situations. Remember that appropriate decisions for primary schoolers are different from adult choices. Your children still need you to be in charge. Don't make the mistake of overburdening them with grown-up issues.

▶ Treat children with respect by listening to their feelings and ideas

Truly listening to your children is perhaps one of the most meaningful ways you can build their self-esteem. Taking time to hear what they have to say or giving them your full attention when they share ideas is incredibly important. The gift of your time and attention reinforces for your children that they are valuable. For more information on how to be a better listener read Chapter 24.

▶ Set a good example

Children learn by example. If you are overly critical of yourself, expect that your children will model that same behaviour. Teach children the lesson of self-acceptance by speaking positively about yourself, acknowledging what you do well and forgiving yourself when you mess up.

Developing skills and talents

When it comes to skills and talents, there are so many ways children benefit from being involved in activities outside the home.

Along with building self-confidence, developing skills also helps children:

- Build relationships with peers
- Learn to connect with people outside of the family
- Create a support system
- Develop important values and social skills (such as sportsmanship, honour, respect, compromise and teamwork)
- Challenge their abilities and grow stronger

All too often when divorce enters the picture many children end up having fewer resources and opportunities available to them. Instead of both parents contributing their time and energy to one home, now your children have two separate homes that have to be sustained. This often leaves you with less time, possibly less money, and less energy to give to your children.

What can you do?

Help children feel a sense of accomplishment by supporting activities in both households. When possible, discuss options with the other parent before involving your child in activities. This will ensure that your child receives the support she needs from both homes. The value of parents being involved in children's school events and activities is immeasurable. It's no great surprise that kids who have involved parents tend to perform better academically, have fewer discipline problems and show higher levels of self-esteem.

Greater sense of sadness

Children between the ages of six and nine tend to view divorce differently from younger children. They realise the extent of the loss and, as a result, may feel a greater sense of sadness over the loss of the family. Although there are lots of families that experience divorce, your child may feel differently from other children, or isolated during this time. He may think no one else in the world has ever felt the same way he does. Also, because primary school children are more aware of how others see them, they can be very concerned about what their friends think.

Sometimes it may be difficult to know how your child is managing sadness. Different children can process their feelings of loss in a variety of ways. Some may avoid the topic, whereas others will tell you it's no big deal. Some kids will give the outward appearance that everything is okay, but others may start having emotional meltdowns at the drop of a hat.

To complicate matters, lots of children worry about making things worse. Therefore your children may try to hide how they are feeling or choose not to talk about what's going on.

What can you do?

As often as possible, try to normalise divorce for your child. Often primary school children really benefit from talking with other kids. It may be helpful to contact your local school to find out what types of resources (counselling, peer support or groups that deal with divorce-related issues) are available. If you feel your child would do better talking at home, consider other resources, such as books, DVDs, movies or television programmes as a way to initiate discussions. Often it is easier for children to talk about what has happened to a character in a story than about what is happening in their own lives.

Even though you may be a great parent, understand that your child may be worried about sharing their feelings with you. Again, your child may be concerned about making things worse, hurting a parent's feelings or upsetting one of you. Help your child identify two or three safe people she can talk to about her feelings. Be sure to let your child know you understand that she may feel more comfortable talking to someone else. Of course, you can also let your child know that it's okay to ask questions and that any time she wants to talk you will be ready to listen.

WHAT TO LOOK FOR	HOW TO HELP
Greater sense of sadness over the divorce	Give children an opportunity to talk about feelings and to know they are not alone.
Fantasies of reuniting or saving the family and getting Mum and Dad back together	Tell children they cannot change what has happened; make sure they know divorce is a grown-up problem.
May personalise the divorce and feel they are to blame	Provide children with the opportunity to build self-esteem.
Worried about being replaced, losing their relationship or being rejected by a parent; concerned about someone else becoming more special to Mum or Dad	Offer reassurance that they are special and their relationship with both parents is permanent.
Can experience regression (become excessively clingy, engage in baby talk or want you to do things you did when they were younger)	Provide support by gently bringing regressive behaviour to your children's attention; help them develop more age-appropriate ways of managing stress.

IDEAS FOR PARENTING YOUR PRIMARY SCHOOL CHILD

▶ Spend one-on-one time with your child

After divorce, school-age children often worry about someone taking their place or perhaps losing the special relationship they have with Mum or Dad. Between the ages of six and nine they may feel unsettled by situations that involve new relationships, remarriages, births of new children or blended family situations. Keep in mind that feelings of vulnerability may be more significant with the parent who has limited time with the children.

To calm their worries, make spending one-on-one quality time with your children a priority. Even in well-adjusted newly formed families children still need individual time with their biological parents. The time you spend with your children will help restore their confidence regarding how important they are to you and perhaps even give them the security they need to adjust to future changes.

You can also strengthen your children's sense of connection by making sure they have their own physical space in each home. If you cannot give your children their own rooms, consider creating an area that is designated as their space where they can keep belongings such as toys and clothes.

▶ Stay involved in day-to-day lives and activities

At this age your children will most likely be able to tolerate longer periods of time away from a parent (such as weekends and holidays). Although they are older, your children will still need regular contact from the parent they are not with (through phone calls, emails or by sharing a dinner during the week). Be sure to check in regularly with your children to find out how their day was or what's going on with friends; show your support by attending school activities and special events.

▶ Help your child learn how to talk about feelings and develop skills

While your children are better able to put their feelings into words, they still need help figuring out how to handle them. When emotions are strong, their first reaction will usually be to play them up. At this age you may still see outbursts, sulking, pouting and occasional tantrums. Help your children identify positive ways to handle their frustration and upset. For ideas see Chapters 25 and 26.

Also, it is possible that when your children become overwhelmed or stressed out they may resort to regression. Regression is when children return to a behaviour or set of behaviours that occurred at an earlier developmental stage. Older children may become excessively clingy, engaging in baby talk, or asking you to do things for them that you did when they were much younger. While this can be frustrating, remember to be patient with your school-age children. Regression is a way of coping with change and stress for some children. If your children are engaging in these types of behaviours, it's best to raise the issue gently. Let them know that, while you understand this is a difficult time for them, behaving in this way is not okay. Talk with them about other things they could do when they are feeling anxious, upset or stressed.

WHEN CHILDREN HAVE A DIFFICULT TIME TALKING

Despite your best efforts, you may find that your child just doesn't want to talk about the divorce. While talking is important, forcing him into a discussion is probably not your best bet. Instead of having a series of sit-down talks, consider being creative and become your child's pen pal.

Children of primary school age love sending notes and receiving letters. Use this to your advantage and find a regular school-size spiral notebook or bound diary. Put it in a specific area of the house where your child can easily access it. Let your child know this notebook is a special and private place for the two of you to write notes to each other. Start out by writing things that will engage your child (for example, tell him about your day, ask what was important about his day or how school is going, or include short notes that tell your child he is special).

Be sure to check your pen pal notebook at least once a day. After you have made a couple of successful entries consider including questions like these:

- Three things I like about my family are ...
- Three things that could be better in this house are ...
- I am most upset about ...
- I am worried about ...
- I wish ...

Be sure not to judge or criticise his responses. It is also important that you do not show what he has written to anyone else without permission.

12.
PRE-TEENS (9 TO 12 YEARS)

Small children disturb your sleep, big children your life. – Yiddish proverb

The pre-teen years can often feel like the beginning of the end. Your child is now entering the first stages of young adulthood. Aside from wondering how in the world you are going to keep him in clothes and shoes that fit, you will notice lots of other changes too. Girls move from playing with dolls to asking things like, 'When can I shave my legs and wear make-up?' Boys go from being totally clueless to really concerned about fitting in and looking cool. Let's face it: from this point forward there's no looking back.

Just as their bodies change, so do their feelings. During this time it may seem like your children are riding a rollercoaster of emotions, going from happy-go-lucky one minute to on the verge of a major meltdown the next. Although it can be difficult, keep in mind this is normal behaviour for children in the pre-teen years. However, when separation and divorce become part of the equation, understand that your children's mood swings may become much more intense.

These years can probably best be described as a time filled with pushing and pulling. Your children start pushing towards independence and pulling away from you. Even though they are giving you every indication that they want their space, don't forget they still crave your time and attention. Along with their sought-after independence, children begin to question your decisions as they struggle to understand a more complex world. Initially in this stage your child is thinking about the world in all-or-nothing terms. When it comes to divorce, this way of seeing the world makes them vulnerable to taking sides or seeing one parent as all right and the other as all wrong. When they reach 11 or 12 years old your children's thinking begins to shift. Developmentally they enter the realm of reason and abstract thinking, where the world is no longer defined by absolutes.

Just because your children are beginning to physically look more like adults, don't overlook the fact that they will continue to need a lot of guidance, structure and love from you as a parent. To support the multitude of changes your pre-teen is going through, it helps to have a good understanding of how divorce and separation affect your children as they head towards the uncharted waters of adolescence.

DEVELOPMENTAL ISSUES FOR PRE-TEENS
Changes in thinking

In the early pre-teen years (9 to 11 years old) children believe that the world should operate by a set of rules. This is a time when words like *never* and *always* get used a lot by your kids. They really can't help it. From their perspective the world exists in absolutes, all or nothing, right or wrong, black or white. For this reason, young pre-teens can easily end up in the middle of adult issues or feel a strong need to side with one parent over the other. Some children may become very critical of a parent for his or her actions – particularly if they view that parent as the one who is responsible for the divorce. Others may swing the opposite way and feel a strong need to defend or protect a parent, especially if they think that parent has been treated badly or wronged.

To give you an idea of how a young pre-teen thinks, let's see what a nine-year-old might say about his parents' break-up:

'I hate my dad for leaving my mum. When you get married you are supposed to stay together for ever, not get divorced. Why didn't Dad keep his promise and try to work things out? I don't like going to his

new house, and if he ever tries to bring his new girlfriend over I will never go back. If she weren't around, then I know my parents would get back together. It's all her fault. Why did he have to choose her over my mum? It's not fair.'

As children move into the early stages of adolescence (11 to 12 years old) their thinking takes another turn, and they start looking at the world a little differently. Instead of seeing things as black and white, they begin to notice shades of grey. Things are no longer cut and dried. Instead of dealing with the here and now, older pre-teens start developing the ability to connect past, present and future events while taking in the opinions, perspectives and feelings of others.

In comparison to a younger pre-teen, here's how a 12-year-old might view separation:

'I feel really confused. I am angry with my dad for leaving, but I still love him. I'm really worried about how Mum is handling things. I know there were problems and both of them tried to work things out. I just wish they could have tried harder. Dad says he would like me to meet his new girlfriend, but I don't know if I want to, I really don't want to upset Mum. I just want both of my parents to be happy.'

Understand that changes in your child's thinking don't happen overnight and there may be a period of time when your pre-teen moves back and forth between all-or-nothing thinking and mastering the bigger picture. Although your child is gaining the ability to reason, she will still need your support in maintaining a balanced view of both parents.

What can you do?

Although it can be tempting to jump on the bandwagon when your child is angry with the other parent, it's best if you don't. Today you might be the good guy, but remember with kids the tide is always changing. Chances are when you tell her to go to bed or to pick her clothes up off the floor, you could easily become the bad parent.

Instead of setting up one parent to take the fall, give your child an opportunity to express how she feels without adding your own judgements or opinions. After your child has had a chance to voice her feelings, help her gain a more objective point of view. If she seems to be holding one parent responsible for the divorce, reinforce that it takes two people to make a marriage successful. Whether you initiated the separation or not, it is important for your child to understand that you each had some responsibility for problems in the marriage.

Some key messages pre-teens need to hear are these:

- 'You don't have to stop loving Mum or Dad just because you are feeling angry.'
- 'It's not your responsibility to figure out who is right and who is wrong.'
- 'Your feelings don't have to be the same as Mum's or Dad's.'
- 'Both parents had some part in things not working out.'

Physical changes

Over the next few years your child will go through a tremendous number of physical changes. As your child's body begins to change, be aware that she may become more sensitive to what others think or she can be overly critical of herself. Since development varies greatly, there undoubtedly will be times when she may feel awkward or uncomfortable with some of those changes. You've probably already noticed your pre-teen is developing a greater need for personal privacy. When parents separate, normal developmental transitions can either happen faster or be delayed. Because lots of changes are taking place it can be challenging to make those necessary adjustments, especially if you are not seeing your child every day. The pre-teen years are often a very awkward time for kids. Therefore it is important for both parents to stay mindful of their child's developmental needs during this time.

What can you do?

Be aware of your child's growing need to fit in and feel accepted. Realise he may be especially sensitive to teasing or criticism of how he looks or what he wears. Remember to be patient, flexible and, most of all, understanding.

During this time in your child's life he or she may really need the support of the same-sex parent. As his body changes and grows, a boy may feel more comfortable talking with Dad and having him answer questions, rather than Mum. Likewise a girl may feel awkward discussing changes in her body with Dad and feel more at ease with Mum.

If the same-sex parent is not involved, is not readily available or is not talking to your child about important changes, then find a way to bridge the gap.

- Get educated about the physical and emotional changes your child is going through.
- Set aside time to talk with your child.
- Let your child know you understand it may be difficult for him or her to talk with you.
- Reassure your child that he or she can always ask questions. If needed, find someone of the same sex for your child to talk to, such as an aunt, uncle, cousin or close friend of the family.

Books can also be an excellent way to connect and get kids talking.

Emotional changes

As if all this weren't enough, when your child's body starts to change, so do her hormones. Pre-teens can easily experience a wide range of feelings from one minute to the next. While you are going through the process of splitting up, expect that your child's feelings may intensify. Highs will be higher, and lows will be lower. Keep in mind that the stress that you feel during this time can also significantly contribute to the intensity.

As mentioned earlier, children can be very vulnerable to taking sides. Pre-teens may also deal with the divorce by taking the moral high ground, especially if they view one parent as a victim of the situation. Because they struggle with all-or-nothing thinking, it's easy for their emotions to mirror their thoughts. From a pre-teen's perspective, if you are angry with someone you deal with it by rejecting that person. Therefore it is helpful to introduce and rein-force with your children that you don't have to stop loving some-one just because you are feeling angry.

When issues of privacy start to emerge, you may find that your children are not only interested in having their space but may also be very private emotionally. You may find that your once over-talkative child's conversational skills have now been reduced to one-word answers.

What can you do?

When your children move into this phase of their lives, your skills in the being-patient-and-understanding department will be taken to a whole new level. Believe it or not, your child isn't trying to drive you crazy. Often your child doesn't understand why he feels the way he does. While in many ways more mature, your pre-teen still needs your help in identifying what is going on and how to handle it. Work with him on developing healthy ways to manage his feelings, especially when he is feeling overwhelmed or very upset.

Of course, being a good role model will have the most influence with your 12-year-old. The *do as I say, not as I do* philosophy doesn't tend to work particularly well with pre-teens. Remember, as a parent you may be struggling to understand your own feelings. As a result there may be times when you don't do the best job of managing those feelings or set the best example for your kids. When this happens, be willing to admit your mistake and talk openly about how you could have handled a situation differently. By doing so you will teach your children that it's important for everybody in the family to pay attention to how he or she is handling feelings.

Because of the enhanced need for privacy, remember your pre-teens may feel embarrassed or reluctant to share how they feel with you. Given that life as your children have known it has come to an end, the strain on communication you may normally expect becomes that much more challenging.

Rather than letting them wander through this unfamiliar territory, it may be helpful to talk with your pre-teens early on and set the stage.

▶ Prepare your child

Let your children know that change is a part of growing up. Explain that going through many changes all at once can often make things harder. Let them know you understand that they may feel lots of different feelings, especially given what has just happened in the family. It's also possible they may feel certain feelings and not even know why. Reinforce that they can always talk to you if they are having problems with managing some of those changes and that you plan to be available when they need to talk.

▶ Normalise their experience

To minimise possible embarrassment or worry, reassure your children that all kids at some point experience lots of changes physically, mentally and emotionally. It is important for them to understand, however, that everyone goes through those changes in different ways. If they are developing differently, it doesn't mean anything is wrong. You also may want to give them a heads-up by telling them that when families go through a divorce feelings may be stronger.

▶ Teach your children to identify their feelings

When feelings are at their strongest, your children may have trouble identifying what they are feeling and why. More often than not, kids feel something and then immediately move into reacting. Help your children find ways to identify how they feel by reflecting back what you see and hear. For example, if Oscar is ranting about how Dad didn't show up to his football game, then you may say something like, 'Sounds like you are really disappointed Dad didn't show up,' or 'The way you're shouting makes me think you're angry at Dad.' By reflecting back, you can guide your children towards making those connections on their own. This can also help your children learn how to avoid reacting impulsively (see also Chapter 24).

▶ Help them learn how to manage their feelings

Work on helping your pre-teens build good coping skills. As suggested in Chapter 25, consider making a list with your children

WHAT TO LOOK FOR	HOW TO HELP
Sides with one parent over the other	Tell children they don't have to pick or choose between Mum and Dad.
May have strong opinions about what is right and wrong	Support children in seeing more than one perspective.
Can easily move into a more adult-like role (feel the need to take care of a parent or the family)	Avoid placing children in the middle of adult issues.
Feelings may seem more intense and unpredictable	Guide pre-teens in safely managing their feelings and help them understand it's normal to have mood swings.
Can be anxious about the future	Consult your children on things that affect their lives; the final decision, however, rests with the parents.

of acceptable ways to handle their feelings. While they may balk at it or tell you they are too old for that, ask them to humour you. You may even consider making a list for yourself to show them that everyone needs reminding.

IDEAS FOR PARENTING YOUR PRE-TEENS

▶ Provide opportunities for developing independence

During this stage your children may test their independence by questioning your choices and decisions as a parent. They want to know why things are the way they are, why you have different rules from other parents, and most important, why you have different rules from each other. When there are significant differences between households, enforcing limits or rules can be a real challenge with pre-teens. For example, 12-year-old Claire may battle over the length of her skirts. Mum understands what's in style, why can't Dad? Or 11-year-old Dylan may argue with Mum over his need for a mobile phone; after all everybody else in his school year has one. Besides, Dad bought him one. Why can't he have it at Mum's house?

Do your best to support your pre-teens in developing their sense of identity and independence. If they are challenging a rule or questioning a decision you have made, give them a chance to voice their opinion. Be sure you set limits on how that opinion is shared. Now more than ever, your children need to learn how to share their ideas while remaining respectful. While you are still an authority and the one in charge of making final decisions, giving your pre-teens a chance to think out loud can be beneficial.

Allowing your pre-teens to express their opinion helps them:

- Develop critical thinking skills
- Form and test their own opinions about the world
- Feel respected and valued
- Learn problem-solving skills

Because this is a time when communication can easily shut down, listening to your children's ideas or opinions may be your saving grace. It not only lets you know what they are thinking but it also gives the two of you something to talk about.

▶ Support your children's friendships

Support the development of friendships and positive social activities by being involved in your children's lives. Sometimes getting to know your children's friends can be difficult when parenting out of two homes. If you are the parent who is not as involved in your child's day-to-day life, you may need to be more creative. Healthy friendships are an incredibly important part of your child's development. Think about ways you can stay connected and help your children maintain friendships that are good for them. If you are the parent who has more involvement in your child's daily life, consider ways to keep the other parent in the loop.

▶ Stay involved and maintain family connections

You have probably discovered by now that your super-cool, infallible status has become a thing of the past. Your children are moving away from wanting you involved in everything they do to

---

HELP YOUR CHILDREN MAINTAIN AND DEVELOP HEALTHY FRIENDSHIPS WHEN THEY DON'T LIVE WITH YOU FULL-TIME

- Attend school events or activities.
- Offer to volunteer time, chaperone or help out at events that involve your children.
- Let your children invite a friend along for an overnight or family event.
- Be flexible about scheduling if your children have an important event with friends.
- Get to know the parents of your children's friends.

doing things on their own. Although kids at this age may give you the impression that they want to go it alone, they still very much need and want parents involved in their lives. Make it a priority to regularly contact them when they are not with you through phone calls, email or texting, or by participating in important activities.

As a parent, you may need to be more creative about how you stay connected with your pre-teens. Although it may not be cool to have lunch with Mum or Dad at school, they may be willing to have one-to-one time with you doing something else, such as going to a local coffee shop or catching a film. Still plan special family trips and events and continue holiday rituals. The time you invest now helps build a stronger foundation for children long term.

13.
TEENAGERS
(13 TO 18 YEARS)

You know your children are growing up when they stop asking you where they came from and refuse to tell you where they're going. – P. J. O'Rourke

Once your children enter their teenage years, you can pretty much expect that life will never be the same. Most parents experience this as both a blessing and a curse. On the one hand, you may relish the fact your child is moving towards an age where you no longer have to be her personal chauffeur. On the other hand, you may feel a great sense of loss, longing for those days when you knew exactly where your child was and what she was doing at all times. While the pre-teen years are riddled with a push–pull kind of relationship between you and your kids, with teenagers it may feel like one huge push after another. As they transition into young adulthood, they begin pushing away from Mum and Dad and pushing themselves out into the world.

Be mindful that your teens are in the process of putting together their own ideas about life – ideas that, at times, may be very different from your own. While you may feel a strong urge to share your years of wisdom, keep in mind your words will probably fall on deaf ears, especially now. It's not unusual for teens to feel as if they have everything worked out. From their point of view, parents don't have a clue about the real world. Now that you are getting a divorce, don't be surprised if your teens have the impression that you've really screwed things up. So why should they listen to you? Remember, as you're going through this process there may be times under the scrutinising eye of your teens that you don't look like you have it all together. Your splitting up may be viewed by your teens as reason enough for being even more judgemental of your decisions, actions and choices (especially if there are significant differences between households).

Teenage years are often branded as a time filled with lots of drama and turbulent emotions. Quite personally, I don't buy into the idea that teens have to be emotionally unstable. Yes, it is a challenge to parent teens. Parents who have a hands-on approach to parenting and who have invested time as well as energy into building a strong relationship with their children tend to experience smoother sailing during these years. However, when you mix in the crisis nature of divorce, expect that the waters may get pretty choppy.

Just like younger children, teens can react to divorce in a number of different ways. Some may become over-cynical about their future and avoid relationships altogether. Others may try to get back the family they've lost by rushing into a serious relationship and creating a family of their own. Some teenagers may respond by testing limits, withdrawing from the family or acting in dangerous ways. Others may compensate by moving into a caretaking or parent-like role. These ultra-mature teens often feel a strong urge to care for and protect a parent they view as vulnerable or in need of emotional support. While, in some ways, this can lead to teens becoming more responsible (typically viewed as a good thing), it can also cause delays in their development (such as social skills and emotional maturity) and affect future relationship choices. Although they are like young adults in many ways, teens should never feel emotionally responsible for parents or be involved in parental issues and conflicts. Teens still very much need you to be their parent.

Probably the most appropriate word to describe the art of successfully parenting teens is *balance*. Essential elements in maintaining a strong relationship with your teen involve:

- Providing them with flexibility, yet finding ways to have quality time
- Offering enough information about how life will change, without overexposing them
- Involving them in important decisions about the future, without drawing them into adult issues
- Giving them the ability to develop responsibility, but maintaining your role as a parent

Although parenting teens through divorce can feel hugely challenging, it's not impossible. Having an understanding of these primary developmental issues will help you guide your teens in the right direction.

DEVELOPMENTAL ISSUES FOR TEENS

Role confusion

In many ways divorce presents a different set of hardships for teens than for younger children. Because teenagers have the ability to intellectually understand adult concepts, boundaries between parents and teens can easily become blurred. While your teens may seem more like grown-ups than children, don't lose sight of the fact that they are still kids who need your guidance and support.

What can you do?

To avoid putting your teen in a compromising position, follow these tips.

▶ Deal with your feelings in a responsible way, and address your needs

While all children pay close attention to how their parents are managing the divorce process, teens may try to counterbalance parental distress. If your teen views you as overwhelmed, depressed or vulnerable she may feel a strong need to be the shoulder you lean on. Certainly being supportive of one another is an important part of being a family. However, no matter how old your children are, they should never be your only source of emotional support. If you are having trouble managing your feelings or coming to terms with your divorce, be sure to seek help and support from other adults (for example, family members, friends, support group, counsellor, therapist or life coach). For more information on how to balance divorce-related stress, see Chapter 1.

▶ Offer your teen a balanced perspective about relationships

Teens can easily develop an overly cynical or distrustful view of relationships when parents split up. ('I'll never get married and screw things up like my parents did'; 'Why bother getting married? It will never last anyway.') Although you probably can't talk them out of those feelings, you can offer them another perspective. Teens need your help understanding that even though things didn't work out for you they will probably be able to have a successful relationship of their own some day. Actually, children of divorce can learn from their parents' mistakes and develop important skills that help them have meaningful and committed relationships later in life. Be sure to see the resources at the back of the book for recommended reading in this area.

▶ Continue to be a parent

As you go through the emotional process of divorce it's very natural to feel vulnerable and isolated. When parents don't pay attention to how they themselves are coping, unhealthy parent–child relationships can develop with teens. Although these roles often develop in very unintentional ways, they are still harmful to children.

The new best friend: After your divorce you may find you and your teen are going through similar life experiences (for example, entering the dating scene, discovering new interests, and defining and redefining who you are). While these shared experiences have the ability to bring you and your teen closer, it's probably best to avoid becoming your teen's new best friend or double-date mate. Despite how cool it might be to hang out together, your teen still needs you to provide him with structure and discipline (that is, being a parent). Besides, best friends don't usually tell you what time you have to be home or take away your mobile phone when you fail your chemistry exam.

Also, keep in mind as you begin dating again that your teen will be watching your every move and taking notes. How you handle dating situations and new relationships will definitely set the bar for your teen. Make sure you are playing by the same rules you want him to follow.

The other parent: When you have children of different ages, parenting on your own can be really tough. Even though older children can be enormously helpful when you are short-handed, steer clear of making your teen second-in-command. Sure, there may be times when you need her to pitch in and help cook dinner, baby-sit or look after the younger kids. However, teens should not be the primary disciplinarians or someone you consult regarding parenting matters.

The confidante: Parents can make the mistake of overexposing teens to the adult details of divorce. While you may feel that your teen is old enough to hear the truth or know the whole story, don't forget the person you're talking about is still your child's mum or dad. Will teens want to know why things didn't work out? Certainly. However, just because they are beginning to look like grown-ups doesn't necessarily mean you need to give them more information. Exposure to adult information and conflict between Mum and Dad can be as unsettling for teens as it is for younger children. Although intellectually teens view divorce differently from younger children, emotionally they are not prepared to handle the adult details of divorce. I knew a teen once whose mother told him very candidly that the marriage didn't work because his father wasn't exciting in bed any more. Needless to say, this teen was floored by what his mother said. Even when teens press you for information about situations between you and your ex, don't take the bait. Remember, your teen still needs you to shield him from intimate details about the difficulties between you and the other parent.

The decision-maker: As teens become more independent it's natural to consult them about important issues and future decisions that will affect their lives. Yet when parents no longer live under the same roof, teens may inadvertently get placed in the role of decision-maker. While giving teens the power of choice may mean you don't have to talk to your ex as much (a plus for you), at the same time your teens get stuck with trying to walk both sides of the fence and taking on a lot of unnecessary stress (definite negative for your kids). Even worse, when significant disagreements occur between Mum and Dad, parents may make the mistake of wanting their teens to take sides and become leverage to use against the other parent. ('It's not about what I want, it's about what the children want. Karen's old enough to make her own decisions, and she agrees with me. You should respect her choice.')

When teens are left to call the shots, they end up becoming responsible for most (if not all) of the communication between the households. When this happens, teens are handed carte blanche to work both ends against the middle. Take Amy, for example.

Amy wants to go to a concert in town with some friends but knows there's no way her parents would approve. Since it's her weekend with Dad, Amy decides to call him and tell him she wants to spend the night with Susan. She adds, 'By the way, Mum doesn't have a problem with it.' Amy then calls Mum and says, 'Dad told me I could spend the weekend with Susan.' Mum responds, 'Fine as long as you've worked it out with your father. What you do on your weekends with him is between the two of you.' Because Amy's parents avoid talking

to each other and don't share information about their households,
Amy's off to the concert and left to do whatever she wants.

Don't lose sight of the fact that your children are still children.
It's okay to ask for their opinion regarding choices that affect
them, but final decisions should still be left with parents. While
you probably don't need to consult each other daily, make sure
you and your ex are exchanging information about details that
involve your teens. If differences crop up, find some way to work
things out. Don't leave it up to your children.

The messenger: When children are older, parents may naively fall
into the trap of relaying information to one another through their
teenagers. It often starts with small things like, 'Let Dad know
you have a netball game next week,' 'Be sure to tell Mum we're
planning to go on holiday the first week in July.' While it all seems
fairly harmless, it has the potential to develop into a minefield of
problems for both you and your teenager. When disagreements
come up, teens who have been given the job of messenger quickly
find they have a new set of problems. This once simple exchange
of information quickly transforms into a series of settlement
conversations and negotiations.

Consider 17-year-old William and 15-year-old Andrew:

As the boys have got older, their parents talk less. Both parents feel
that the boys are old enough to work things out with each parent; after
all they're almost adults. When the boys ask their mother about the
arrangements for Christmas this year, she says she wants to take them
skiing. Both boys are incredibly excited; they hadn't been skiing in
years. However, and here comes the catch, Mum lets them know they
need to discuss it with their dad because part of the trip would fall
during his time. When Andrew and William approach Dad about
scheduling, their initial excitement takes a sharp nosedive. Dad
wants to know why their mother couldn't schedule it for another time.
Why did he always have to give up his time with them? Of course, the

boys didn't know what to say other than, 'I suppose that's just how it worked out.'

Dad, now feeling more than a little worked up, then launches into a series of questions such as, 'How can your mum pay for such an expensive trip? Didn't she tell me last month she couldn't afford to help out with your school fees? Why can't you go for seven days instead of ten?'

When William and Andrew get back from Dad's, Mum starts in and immediately wants to know what Dad had to say about their trip. As expected, Mum had her own series of questions and comments about Dad. Trying not to make the situation worse, both boys walk on eggshells as they answer Mum's questions. Despite their best efforts, Mum gets angry about Dad and ends the conversation ranting about what a selfish git he is. Later, Andrew tells William he no longer cares if they go skiing. 'Why does everything have to be so complicated?' he asks. 'Why can't they just work things out?'

Poor kids. Instead of getting to be excited about an upcoming family trip, they both ended up being caught in the crossfire.

So how could this have been avoided?

Let's look at Mum's role first. One way she could have shielded her sons was to talk with Dad before mentioning the ski trip to the boys. Yes, Dad still might have been upset, but at least Mum would have been the one dealing with his reaction, not William and Andrew. It also might have helped if Mum had offered to be flexible about the time arrangements. If the ski trip dates were set, then perhaps she could have offered to adjust the schedule so Dad and the boys could have extra time after the trip.

Now, what about Dad? When William and Andrew told him about the trip he could have done a better job of controlling his reaction. While he may have been upset, he could have let the boys know the arrangements for Christmas are really something he needs to discuss with Mum. Instead of putting the boys in the interrogation seat, Dad could have chosen to call Mum and address his concerns directly with her. Even if the situation didn't feel fair, Dad could have chosen to be flexible and focus on how exciting it must be for the boys to go skiing.

When teens become the messengers between Mum and Dad, it:

- Increases miscommunication and conflict between parents
- Leaves teens feeling disloyal to one or both parents
- Places teens in the middle of adult problems
- Provides teens with an opportunity to play one parent against the other
- Leaves teens to deal with the other parent's reactions

Don't put your teens in the position of having to be a negotiator, mediator or peacekeeper between yourself and your ex.

New experiences

Parenting teens takes a lot of commitment and patience. The leap between being under the protective arm of Mum and Dad to being an independent adult who is responsible for his or her own decisions is considerable. It's also a time when your teens are going through lots of changes and are still trying to get their feet on the ground. Over the next few years your children will be experiencing a multitude of challenges and first experiences at a rapid rate. Some of those experiences can be exciting and rewarding, whereas others may test your teen's moral character and ability to make sound choices.

Think about some of the experiences your teen will encounter:

- Going to high school
- Dating
- Learning to drive and possibly owning a car
- Having an after-school job
- Managing money

- Owning a mobile phone
- Accessing social-networking sites
- Enjoying a greater degree of privacy
- Feeling pressure to drink or use drugs
- Falling in love
- Experiencing heartbreak
- Being increasingly exposed to sex
- Attending a school disco or dance
- Graduating
- Getting a flat
- Going to university
- Travelling without parents

Unfortunately when parents live apart many of these first experiences for teens can become complicated and riddled with power struggles between Mum and Dad. Consider the following scenario:

Katherine, 17 years old, is in her final year and wants to start looking at universities. When her mum and dad were together they frequently talked about Katherine's future and the importance of attending a good university. Now when Katherine brings up the subject her dad says, 'I don't know. I suppose you'll have to talk to your mum about it. I think we need to find out how much she's willing to pay before we make any decisions.' Last time Katherine brought up the issue with Mum she got an earful of complaints. When Mum replied, 'Your dad never pays for anything. Maybe he should get a real job instead of trying to bleed me dry,' Katherine started thinking maybe university isn't worth the hassle.

Katherine is facing a major life change that is made all the more overwhelming and complicated by her parents' contentious relationship. What can her parents do to make this life transition easier for their daughter? Perhaps when Katherine tells Dad she would like to start looking at university, he could ask if she has anywhere specifically in mind. After they discuss some ideas, Katherine's Dad

could email his ex to tell her how excited Katherine is about looking at university. He also asks if they can schedule a time to talk
about how they can both support Katherine in finding the right
place. Mum and Dad might still argue and have conflict, but at
least now Katherine is not in the middle and can experience the
excitement that usually accompanies this time in a teen's life.

What can you do?

▶ See the situation through your child's eyes

When issues arise with the other parent, do your best to stay
focused on how the situation feels for your teens. Think through
what you can do to safeguard what is most important to them. It
may also help to consider what kind of memories you want your
children to have when they look back on this time in their lives.

▶ Don't undermine the other parent's authority

Teens are more apt to be drawn into disagreements and feel the
need to take sides when parents clash. While it may feel good to
have your teen side with you, you are sending them a very dangerous message when you join forces against the other parent. Undermining the other parent communicates to your teens that they
don't have to respect the other parent's authority. Be aware it may
only be a matter of time before they apply that same kind of logic
to you.

▶ Voice disagreements without slamming the other parent

At times your teens may share in your anger at the other parent,
especially when there are disagreements about rules or values. If a
disagreement arises, avoid sharing your personal opinions or crit-
icisms of the other parent. It's okay to let your teens know you
and the other parent don't see eye to eye. However, when issues
crop up stay focused on the problem, not the person.

Don't forget, when you openly criticise the other parent you
are ultimately chipping away at your children's self-esteem.
Although your teen may roll her eyes and say 'Whatever,' the truth

is parents are an enormously important and influential feature in a teen's life. Eventually she may grow to resent your negative comments, and you. While you may be justified in feeling the way you do, don't sacrifice your teen's self-esteem.

Do your best to handle disagreements with integrity. While you can't control the other parent's reaction, your teens will notice how you choose to handle the situation.

▶ Live by example

How you manage your relationship with the other parent under the watchful eye of your teens definitely has a domino effect. First, it sets a clear example (good or bad) of how to handle problems with others and, more important, with others you once loved. I can't tell you how many parents I have heard complain about today's youth. Comments range from saying teens have no respect for authority to complaining that they're rude, lack manners and feel entitled to do whatever they want. In dealing with your ex, what kind of example are you setting for your teen? If you want to teach respect, act respectfully. If you want to instil your teen with a sense of integrity, then behave with integrity without excuses.

Remember that terms such as *respect* and *integrity* have different meanings for different people. Think about what each of these terms means for you. What does respect look like for you? In your opinion, how does one act or speak with respect and integrity? Knowing your own expectations not only helps you communicate them to your children better but also allows you to be a better example.

Risk taking

As mentioned earlier, the teenage years are loaded with new experiences. Along with those new experiences comes experimentation and risk taking. Risk taking is a normal and healthy part of growing up for teens. When teens are engaged in healthy risk taking, it helps them move towards defining who they are and what they value in life. Yet, when paired with the strong emotions brought on by divorce, risk taking can take a dangerous turn. Much like when they were younger, your teens may choose to play out their feelings in some very unsafe ways.

Negative risk taking may involve:

- Drinking and driving
- Using drugs
- Inappropriate sexual behaviour
- Excessive dieting or eating
- Self-mutilation (secretly cutting themselves)

WHAT TO LOOK FOR	HOW TO HELP
May withdraw from family by spending more time away from home	Be responsible for checking in with teens and stay involved in their lives and activities.
Can easily move into a more adult-like role (feel the need to take care of a parent or the family)	Avoid placing children in the role of confidante, best friend or putting them in the middle of adult issues.
Reaction or management of feelings becomes more intense	Maintain your role as parent by providing nurture and structure. Keep communication open and help teens explore healthy ways to express feelings.
Involvement in negative risk-taking behaviours (smoking, drinking, being disrespectful of authority, drugs, having unsafe sex, unhealthy relationships with food)	Help children identify healthy risk-taking behaviours and support their involvement in positive activities (sports, volunteering, making new friends, developing new skills, travelling).

When teens are left without appropriate supports or coping skills they can easily be lured into engaging in high-risk activities. Make sure to pay attention to how your teens are managing their feelings about the divorce. Help them develop opportunities to engage in healthier outlets such as playing sports, enhancing their artistic abilities, volunteering time to a worthy cause or learning a new skill.

It's equally important that you, as a parent, are helping your teen learn how to:

- Evaluate risks
- Consider the consequences of their actions
- Develop and implement positive coping strategies

Of course, nothing will speak louder to your teens than your own actions. Be mindful of your own risk-taking behaviours and what kind of example you are setting for your children.

IDEAS FOR PARENTING YOUR TEENS

▶ **Be flexible about schedules without letting your teen off the hook**
While in the past you may have been used to seeing your children on a fairly regular basis, now that they are entering the realm of adolescence things have changed. Instead of negotiating scheduling issues with your ex, you'll also need to consult your teen when coordinating dates or making plans. You may also be feeling a great sense of loss and looking to spend as much time as possible with your teen. However, your teen may have other ideas about that.

Most teens have jobs, become interested in dating, hang out with friends or get involved in other activities. This is why traditional schedules don't typically work very well with older children. Spending quality time with Mum or Dad on the weekends tends to be pretty low on their list of priorities. Do your best not to take it personally; moving away from the family is normal at this age.

During this time flexibility is an important part of parenting. Of course, that doesn't mean you let your teens off the hook. Time as a family shouldn't take a back seat to everything else in your teens' lives. Be creative and offer to negotiate times. Perhaps instead of asking for a whole weekend you can make arrangements to have a sit-down dinner together on Saturday or spend Sunday together having brunch and watching a film.

Take heart. While the teen years can be tough, they're actually not all bad. Although you will probably be spending time differently with your teens, approach the time you have with creativity. Building opportunities for connecting will in the long run mean a lot to your children.

Also, when kids get older it's easy to think that if they really wanted to talk with you they'd give you a ring or seek you out. But typically teens don't initiate conversations with their parents. Therefore make a point to check in with your kids regularly. In this day and age there's no shortage of ways to get in touch with one another. Teens usually have mobile phones, access to email and lightning-fast texting skills. Continue to make an effort to stay connected to your teens. While an occasional voicemail message or email doesn't seem like much to you, it lets your teens know you're thinking about them.

▶ Keep asking with whom, when and where

Whether your teens live with you full time or not, be sure to provide them with structure. Although you may not feel as if they are paying any attention to you or what you say, your active presence in their lives makes a difference. Don't be afraid to set limits, have expectations and set standards with your teens. Keep track of what they are doing, who their friends are and what's important to them. Make time to attend important events and ask questions about school. True, your interest may sometimes be met with reluctance, but it lets your teens know you care.

▶ **Talk to your teen about how life will change and future concerns**

In the early stages, consider structuring holidays and special events rather than leaving it up to your teens to work out how to manage their time with each parent. Do your best to work with the other parent to share these times in a way that feels comfortable for everyone. Don't put your children in the position of deciding who they want to be with when, or worrying over how they should divide their time when celebrating important events. When children are younger, parents are usually more attentive to maintaining holiday rituals and traditions for their children. Now that your children are older it's really no different. Although teens are not particularly good at showing it, holidays and special occasions still matter. Be sure to make arrangements with the other parent and then talk with your teens about how they will celebrate important events and occasions with both families. While these situations may be hard for you as a parent, remember not to let your issues with each other overshadow your children's special days.

PART THREE

A Guide to the Most Common Probelms and Issues for Divorced or Separated Parents

14.
HOW TO TELL YOUR CHILDREN YOU ARE GETTING A DIVORCE

There are a lot of things about divorce that you can't fix, change or make better for your kids. The real question is: Are you willing to do what you can not to make it worse? – Christina McGhee

Telling your children that you have made a decision to separate or divorce is never going to be easy. Deciding how to handle your very first conversation can stir up a lot of anxiety for even the most capable parent. Keep in mind this is probably one of the most important conversations you'll have with your children, as it will set the stage for future discussions.

It's natural to feel some guilt about the hurt and distress your children may experience when they hear your news. You may even be struggling to find the right words, perhaps wondering what to say and what not to say. Like many parents, you're probably very concerned about making an already difficult situation even worse for your children.

To complicate matters, in the early stages of a separation you may feel emotionally overwhelmed as your relationship comes to an end. The situation can be even more challenging if:

- One of you is uncertain of your feelings
- One or both of you are having difficulty managing your emotions

- You each have significantly different opinions about why the divorce is happening
- One parent is committed to blaming the other for the divorce

Given all the different issues parents have to face, it's no wonder that so many of them have a difficult time telling their children that Mum and Dad are no longer going to live in the same home.

This chapter provides some helpful information and encouragement on how to talk with your children about divorce. Keep in mind that what you might say to a three-year-old will be different from what to say to a 13-year-old. You'll also find tips for talking to children of different ages and in different developmental stages.

WHY YOU NEED TO TALK TO YOUR CHILDREN

In addition to informing your children that life is changing, talking with your children about divorce is incredibly important because it:

- Helps children understand that divorce is not their fault
- Minimises the possibility of children feeling they can change what has happened in the family
- Lets children know that it is okay to talk about divorce now and in the future
- Decreases the anxiety of children about how their lives are changing

Throughout my career, parents have often told me they really want to talk with their children about divorce, but they don't know what to say or how to say it. When parents become over-concerned with saying the wrong thing, they often make the mistake of not saying anything at all. Not talking about separation and divorce is a common problem for lots of families. Research shows that 95 per cent of surveyed children reported feeling like their parents gave them little or no information about their separation or divorce.

The problem with saying nothing (or very little) to your children is that you put them in the position of having to work out on their own what is going on. Children deserve an explanation, and in the absence of one they will find some way to explain the situation to themselves. Often those explanations are based on neither logic nor reason, and they usually have more to do with how the children view the world around them than with the actual situation. This leads many children to feel responsible for what has happened between their parents.

The following are a few examples of things children may do and say when they are feeling responsible or are trying to change what has happened:

- Promising to behave better and follow all the rules if Mum and Dad promise to stay together
- Trying to become the perfect child, thinking, 'If I am really good then Mum and Dad won't have anything to argue about.'
- Creating a crisis by getting into trouble at school or causing more discipline problems in an attempt to give parents a common cause – their child's behaviour
- Planning events or activities in which parents have to interact – for example, asking both parents to go to dinner, sit next to each other at events or share time with the child together
- Developing physical symptoms, such as faking an asthma attack, complaining of stomach aches or showing a loss of appetite, thinking, 'If I get sick both my mum and dad will have to work together to take care of me.'
- Older children may act out by drinking, being verbally abusive, becoming a discipline problem at school or testing limits

Providing children with a reasonable, honest, non-blaming explanation of why the family is changing will allow them to make sense of the situation and make it less likely that they will feel they can fix it. Appropriate information can also significantly reduce the anxiety your children feel as they face major changes in their lives.

WHEN IS THE BEST TIME?

While there are some common experiences, divorce is essentially a unique process for each family. The decision when to tell your children is a very personal one. Some parents may choose to have a conversation with their children before anyone moves out. For others, it may not happen until after a period of separation.

You may also choose to talk to your children with your partner or individually. One parent may want a divorce, whereas the other parent may still be interested in saving the marriage, or perhaps the decision was a surprise for one parent. In these circumstances the conversation may be driven by necessity rather than by careful planning. Regardless of the situation, once you have made a firm decision and are certain it is not going to change you should talk with your children as soon as possible.

Sometimes parents put off telling their children about the divorce because they hope that, as time passes, it will become easier to tell them. Or they choose to wait for a better time, such as after the holidays or at the end of the school term.

For some parents, talking to their kids about a divorce or separation makes the decision that much more real. Admitting that a relationship is over can be even more difficult than telling the children.

But keep in mind that if you delay talking about the divorce you risk:

- Supporting your children's fantasy that things may not change

- Keeping your children confused about what is happening in the family
- Prolonging your children's anxiety
- Unnecessarily exposing your children to tension between yourself and the other parent

Children are often very intuitive. If there have been problems in a marriage, they will often sense it, even if they don't understand it. Even when kids suspect things are not okay between Mum and Dad, this does not mean that it will be easier for them to accept your decision. Actually it's common for children to hang on to the hope that things may change.

Gaining clarity is another important reason for your children to be informed about your decision. It is never easy for children to hear that their parents are splitting up. However, when you have made a firm decision it's time to have that talk.

HOW TO TALK ABOUT DIVORCE

When talking with your children, be direct and use the words *divorce, separation* and *splitting up* as a way of explaining the change in the family. Don't try to soften the blow by not using the appropriate words. Using different words may give children a false sense of hope that things will go back to the way they were. It's also important to talk about the divorce, separation or split-up as a permanent change.

Understand your children may have a variety of reactions. Some children will be sad or disappointed, while others may react to the news with anger or shock and disbelief. If there has been a significant level of conflict between parents, a child can also feel a sense of relief. A parent once told me that, after she told her children that Mum and Dad were getting a divorce, the kids wanted to know why it had taken them so long to make the decision.

Some children may not show a reaction at all. This can occur when a child is not ready to accept the reality that life is changing or if they're shocked by the news. If your child does not show an immediate reaction, be patient. Once you have had an initial conversation, keep talking to them. Make sure you tell your children that they can always ask questions or talk with you about their feelings.

One parent or two?

Ideally, it's best if both parents can have the first divorce conversation with their children together. However, this is a good idea only if both parents are capable of managing their own emotions and can shield children from existing tension or conflict. To ensure that children hear consistent messages, it is best if you and the other parent discuss what your children will be told before any conversations take place. This will minimise confusion and keep your children from feeling caught in the middle as well as making a successful and healthy adjustment more likely.

If both of you cannot talk to your children together, work on reaching an agreement with the other parent about what will be said. While you may have separate conversations, it is beneficial if your children can hear the same information from both parents.

If you can't agree about what will be said

▶ Avoid the temptation to blame the other parent

When parents blame each other they create a very confusing and difficult situation for children. Children should never have to side with one parent over the other or be placed in the position of having to decide who is right and who is wrong. Placing blame – no matter how well intentioned – often exposes children to adult information, which increases the chance of their misunderstanding the situation. Access to adult information will also increase a child's level of anxiety and can be overwhelming. For more information on why blaming the other parent is damaging to children, see Chapter 28.

▶ Manage your emotions and stay focused on the needs of your children

It may be very difficult for you to manage your own feelings about the divorce or separation. However, for the sake of your children it is vitally important that you find some way to handle your own feelings in a healthy, adult way. How well parents are able to adjust is a key factor in influencing how well children adjust to divorce and separation. In short, if you want your children to be okay, *you* need to be okay.

▶ Keep your explanation short

Avoid lengthy explanations and excessive detail, or children may quickly become overwhelmed. Stay focused on your children's feelings and the issues that are most important to them, such as how their lives will change and when they will be spending time with each parent.

▶ Avoid contradicting what has already been said

If your children have already received information from the other parent, minimise the confusion and don't directly contradict what they have already been told. Offer them a consistent message, if possible. Even though they may have received incorrect information from the other parent, you can help your child more by offering support for his or her feelings. For example, imagine Jamie is very angry about Emma's decision to end their 14-year marriage. As a result Jamie has told seven-year-old Tess that Mummy is breaking up the family and she didn't try hard enough to make things better. Instead of directly contradicting Jamie, Emma could say something like this to Tess: 'It sounds like Dad is very upset about the divorce. I can understand why he feels that way. This is difficult for me too. Both Dad and I want you to understand that no matter how we feel about each other we will both always love you.'

▶ State your disagreement clearly

It is okay to let children know you don't agree with something the other parent said, but do your best to avoid setting the record straight with your child. Simply say, 'I don't agree with that,' or 'I see it differently.' Justifying your position only puts your child in the middle of a no-win situation. Children should be neither judge nor jury.

What can you do?

Acknowledge the validity of your children's feelings by letting them know you understand how confusing it must be for them to hear different things from each parent. Here are a few examples of things to say to children:

- 'How do you feel about what Mum or Dad has said?'
- 'I am sorry this is so hard for you.'
- 'I understand how confusing it must be to hear different things about the divorce from two people you love.'
- 'It is important for you to understand you do not have to pick or choose who is right or wrong. This is a grown-up issue that has to be solved by Mum and Dad.'

AGE-SPECIFIC CONVERSATION

Overall, conversations with children need to be kept age specific.

Very young children (between birth and five years old) clearly will not be able to comprehend divorce in the same way as older children. However, even though they don't understand it they will still respond to changes in the family. Because they don't always have the ability to put their feelings into words, expect your little ones to show their upset and stress through their actions. Their distress may be expressed through behavioural changes such as tantrums, becoming clingy, not sleeping through the night or being physically aggressive (hitting, biting or kicking).

Because of their developmental limitations, you will need to offer reassurance with both words and actions. While they're not able to mentally process the concept of divorce, it's still important to acknowledge that things are different. Use words and phrases when appropriate in day-to-day conversation that support the idea that parents live apart. Be sure to keep information direct and explanations short and consistent. As young children continue to hear the same messages from you, they will eventually be able to make sense of it all. Keep in mind that just because you say it once doesn't mean they will understand immediately. Young children need consistency and repetition to gain a new level of understanding. See also the information in Part Two.

WHAT TO DO AND SAY: INFANT TO TWO YEARS

- Keep your child's home environments consistent and predictable.
- Stay mindful of your emotions and how they affect your baby's behaviour.
- Give your little one lots of physical reassurance (hugs, kisses, cuddles and direct eye contact).
- Openly acknowledge differences when they come up. For example, if your little one is asking for a parent you can say, 'You miss Daddy. Daddy isn't here right now. He and Mummy live in different homes,' or 'You will have special time with Mummy tonight when she picks you up.'

WHAT TO DO AND SAY: THREE TO FIVE YEARS

- Provide ongoing structure and predictability.
- Use words and phrases to reinforce that things have changed:
  'You have two homes. A home with Mum and a home with Dad.'
  'Our family has changed. Mum and Dad live in different homes.'
  'This is the way we go to bed at Mum's house.'
  'Mum and Dad are divorced. That means Mum and Dad are not husband and wife any more but we will always be your parents.'
  'Divorce is one way some families change, but you will always be a part of your family.'

Consider using books and stories to help children come to terms with the divorce. Books often provide younger children the opportunity to take information in over time.

Slightly older children (between five and eight years old) will naturally be more concerned with concrete, practical issues and may need more physical reassurance. Some possible questions they may ask are, 'What will happen to my house (my pets, me)?', 'Will Mum/Dad stop loving me?' Keep your answers simple and short.

It will also help young children if you can maintain some predictability in their lives. Minimise significant change to their routines and surroundings as much as possible. Don't be surprised if they choose not to talk about the divorce or separation. It may take some time before they are able to accept the reality that life is changing.

WHAT TO DO AND SAY: FIVE TO EIGHT YEARS

- 'A divorce is when a mum and a dad decide not to be husband and wife any more. Instead of being a family in one home, you will have two separate homes, one with Mum and one with Dad.'
- 'Things have changed in our family. We feel we would be a better mum and dad in different homes.'
- 'We know this will be hard for you, and we are sorry.'
- 'Divorce is never a child's fault. You did not cause this.'
- 'Divorce is a grown-up problem between Mum and Dad that you cannot change.'
- 'While things have changed between Mum and Dad, we will always love you.'
- 'The other important people in your life, like your grandparents and friends, will still be around for you.'

With older children (9 to 18 years old) things can be a little trickier. Usually saying, 'We feel we'd make a better mum and dad

WHAT TO DO AND SAY: OLDER CHILDREN (9 TO 18 YEARS)

Keep in mind that you need to customise what you say and how you talk to your children based on your family's situation.

- 'In a marriage it's important for both parents to be happy together. As hard as it is to understand, we've decided we're not happy together any more. It doesn't mean that anyone has done anything wrong. Two good people aren't always good for each other. That's the way it is for us. We've decided we need to live apart, which means we will be getting a divorce. We want you to understand you're very important to us and how much we love you will never change.'

- 'Sometimes in a marriage how a husband and a wife feel about each other changes. Usually it's not just one thing but lots of small things that happen over time. We know it's probably hard for you to understand how that could happen, and we hope you know our decision to split up wasn't an easy one for us to make. We're really sorry our decision has hurt and upset you.'

- 'Even though we don't want to be together any more, we'll always want to be your mum and dad. You'll probably have questions about how things are going to change, and we want you to know it's okay to talk to us.'

- 'Trust is an important part of a relationship. When a husband and wife stop trusting each other it changes how they feel about sharing a life together. We've stopped trusting each other. The kind of trust needed to make a marriage work, we can't get back. Because of that, how we feel about staying married has changed, and we've decided to get a divorce. No matter how we feel about each other we will always love you.'

- 'When we got married we hoped for the very best. We felt like we would be happy together, and we wanted to be parents. We hope you understand we've tried very hard to make things work. Over the years we've both changed. At first the changes seemed small, but those changes have become bigger, and we now realise that we want different things. While we both want to be your parents, what we each need to be happy isn't the same any more.'

- 'We want you to understand this wasn't an easy decision for us to make. While we've made the choice to end our relationship, we'll always be your mum and dad. Divorce ends a marriage, but doesn't mean the end of your family. It just means your family will change. Instead of being a family in one home, you'll have two separate homes. We also know this will be hard for you, and you will probably have a lot of different feelings about this decision. It's okay to be upset or sad about the divorce. When you feel like talking about it, we're both here for you.'

in different homes' isn't going to satisfy kids in these age ranges. However, don't make the mistake of thinking that because they're bigger they should be given more information about what has happened between Mum and Dad. While older children will need different information than younger ones, they still need to be protected from adult details. Don't discuss adult concerns, do not reveal intimate details about marriage problems, do not mention court matters, and do not ask them to make adult decisions (such as who they want to live with and when they would like to spend time with each parent). When you break the news to your children, it's certainly appropriate to ask your children what they think or how they feel about changes that affect them. Parents, however, still need to be the decision makers. See Part Two for more tips.

A PARENT'S CHECKLIST

▶ Decide what you want to say and how you will manage your feelings before you have any discussions with your children

Be aware of issues that you feel strongly about and give thought to how you'll speak to your children about these issues. It's best if you find some way to address your feelings before talking with your children or work on some way to minimise or manage your reaction. Children will be concerned about how their parents are feeling or handling the divorce. If your children sense that you are not okay, they may become focused on your needs instead of their own. When this happens, emotional boundaries can become blurred, putting children in a position of caretaker. In addition, if you are not managing your emotions well your child's sense of security can easily become compromised (see tips in Chapter 1). How can your children believe that they are going to get through this if *you* are falling apart? If necessary, get professional help in managing your emotions. Children should never be emotionally responsible for a parent. It impairs a child's ability to move forward with his or her own healing process.

▶ Address the concerns of the children

Spend time discussing what is most important to your children, such as when they will see each parent, where will they live and how this change will directly affect their lives.

▶ Plan on a series of discussions

Keep the first conversation focused and brief so that the children do not become overwhelmed. The initial discussion doesn't have to be a formal meeting or talk. It should primarily concentrate on the fact that parents are getting a divorce and how life will change for now. Be sure to leave the door open for children to approach you in the future.

▶ Reassure children that it is not their fault

At one time or another most children will struggle with feeling responsible for their parents' divorce. They need to hear from you that a divorce or a separation is never a child's fault. They will also need to know that there is nothing they can do to fix or change what has happened in the family.

▶ Reaffirm your love for your children

Children often think that if their parents can stop loving each other, it might mean that some day their parents may stop loving them. They need reassurance from both Mum and Dad that the love shared between a parent and child never ends.

▶ Encourage children to ask questions and talk about feelings

Be prepared to accept the wide range of emotions that your children have about the divorce. It can be incredibly difficult to see your children suffer, and instinctively you may want to shield or protect your children. Don't try to fix, change or explain away your children's feelings. It is necessary for children to be able to share how they feel, and your support and validation are critical. Be sure to give children the space and freedom to express their feelings, particularly those of anger and sadness. More information is given in Chapter 24.

▶ Don't pretend you have all the answers

If an issue comes up and you are not sure how it will be handled, it's fine to tell children that you don't know. You can reassure them that once you work things out they will be the first to know.

No matter how great a parent you are, there is no way to take away all the hurt your children may experience as they go through this transition. By providing them with good information and being available to support their feelings you can help to minimise the negative effects.

If you feel you are still having trouble finding the right words you can also go to your local library or bookshop to review children's books or other media resources about divorce before you talk with your children. This will help you:

- Choose the most appropriate resources for your children
- Learn what kinds of language and concepts to use when talking about difficult subjects

- Find alternative tools to help you start discussions with your children, particularly if they are kids who don't like to talk
- Consult with a specialist (a divorce coach, counsellor or psychotherapist experienced in separation and divorce)

IF YOU SAY THE WRONG THING

As they say, to err is human. Expect that as you forge ahead you will make some mistakes along the way. You may wish that you had said something different to your children or perhaps wish you hadn't said anything at all. If you've said something inappropriate or perhaps blamed the other parent, don't panic. However, remember how you handle your mistake is important. Here are some things to keep in mind:

- Realise that you've made a mistake and vow not to repeat the behaviour.
- Apologise to your children. Let them know that you realise that you made a mistake and you're truly sorry for what you did. You may even want to give them permission to let you know if they notice similar behaviour in the future.

In addition to validating your children's feelings, apologising sets a good example. It teaches the valuable lesson that not only is it okay to make mistakes, it is also important to take responsibility for them. When parents are willing to admit they are wrong, a greater sense of trust is established between parents and their children.

15.
WHAT TO DO WHEN CHILDREN ASK WHY

There's a fine line between not saying enough and saying too much. While it is important to think before speaking, it is equally important to think about what your children need to hear.
– Christina McGhee

Not so long ago my husband and I decided to update our wills. Out of convenience, our lawyer stopped by our house to discuss the final details. Since death was a very touchy subject with one of our daughters, we chose to bypass the upset and told the children a lawyer was coming over to talk with Mum and Dad about some grown-up stuff. While we were having our private grown-up chat we told them they would need to play in the other room. Now our youngest has a very strong need-to-know streak. As a result, throughout the meeting she kept popping her head in and out of the room to ask a series of completely random questions. While we knew she was up to something, we dismissed her each time with a customary, 'Not right now, sweetie. We'll talk about it when we're finished.' Once we finished reviewing the legal documents the conversation shifted and our lawyer began sharing a story about a tough case he once worked on.

Shortly after that my daughter walked into the room and whispered quietly in my ear, 'Mummy, can I talk to you right now, please? It's really important.' By the look on her face I could tell it was urgent, so I politely excused myself from the conversation and walked into the other room with her. Looking up at me with huge crocodile tears in her eyes she asked, 'Mummy, are you and Daddy getting a divorce?'

Needless to say, I was gobsmacked. Due to my professional life my kids are no strangers to the topic of divorce. However, I couldn't even begin to imagine why my daughter was worried that her parents' relationship was hanging in the balance. 'Why in the world would you think Daddy and I are getting a divorce?' I asked. 'Because,' she said, 'I heard Daddy tell the lawyer, "It's a very sad situation."' From one simple statement combined with bits and pieces of information, my daughter had constructed a

EXPLAINING WHY TO YOUNGER CHILDREN

Bobby, an eight-year-old in one of my children's groups, was really struggling with why his parents had chosen to divorce. 'Why can't they just work it out and get along?' he asked. Like lots of children, Bobby just couldn't understand how the two people he loved the most didn't love each other.

In an effort to help him understand I asked Bobby, 'What's your favourite food?' He quickly answered, 'Pizza.'

'Do you have another favourite food that you really like? Maybe something sweet like a dessert?' I asked. Without hesitation, Bobby said he really liked doughnuts.

'So what would you think if we put both of your favourite foods together and made a pizza doughnut sandwich?' I asked.

Bobby's response this time was much less enthusiastic. He looked at me as if I were one of the stupidest people on the face of the planet for suggesting something so weird. Patiently and with a great amount of restraint, he explained to me that while pizza and doughnuts were both really good, it doesn't mean they belong together. I suggested that perhaps the same was true with Mum and Dad. Like the pizza and doughnuts, maybe Mum and Dad weren't so great when you put them together. However, when you took them apart they could be really amazing.

story that suddenly sent her anxiety level through the roof. And that's what children do. When they don't have access to information they fill in the blanks on their own.

Now think about your kids. What have you told them about your separation? Do they understand why things didn't work out?

When parents break up, kids naturally struggle to understand why. The idea that love can be conditional and is not always permanent is a tough pill to swallow. At some point their next leap of logic may be, 'If my parents have stopped loving each other, then what would it take for one of them to stop loving me? After all, didn't Mum and Dad once love each other?'

This, of course, is a really important point. Just like the situation with my daughter, when kids are left to fill in the blanks they'll find a way to make sense of what's going on around them. Usually they do this by piecing things together based on their own perception of the situation. This is why your children need to understand in an age-appropriate way why things did not work out between their parents. Without your guidance or an explanation, your children will be left feeling very vulnerable and confused. Keep in mind, however, *how* **you answer your children's questions about your separation is equally important.**

THE HARD QUESTIONS
So whose fault is it?

Children will inevitably want to know more about what happened and why parents are choosing to split up. Initially, it's best to offer children a short explanation that does not place blame exclusively on either parent. For ideas about what to say to children when answering the question why, review the sample statements offered in Chapter 14. Remember this may be a question your children struggle with, so a one-time conversation will not do the trick. Best to be prepared for a series of conversations and to answer this question repeatedly.

Why do your children need to talk about why more than once?

There are lots of different reasons why your children may have trouble embracing your decision to separate. Coming to terms with why is a normal part of the process and happens over time. In the early stages children may wonder:

- **How could this be happening to me?**
  Even once you've told them the situation, your children may not believe you or they might not want to believe you.
- **How long is this going to last?**
  In the early stages children will need you to reinforce that this is a permanent change. Because they may not be ready to accept the reality of your decision, ongoing conversations may be necessary.
- **Did I do something wrong?**
  Separation and divorce usually threaten a child's sense of safety and security. While you may tell your children you will always love them and they are not to blame for what has happened, these messages need to be reinforced. Understanding why also helps children resolve feelings of guilt.
- **Can't you work it out?**
  Children are taught at a very early age that when you have a problem with someone you find a way to work it out. Expect your children to follow the same lines of logic when it comes to divorce. After all, if your children weren't getting along with each other they wouldn't get a divorce, would they? Also, be aware that children may be under the impression that if they can understand the problem they can find a way to fix it. Providing a simple explanation for the break-up can also reinforce that divorce is an adult decision that children can't fix or change.

- **Who's telling me the truth?**
  If your children hear different reasons or receive contradictory information from each parent they may feel very conflicted. This situation puts children in a position of having to decide who is right and who is wrong. Children need to know they should never have to pick sides. Likewise, when Mum and Dad cannot work things out, children need to understand that parents don't always agree.

How much information is enough?

Children are naturally curious. Expect that they'll ask for more specific information. However, don't assume that you need to provide it. When your children ask questions about the divorce, keep in mind that they may have another agenda that isn't so obvious.

To illustrate, let's consider the story about little Toby who comes home from school one day and asks his mother, 'Where do I come from?' She hesitates but decides that, if he is old enough to ask, well, he deserves to know the truth. She quickly runs to the bookshelf, grabs a book and sits Toby down on the couch with her. She then proceeds to have an in-depth conversation with Toby about the birds and the bees and where babies come from. Finally she finishes and says, 'So that's where you came from. Do you have any other questions?' Wide-eyed and looking a little distraught Toby said, 'No, I was just wondering. My friend Anna says she's from London.'

Before providing an answer, consider asking your child some additional open-ended questions like, 'Tell me more about your question,' 'Why are you curious about that?' and 'What do you think?' By doing so you will gain a clearer understanding of your child's need to know.

Consider the following conversation, for example.

SHANNON: Why did you stop loving Dad?

MUM: The feelings Dad and I had for each other changed.

SHANNON: Yes, but why did you have to divorce him? Can't you get those feelings back?

It's possible that Shannon's not just worried about the break-up between Mum and Dad. She may also be worried about what this break-up means for relationships in general or if it's possible that one day Mum or Dad might stop loving her too. Be aware of this issue and make sure to reassure your child that you will never stop loving her.

The conversation could continue as follows:

MUM: No, those feelings are not going to come back. It sounds as if you are wondering how two people could stop loving each other.

SHANNON: If you love somebody, shouldn't you love them for ever?

MUM: When Dad and I married we hoped it would be for ever, but things changed, and we have figured out that we are a happier mum and dad in different houses. It is important for you to understand that the love Dad and I have for you will never change. The love between parents is different from the love between a parent and a child. The love we have for you is for ever.

If one parent wants to stay in the marriage

One parent may not be ready to face the reality that the marriage or relationship is ending. If one parent shares that wish with children it can be very confusing. First, it puts children in the middle and in a position in which they feel they should take sides.

Second, children can easily misunderstand or misperceive a situation. Painting one parent as 'the leaver' may also lead to the other parent being viewed as 'the victim'. This situation may place unnecessary stress on children to protect or defend one parent and reject or punish the other.

Parents who struggle with this issue may say the following things to their children:

- 'I hope that Mum will change her mind.'
- 'He broke up the family.'
- 'I don't want the divorce either, but I can't make Mum come back home.'
- 'I wish Dad wouldn't leave us.'

If you hear yourself saying things like this, regardless of whether you believe them to be true, it is damaging to your children. It is understandable how hurtful and frustrating it is to be in a situation with a partner who is not willing to work things out. However, it is important that you find some way to sort through your feelings about this issue without involving your children.

I have often been asked, 'How do you respond to a child who has been told that the divorce is all one parent's fault?' While it might be tempting to go into all the reasons why the divorce was initiated and tell the children everything that went wrong, it will certainly not be helpful to them. Whether you are the parent who wants to stay in the marriage or the one who wants it to end, it is best to agree to disagree, without blaming one another.

In this situation I recommend that parents give children a comparable example. For instance, you might say to your child, 'When you are in school, has the teacher ever asked the class a question and you knew the answer before everybody else?' Chances are your child will probably say yes (if they say no, ask if somebody else knew the answer before everybody else). You can then let the child know that's how it is with Mum and Dad right now. Sometimes in a marriage one parent might work out how unhappy things are before the other parent.

It's okay to explain to children that, in a marriage, things need to work for both parents. Sometimes things may change in a marriage, and one parent may no longer be happy. But do understand that children may still have feelings about one parent wanting the relationship to work and could be angry with the parent they perceive as leaving the marriage.

When a parent has made bad choices

If the reason for the split is because one parent has been abusive, is dealing with an addiction, has been imprisoned or has engaged in some other inappropriate behaviour, it is best to be honest about the situation.

Remember that being honest does not give you permission to disparage your child's other parent. There is a big difference between portraying your former partner as a bad person and saying, 'I am sorry that Dad is not making safe choices at the moment. I know it must be hard for you to understand why an adult would behave this way.' Help your children separate the behaviour from the person. Children literally view themselves as half Mum and half Dad, so when they hear negative comments about one of their parents their tendency is to view those statements as something bad about themselves. For example, when hearing negative comments about their mother they may think: 'If my mum is a really horrible person, then what does that make me?'

Speak truthfully to your children without exposing them to adult details that will overwhelm them. It is also important to frame information with a child's age in mind. For younger children it is best to keep the language simple and put it in concrete and straightforward terms. For instance, if a parent is an alcoholic you may need to say to your children, 'When Daddy drinks too many beers he does not behave safely.' Older children should have information that can help them identify the parent's unhealthy behaviour.

Ultimately, your *children need to know that their safety is your number one priority*. If a child is confused about why he can't see one parent or why the visits are supervised, you can explain that the other parent is not making good or safe choices at the moment, and until that parent makes better choices the time spent with them will be different.

Children may sometimes feel that fixing a situation is their responsibility, so it's also important to help them understand that a parent's poor choices are not the result of a lack of love, but rather the result of a parent being unable or unwilling to make better choices. Help your children separate themselves from adult choices by reiterating they are not to blame and cannot fix or change the situation with their other parent.

Let your children know that not all adults behave this way. Children need to be reassured that there are reliable adults available other than Mum or Dad whom they can count on or talk to about the situation. Even though you may be a very approachable, supportive parent, sometimes children will worry that if they share their feelings with you they may make the situation worse or upset you. Help your child make a list of safe and dependable adults with whom they can talk. Provide your children with other positive, healthy role models, such as extended family members and teachers. Your chief task in this whole process is to be the most nurturing, stable, supportive parent that you can be.

On the flip side, avoid the temptation to sugar-coat the situation when talking with your children about a parent's bad behaviour. Sometimes in an effort to protect a child from further hurt a parent will choose to misrepresent a situation. When this happens they may build a parent up to be something he or she is not or even give the child unrealistic excuses to pardon a parent's bad choices.

A mother once told me that when her divorce process began, the children's father stopped having contact with their two teenage sons. The boys were very upset by this, and to spare their feelings Mum continually made up excuses and justifications, such as, 'Dad has to work long hours, but he really wishes he could spend time with you.' Eventually, the children learnt that their dad was choosing not to be involved in their lives and they were infuriated with their mother. They felt betrayed, and demanded to know why she had lied to them. While the mother's intentions were motivated by a desire to protect her children, she ended up compromising her own credibility.

Children need honesty in an appropriate and supportive way. It may be difficult to see your children feeling sad or upset. It is quite normal to want to heal the hurt by either setting the record straight or trying to shield children from painful truths. Either way, we deprive our children of the opportunity to build important skills. It is more helpful to our children if we use these opportunities to help them learn how to deal with difficult situations, and – most important – to learn how to recognise unhealthy behaviour in adults.

See Chapter 22 for more information on dealing with difficult situations.

TIPS FOR ANSWERING WHY

▶ Avoid having an impulsive conversation

If your children ask why and you don't feel prepared to answer them, then don't. It's perfectly okay to say you're not ready to answer their questions or you would like some time to think about your answer. Let your children know you understand they feel curious and it's natural to want to know why things didn't work out between Mum and Dad. If you delay the conversation, let your children know when you will talk to them. However, don't wait too long or use delay as a way to put off the conversation altogether. It's probably best to revisit their questions in a day or so.

▶ Help children have a balanced perspective

Because children's self-esteem and identity are closely linked to their relationships with Mum and Dad, help your children maintain a balanced perspective on why things didn't work. Whether you initiated the divorce or not, it's important to remember that in most situations each parent has some responsibility for the relationship not being successful. Do your best to take responsibility for your part and do not place blame on the other parent. Placing blame only puts children in a no-win situation.

▶ Avoid offering children too much information

Children are naturally very curious and at times may press you for more details about why you couldn't make things work. Don't make the mistake of thinking that more information will make your children feel better. Usually it has the opposite effect. Instead of decreasing their anxiety it often increases your children's stress and worry.

Overindulging children with additional details also often leads to exposing children to adult information. While your child may seem capable of understanding the information intellectually, they may not be capable of processing it emotionally.

TELLING CHILDREN THE TRUTH

Remember there are almost always at least two different perceptions of the truth when a relationship breaks down. Rest assured your children will come to their own understanding about why things didn't work between you and your ex in their own way and in their own time.

Often the desire to speak your perception of the truth or to set the record straight has more to do with how you are feeling about the situation than with your children's needs. If you are feeling a strong desire to tell your side of the story, consider asking yourself the following questions first:

- How is this information going to help my child?
- How could this information hurt my child?
- Have I dealt with my own feelings about the situation (see Chapter 3)?

Even though you may take higher ground, it's possible that your ex may not play by the same rules. If your ex is telling children his or her side or perhaps giving children inappropriate or misleading information, don't fight fire with fire. Rest assured your children are smart enough to work out what's true and what's not true about who you are.

If your ex is saying something you don't agree with, it's okay to disagree with the other parent's perception. You can say things like:

- 'I don't agree with what Dad said.'
- 'I have a different opinion.'
- 'That's not the way I see things.'

You can also use the situation as an opportunity to help your children gain some insight. You may want to ask your child, 'How do you feel about what Mum said?'

REVIEW POINTS

- Answer your children's questions honestly in an age-appropriate manner.
- Be sure to shield your children from adult problems and issues.
- Children benefit most from a short explanation that does not place blame exclusively on either parent.
- Answering why provides children with reassurance that they're not to blame for what has happened between their parents.
- When a parent has made bad choices, be honest without disparaging or making excuses.

16.
SUPPORTING THE OTHER PARENT'S RELATIONSHIP WITH YOUR CHILDREN

Love your children more than you hate your ex.
– Christina McGhee

Leonard hated his ex-wife, Judy. In his opinion she didn't even deserve to breathe the same air as he did. She had abandoned the family and ruined him financially when they got divorced. His bitterness was so intense that Leonard frequently shared his less than glowing opinion of Judy with their 10-year-old daughter, Bridget. He often called Judy degrading names and made incredibly demeaning comments about her to Bridget.

Judy, it seemed, was no saint either. While she said she wanted to have an amiable relationship with Leonard, she frequently did things she knew would set him off like a rocket. Judy made it a regular habit to engage Bridget in activities during Leonard's scheduled time. Judy would then tell Bridget about the event before talking with Leonard. Judy explained to Bridget that if her dad really cared about what was important to her he would make arrangements to take her. Due to the distance between their two homes, most of these activities were not feasible for Leonard unless he forfeited his time with Bridget. Judy, while not overtly aggressive, sent a very clear message to Bridget that she did not value Bridget's time with her dad. As a result Bridget was frequently exposed to her parents' vicious arguments and cruel jabs at one another. Neither parent seemed to understand how their constant undermining of one another was damaging Bridget, not the other parent.

Carla, on the other hand, never openly discredited her ex, Jim, in front of the children. She prided herself for always being supportive of Jim's relationship with Sadie and Josh. In her eyes she had never done anything to disrupt the children's relationship with their father. From her perspective she was a good mother and an excellent co-parent. Carla, however, didn't back her words up with action. She regularly made important parenting decisions without consulting or informing Jim. Consistently, he received second-hand information from the children (usually after the fact) about significant issues, such as educational matters, doctors' appointments and other impor-tant events.

While it is to Carla's credit that she never said anything directly critical about Jim to the children, she frequently made negative comparisons between them and their dad. If Josh didn't keep his room clean, Carla would comment, 'You're just like your dad. He never picked up after himself.' If Sadie argued with her mum about a rule, Carla's response would be, 'You're so stubborn and inflexible, just like your father.' Not only did Carla's actions underscore that only negative qualities came from Dad, she also sent a pretty clear message that Dad's involvement in their lives wasn't needed on any level.

WHY DOES YOUR OPINION ABOUT THE OTHER PARENT MATTER?

Without a doubt, you are one of the most important and influen-tial figures in your children's lives. Like it or not, so is your ex. It doesn't take a rocket scientist to realise that how Mum and Dad relate to each other (married or not) plays a tremendous role in children's ability to interact with the world. As a matter of fact, it's a pretty straightforward concept. Essentially, every facet of your children's lives has the potential to be significantly influenced by how you and your ex manage your relationship from this point forward. Positive or negative, what you do and how you deal with each other carries a lot of weight with your children.

NOT-SO-OBVIOUS WAYS PARENTS CAN DEVALUE EACH OTHER

- Not communicating important information to the other parent but sharing it with other family members. (Mum asks Gran to attend Jimmy's school play but doesn't tell Dad about it.)
- Ignoring the other parent's presence at children's events. (Dad says hello to Uncle Ned but ignores Mum even though she is standing right next to him.)
- Disregarding positive comments children make about the other parent. (Jenny tells Mum how much she likes Daddy's pancakes on Sunday mornings; Mum totally ignores Jenny's comment and asks if Jenny is finished with her breakfast.)
- Making negative comparisons between children and characteristics of the other parent. ('You are so much like your mother; she never thinks of anyone but herself.')
- Using language that suggests time with the other parent is a sentence to be served, not time to be enjoyed. ('I'm sorry but the judge said you have to go to Dad's house this weekend,' instead of, 'I think it's important for you to have time with each parent. I hope you have a great weekend with Dad.')
- Asking children to keep information from the other parent. ('I've got a promotion at work and am planning on moving to a new house, but don't tell Mum.')
- Making inside jokes or subtle negative statements about the other parent. ('Boy, Mum has becomes quite tubby. I guess that diet she's on isn't working out for her.')

Keep in mind that how you treat one another also shapes your children's expectations for future relationships. Let's take another look at young Bridget's situation. Without realising it, Leonard is setting the bar pretty low for Bridget regarding how men should treat women and, more important, the value of motherhood. When Leonard insults and devalues Judy in front of Bridget, he is reinforcing a number of damaging concepts. One, it's acceptable for men to treat women in a rude and offensive manner, and two, if someone makes you angry you can justify treating them any way you want. As Bridget becomes older she may very well seek out relationships that mirror her father's attitude. How do you think Leonard might feel when Bridget marries someone who refers to her as a lazy good-for-nothing tart? My guess is he would never tolerate someone treating his little girl that way. Yet what kind of example has he set for Bridget?

However, it's not just the overt lack of support that's destructive; passive undermining also packs a powerful punch. Much like Carla, while you may keep a close watch on what you say, your actions may contradict your words or subtly sabotage the other parent's worth. You can *say* all the right things to children about their relationship with the other parent. However, when your actions don't match your words, children notice. Over time this kind of behaviour can slowly erode a parent's credibility or, worse, children may grow to resent the constant lack of support and negativity. Don't forget children view themselves as half Mum and half Dad. When you reject or devalue the other parent (with words or actions) you are attacking a big part of your child's self-image. Children deserve to love and cherish both parents without worry, restriction or guilt.

WHAT CAN YOU DO TO SUPPORT YOUR CHILDREN'S RELATIONSHIP WITH YOUR EX?

It's no great surprise that when a relationship ends most of us don't have an abundance of warm and fuzzy feelings for each other. After all, clearly there were reasons why the relationship didn't work out. Even when the parting is amicable or civil, usually there are differences and a wide range of feelings about those differences. Those feelings have the potential to rock the boat for even the most dedicated parents. So what's a parent supposed to do? Should you turn the other cheek, and overlook all of your ex's transgressions? Or perhaps, despite how you feel, start singing your ex's praises to your children? Well, yes and no. If the warm and fuzzy feelings aren't there, I don't recommend being dishonest with your children (that is, don't say things about your ex you don't truly mean). When coming up with positive comments proves challenging, it's probably best to say nothing at all. It cannot be emphasised enough that supporting your children's relationship with the other parent is essential. How you accomplish that in words and actions is the tough bit.

Rejecting the custody concept

In my opinion, some of the most destructive concepts to postdivorce parenting ever introduced by the family courts revolve around the ideas of custody, access and contact. Terms like these perpetuate the idea that when parents separate one parent should assume the role of visitor in a child's life. While in this day and age more family courts are supporting the idea of shared parenting, the philosophy of children having one primary parent and one primary home is still incredibly prevalent. Historically, the ideology was that children needed one real home to sufficiently bond and form attachments. Over the past decade this topic has been a hotbed of controversy with family courts and professionals alike. And depending on who you are talking to, there are even more opinions flying around (for and against) about shared care.

From where I sit, however, the way time is shared between parents is not the central issue. From my perspective, supporting each other's relationship isn't about fairly dividing up the minutes and hours of a child's day-to-day life. Rather it is about both parents in good faith facilitating and supporting one another's relationship with children. While we could easily debate for decades the issues of quantity versus quality, the emphasis here is clear. Children have a right to a quality relationship with both Mum and Dad without the pressure of having to view one relationship as more valuable than the other. This idea is also the basis for what I call a two-home concept (see Chapter 17). Although at times it may be difficult to set aside your feelings about one another, remember you're not doing it for your ex, you're doing it for your children.

It may also help to know that avoiding the 'custody' mind-set doesn't just benefit your children but it also has some definite advantages for parents.

BENEFITS OF THE TWO-HOME CONCEPT

THE PARENT WITH *MORE* DAY-TO-DAY CONTACT IS MORE LIKELY TO:	THE PARENT WITH *LESS* DAY-TO-DAY CONTACT IS MORE LIKELY TO:
Receive respect for their role as the primary caretaker in the children's lives	Be supported as an active presence in the children's lives
Get support from the other parent regarding structure and discipline	Gain support for the children having two homes
Experience less stress when the children transition between homes	Have increased time with the children
Receive financial support	Maintain a strong and meaningful relationship with the children
Get cooperation and involvement from the other parent in supporting special events and activities for the children	Be consulted by the other parent regarding important matters

Approach decision making and information sharing as if you were still married

Even though you may have 'lost that lovin' feeling' for each other, your responsibilities as Mum and Dad remain. Whether you feel a decision or activity should involve the other parent or not, be sure to consult or, at the very least, share information. Now that you are divorced, you may feel it's not your job to keep your ex in the loop or believe that what you do in your own home is none of your ex's business. Keep in mind that when you avoid such discussions children often end up in the hot seat.

It usually goes something like this: Let's say Jack called to talk to his 12-year-old daughter, Megan. He asked, 'How was your day?' and Megan started talking about how excited she was to be going to her new school next week. Jack was totally caught off guard; he didn't know anything about Megan changing schools. Instead of being able to share in Megan's enthusiasm, the conversation quickly turned into an interrogation session. Since Megan's Mum, Carol, hadn't bothered to talk to him about the new school, Jack decided to get information directly from Megan. As a result Jack began firing off lots of questions like, 'When was this decided? What's wrong with the old school? How much is this going to cost? Why didn't your mum tell me about this?'

Pretty soon Megan didn't feel like talking any more. Wonder why?

In this case both parents failed Megan. What could they have done instead? Clearly, Carol could have let Jack know about the new school before the decision was made. Possibly sharing information and including him in the decision-making process would have made things much easier for Megan. Even if Jack had been completely unreasonable about the situation, Carol's breaking the news would have saved Megan from getting the third degree.

Although Jack was caught off guard by Megan's news, he could have responded by saying, 'Well, I didn't know about the new school. It sounds like you are really excited. I suppose I should get in touch with Mum. I'd really like to know more about it.' While Jack may have been annoyed that his ex didn't include or inform him, he could have made an effort to shield Megan from his irritation.

Okay, so maybe the idea of talking to your ex about whether your child should play on the school rugby team doesn't exactly thrill you. It doesn't have to. The point here is this: while your relationship has changed, your children's needs have not. Child-centred parenting involves parents making a reasonable effort to share information and include one another in important decisions. While parenting out of two homes is understandably no easy task, do your part by making the opportunity to be involved available to the other parent.

So does that mean you need to send your ex a daily blow-by-blow account of your children's' every waking moment? Probably not. When it comes to the issue of to share or not to share, it may help to ask yourself the following:

- How would I handle this situation if we were still married?
- What will it cost my children not to include or inform the other parent?
- What do my children stand to gain if I include the other parent?

Don't undermine the other parent's authority, even when you don't see eye to eye

Although you may not agree with some of the other parent's perspectives or choices around parenting, avoid undermining their authority with kids. Making critical or contradictory statements about the other parent or their household (rules, structure, etc.) sends children the message, 'You don't need to respect the other parent.' It may not take long before they apply the same kind of thinking to you. In truth, every child on the planet has things she really loves about each of her parents and things she's not so crazy about. You can also expect that, when it comes to enforcing rules or limits, most kids will balk. That's their job. In households in which parents are committed to each other, when one parent sets a limit (usually whether the other parent agrees with it or not), the other backs him or her up. For instance, my husband has a very strict 'tidy your bedrooms before watching TV on the weekends' policy. Me, in theory I'm all for tidy rooms, but I tend to be more lax about it on the weekends and my kids know it. It's not uncommon for them to seek me out and lodge a series of complaints when Dad enforces the rule on Saturday morning. My response? 'If Daddy said you need to tidy your room, then go and do it.' Of course, I realise that when you are parenting out of two homes the differences are often more substantial than whether children need to tidy up. The theory, however, is the same.

Let's say Muhammad wants a mobile phone but Mum says he is too young. When Muhammad is with Dad he complains about Mum being too strict. For good measure, Muhammad adds that Mum's reasons for not letting him have a mobile phone are just plain stupid. All the other kids in school have one, so why can't he? Muhammad then looks at Dad and asks, 'Do you think I'm ready for a mobile phone?' Suppose Dad doesn't have a problem with Muhammad having a mobile phone. Dad could agree with his son and start undermining Mum's decision. While it might be a great way to gain brownie points with his son, jumping on the bandwagon is probably only going to add to Muhammad's frustration, not to mention make things much more difficult at Mum's house. Instead, Dad chooses to back Mum up. He lets Muhammad know that although he doesn't think a mobile phone is a bad idea he respects Mum's decision. Her roof; her rules. Dad also tells Muhammad he needs to respect his mother, even if he doesn't agree with her.

When differences of opinion about rules, structure or general parenting come up, do your best not to undermine the other parent. If it involves a safety issue, certainly those are situations that need to be addressed differently. Yet most differences between households don't involve life-threatening issues. Often it's stuff like should the kids go to bed at 8.30 or 10 o'clock, are crisps and a fizzy drink appropriate snack foods, and/or is it acceptable for Ollie to do his homework in front of the telly? One parent says it's a must, while the other is more laid back. When variations pop up, allow different to be different without criticising or judging the other parent. Look at it this way: The upside is your kids will get two different ways of experiencing life.

POSITIVELY SUPPORT YOUR CHILDREN'S TIME WITH THE OTHER PARENT

Sharing time between households isn't just an adjustment for children. It's also a big adjustment for parents. It can be incredibly hard sometimes to say goodbye knowing you may not see your children for days at a time, or possibly weeks. This is another area in which what you say and what you do come into play. If you feel anxious about your children spending time in the other parent's home, your kids will pick up on it. Even though you may sound as if you are supporting the children's time with your ex, make sure you're not sending your children mixed signals.

Ways to sabotage children enjoying time with the other parent:

- Calling children excessively and/or expecting them to talk on the phone for long periods of time
- Setting children up by saying things like:
  'If you get homesick and need me to come and get you, I will.'
  'I'm sorry but you have to go and see Daddy. There's nothing I can do about it.'
  'I wish you could stay here with me, but the judge said you have to go with Mum.'
  'I will really miss you and think about you every minute you are gone.'

Ways you can support your children's time in the other home:

- Speak positively about the other parent. If you are having a hard time finding something positive to say, focus on making comments about things your children value in the other parent.
  'I can tell you really enjoy going camping with Dad.'
  'I know Mum does a lot of special things for you.'
- Let children know that when they're with the other parent you'll be okay. Emphasise that spending time with each parent is important.
- Help children honour their other parent on special days (Mother's Day, Father's Day, birthdays, family events).
- Display a genuine interest when children share information about time spent with the other parent.

17.
TWO-HOME CONCEPT AND WHAT HELPS CHILDREN

Years from now, when I look back on my life,
I doubt very seriously I will ever regret biting my
tongue, swallowing my pride or taking a higher
road for the sake of my children. But I can
certainly guarantee I will regret the times I didn't.
– Christina McGhee

James has after-school football practice at four o'clock. Unfortunately his practice clothes haven't made it out of the laundry yet. Grace has to be at dance class on the other side of town by half past five. Both kids have a ton of homework, and you find yourself wondering how you are ever going to get it all done. That, of course, doesn't include your own list of to-dos for the evening or week. And what about dinner? Would it really hurt to have a take-away one more night? On your way out the door, both kids hand you notices from school about a series of upcoming events over the next month. You find yourself mentally counting out the weeks as you drive, trying to figure out whether the kids will be with you or your ex. Sound familiar?

The realities of family life do not disappear when parents part. Whether it's sporting events, Boy Scout or Girl Guide meetings, music lessons, science fairs, school programmes or simply sitting down to eat dinner together, life for your children needs to go on. Yet these normal everyday parts of life can become hugely complicated when you are parenting out of two homes.

More important, before your break-up life for your children involved two parents as a part of their everyday life. Now more than ever, your children will need you to support a sense of belonging and connectedness to you and their other parent.

WHY DO CHILDREN NEED TWO HOMES?

Even though I've been talking about a two-home concept for more than a decade, I know from experience that the idea of children having two homes is still not an easy pill for many parents to swallow. Such was the case with a mum in one of my parenting classes a few years ago. A well-dressed, very together-looking woman approached me in the hallway during one of the breaks. She said, 'I wanted to talk with you about this idea of children having two homes. You see, I have always been of the opinion that my children had one home and that home would always be with me.' Upon hearing those words I began mentally gearing up for my standard gentle, yet reaffirming, speech about the importance of children being able to share their lives with both parents. She continued, 'I don't think their father is a bad man. Actually, he's a good father, but I have always been dead set that their real home was with me, and their father's house was some place to visit. Listening to you today I realise that I was wrong about that. I have probably done a disservice to my kids by making sure they felt like visitors with their father. Spending time with him has not been very comfortable for them. I think they've always felt like outsiders looking in. I can't imagine how hard it's been for them to feel like they didn't have a place in their father's life. I can see now that having one home was really more about what I needed than what they needed.'

While your relationship as partners or as husband and wife has ended, your children's need for a family has not. When parents divorce, children often feel as if they have lost their family. However, divorce does not end a family – it changes it. How you handle that change for your children is critical.

Continuing to think of yourself as part of a family with your ex can be very difficult. Right now you are bringing a part of your life to a close. This often involves creating emotional and physical distance between you and your former partner. As you concentrate on your future and seek ways to move forward, keep in mind that your children may be moving in a different direction. Think about the significant role family life plays in your children's lives.

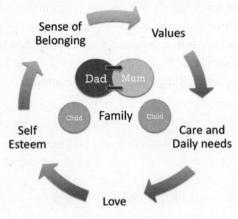

One-home family dynamic

This is where most families start. As two individuals, you choose to become a family and have children. In a healthy one-home family the relationship between Mum and Dad forms the foundation that meets children's needs (self-esteem, values, care, sense of identity, love). Children benefit and grow from their ongoing relationship with both parents and as a family unit.

What do children get from a family?

- Love
- Self-esteem
- Sense of identity
- Values
- Morals
- Security

- Discipline
- Structure
- Food and shelter

While you and your ex are working towards creating separate lives, now more than ever your children need to stay connected to both of you. The challenge then becomes giving yourself the space you need to move away from the marriage relationship while preserving your children's relationship with both parents. This involves promoting a two-home concept and helping children redefine their idea of family.

To better understand the point, take a look at the diagrams below.

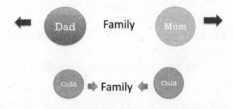

Family dynamic after divorce

After the breakdown of the couple relationship, parents begin to emotionally separate. Soon after, physical separation occurs. Mum and Dad start moving in different directions and distancing themselves from their shared identity as a family. During parental separation, however, children long to maintain their connection to the family and both parents.

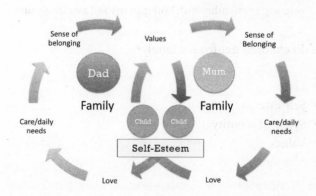

Ideal post-separation parenting arrangement

The two-home concept offers the most potential for children to experience a successful post-divorce adjustment. While Mum and Dad are no longer together, two healthy family environments are established and able to co-exist. Parents provide mutual support for the two households, allowing children to maintain a strong emotional and psychological connection to both parents. Although in two separate homes, children continue to get their needs met by their two families.

The two-home concept has little to do with how much time children spend in each home. Rather this parenting style functions around the idea that, regardless of how time is divided, children feel a sense of belonging with each parent and continue to share a life together.

As you move forward, it may be hard to agree on the best way to restructure life for your children. Each of you may have very different ideas about how life will change in the future. How children spend time with each of you can also become a very complicated and challenging issue. You may find that there is a tendency for one or both parents to view one home as the children's primary home, while the other becomes a place to visit. When parents do not give each home equal value, children experience a number of difficulties:

- It forces children to view one parent as less involved in their lives.
- It contributes to children feeling like an outsider in a parent's life.
- It deprives children of feeling secure about a continuing relationship with both parents.
- It puts one parent in the position of always being the bad guy or disciplinarian, while the other becomes the nice guy or fun parent.

In short, children who are able to feel emotionally, psychologically and physically connected to both homes, regardless of how time is spent with each parent, have the best odds for making a positive adjustment.

Although your relationship has ended, remember your children still need a family.

THE IDEAL SITUATION FOR YOUR CHILDREN

Fundamentals:
- Set aside your differences
- Create a mutual structure between the two households
- Actively support the importance of each other in your children's lives

The two-home concept means:
- Open communication between parents
- Children feel a sense of belonging in each home (they are not visitors)
- Flexible arrangements that meet the needs of the children
- Allowing the children to feel good about their place in both homes

The two-home concept does not mean:
- A 50–50 split in time
- Parents maintain exactly the same structure
- Parents always agree about rules
- Parents spend all special occasions together

HOW TO HELP YOUR CHILDREN ADJUST TO LIFE IN TWO HOMES

Ditch the suitcase

Taking suitcases from one home to the other along with packing and unpacking can create a lot of stress for children. Keeping track of transferring items, what belongs where, and hauling things back and forth are also frustrating for parents. To avoid some of this transitional stress, consider having two sets of everyday items in both homes, such as:

- Pyjamas
- Clothes
- Toiletry items (toothbrush, shampoo, hairbrush)
- Car seats, buggies and nappy bags
- Toys or games

If it is too expensive to purchase two of something do your best to plan ahead and make sure those items are ready for handovers. Avoid getting into power struggles with the other parent over things that make life more comfortable for your children. When you engage in those kinds of battles you are not hurting your ex, you're hurting your children. If one parent sends clothes to help out, try to return them washed, clean and in good condition. If the other parent can't afford to purchase extra toys or items for children to play with, consider allowing the children to pick out several things they can keep at their other home.

When children do not live with you most of the time, you can save money by picking up additional items such as clothes or toys at second-hand shops or car-boot sales. Remember, the effort you put into making children feel comfortable is more important to them than where stuff comes from.

Make sure children have space in each home

It is best if children can have a bedroom in each home. However, for many families divorce can create significant financial constraints. If you are not able to provide your children with their own rooms in your home, consider the next best option. Create a special space where children can keep their things and find them when they are with you.

A dad in one of my parenting classes once told me he put up a tent for his children in his living room with a blow-up mattress. While to the rest of the world it might seem like they were doing without, to his children being at Dad's flat was a great adventure. Remember to be creative.

Change how you talk about each home

While it has been mentioned elsewhere in this book, it is definitely worth repeating: Children and parents should never feel as if they are visitors in each other's lives. Do your best to avoid using words like *contact, visit* and *access*. Instead, talk about time with a parent, your home with Mum and your home with Dad. For more information about why you should avoid this kind of language, see Chapter 19.

Allow different to be different

It's best when parents can establish similar rules, structure and guidelines between the two households, but I have found that for the vast majority of families this is difficult to do. For most people, agreeing on anything in the early stages of separation is hard. Unless a child's well-being is in danger, steer clear of trying to regulate what happens in the other household. When you pass judgement on how your ex manages things in his or her home it makes things very complicated for children. While you may not be crazy about the fact that your ex doesn't make your children brush their teeth every night, chances are nobody's going to die from bad breath. Trips to the dentist may be more frequent, but my guess is that after one filling your children will probably remember to brush their teeth on their own.

Keep in mind there will probably be a lot of things that are different in each home. Even though you may not agree on everything, different isn't necessarily bad. The plus for children is that they learn two different ways of doing things, two different ways of being a family and two different ways of managing life.

The bottom line is: don't make your problem with your ex a problem for your children.

Make your rules and expectations clear

If you and your ex have different rules, remember that your children will need a clear understanding of what the rules are in your home. While it may be very obvious to you that your children aren't allowed to use the computer without permission, keep in mind that if Mum has a different rule it may not be so obvious to your children.

To minimise tension around transitions between homes, it may be helpful to remind children of the rules each time they enter your home. Remember, although you have gone through it once they will continue to need reminders (especially younger children). The use of charts or posted reminders can make remembering easier for children.

Give children calendars

You can often help ease transitional stress for your children by providing them with tangible ways to track time between homes. Your children will have worries about where they are going to be and when. Family events that used to be normal and predictable now leave them wondering where they will be for their birthday, a holiday or next weekend's football game. One simple way to help children manage their anxiety is to post calendars in both homes.

For young children, consider colour-coding two calendars (one for each home). Assign one colour for Dad and one colour for Mum. Mark both calendars corresponding to the appropriate colours with scheduled days for each home. This will help your children easily keep track of which days are with Mum and which days are with Dad.

For older children, you may want to give them a planner with pre-marked dates for the year or at least six months at a time.

Online family calendars can also be a great tool for communicating events more effectively between households. Suggestions for online calendars are given in the resources section.

Transition rituals

One of the big complaints I often hear from parents has to do with managing children's behaviour after children have spent time in the other parent's home. Typically, parents feel frustrated because their children come back either in meltdown mode or bouncing off the walls. Parents report it usually takes them several days to get children back on track after spending time with the other parent. Of course, the same thing happens the next time, and eventually it becomes a source of significant frustration and resentment between households.

Keep in mind that your children are literally shifting between two worlds: Mum's house and Dad's house. In those two worlds there may be different rules, different schedules and different ways of doing things. Often children don't have the emotional space they need to make that kind of transition. Although their behaviour will probably level out over time, in the interim your children may need your help coping with the situation.

If your child is having a difficult time, you may want to consider implementing what I call a *transition ritual*. Basically this means you create a structured, predictable environment for your child every time they either enter or leave your home.

For example, let's say when Nicky gets back from Mum's he is an absolute terror. He doesn't follow rules and has regular meltdowns and temper tantrums. One way Dad could help Nicky is by engaging him in a specific structured activity as soon as he gets back from Mum's house. Suppose he is a very active kid. When he arrives at Dad's house, Dad could take Nicky outside to play catch. After about 30 minutes Dad then transitions Nicky into their regular routine by getting ready for supper or taking a bath. To provide Nicky with consistency, Dad handles his arrivals from Mum's house the same way every time.

Now that Nicky knows what to expect, Dad has noticed that the behaviour problems are starting to be less intense, and Nicky is settling down much more quickly.

STEPS FOR CREATING A TRANSITION RITUAL

- Identify when your child is having problems.
- Pick a specific activity you and your child can enjoy together for about 30 minutes (taking a walk, colouring, putting together a puzzle or playing outside).
- It's important that the activity matches your child's temperament when she gets to your home (if very active, play outside or take a walk; if introverted, play a video game or do some colouring-in).
- Make sure that, whatever the activity, you consistently engage your child in that activity every time.

TIPS FOR MANAGING ACTIVITIES OUT OF TWO HOMES

▶ Support your child's need for both parents to be involved

When you are separated or divorced it can be tempting to avoid the extra hassle and not include the other parent in special activities or events. After all, who wants to deal with more stress? However, think about your child's point of view. When your child has a special event, who do you think are the first people she looks for? That's right – Mum and Dad (notice I didn't say Mum *or* Dad).

The value of parents being involved in children's school events and activities is immeasurable. It's no great surprise that kids who have involved parents tend to perform better academically, have fewer discipline problems and higher levels of self-esteem. Give your kids every advantage and do what you can to support the other parent being involved.

▶ Be responsible for sharing information

In lots of divorce situations one parent often becomes the gate-keeper of information related to children's day-to-day lives. I can't begin to tell you the number of times I have heard parents say, 'If my child wants the other parent at an event then my child will tell my ex about it,' or 'We're not married any more, it's not my responsibility to keep my ex updated about the children's events.' Keep in mind that, while you no longer have a responsibility to your ex, you do have a responsibility to your children.

When you put your children in charge of communicating information to the other household, you are sending the subtle message that the other parent's involvement is not welcome. Think about it: if you were still married, how would you handle the situation? Although your relationship has changed, your children's needs have not.

▶ Share information about both households with others

When children are involved in activities, lessons or school events, let coaches and teachers know your children's schedule and contact information for both homes. It can also be helpful to ask for two schedules and to make arrangements for both parents to participate in scheduled activities. For example, if Henry had football practice every Tuesday and Dad's days are Wednesday, consider altering the schedule so both parents get a chance to take Henry to practice.

This kind of thinking also applies to events like play dates and birthday parties. Friendships are incredibly important to children. When parents do not communicate about these kinds of events, it can create a very awkward situation for kids. Keep each other informed when children are invited to activities and arrange how children will be able to participate.

▶ Avoid creating scheduling conflicts for children

Whenever possible, seek support from both households before involving your children in an activity. This is especially important if an activity takes place during the other parent's scheduled time with the children. It is so incredibly difficult for kids when they are able to attend only every other game or meeting because parents didn't work things out first. If you can't agree on an activity, seek to be creative and find middle ground. When time is an issue for the other parent, consider offering to make an adjustment in the schedule.

If you are a parent who wasn't included in an activity-related decision, focus on how the situation feels for your children instead of how unfair the situation is for you. Although it may feel very one-sided and be inconvenient, find a way to support the activity for your children and work on setting boundaries with the other parent later.

Also, don't engage your children in activities you know they will have a difficult time leaving right before a handover. ('I wish you could stay for the party. I'm so sorry you have to leave and go with your mum now.')

▶ Keep your word

Sometimes, in the early stages, being around the other parent can be tough. However, don't make a tough situation worse for your kids by telling them you will be there and then not show up. As we've discussed, children often worry that if their parents can stop loving each other, then it's also possible that Mum or Dad might eventually stop loving them. While you may tell your kids with your words that you will always love them, you also need to back this up with action. Make every effort to be consistently involved in your children's lives.

▶ Enjoy the moment

When facing significant challenges in life, such as separation or divorce, you can easily lose sight of the important things. The time you have with your children is fleeting, and the moments you spend with them are precious. Make the most of the time you have to cheer at games, applaud performances and work side by side with your child on school projects. I promise you won't regret it!

18.
CREATING A SCHEDULE AND AGREEMENT THAT WORKS FOR YOUR CHILDREN

The greater danger for most of us lies not in setting our aim too high and falling short but in setting our aim too low, and achieving our mark.
– Michelangelo

Working out how to take care of children after you separate is, hands down, an incredibly stressful aspect of uncoupling. If these decisions become paired with the legal process, time spent with children can often become a bargaining chip that, unfortunately, gets thrown in with who's getting the big-screen TV and the dining-room table or – even worse yet – maintenance negotiations. As you move forward it is important to be mindful of two things. First, courts and legal systems only become involved in arrangements for your children if you choose to involve them. The underlying belief is that parents should be able to make reasonable arrangements for children on their own. Second, lawyers and judges are experts on the law, not child development. And they are certainly not the experts regarding your life or the needs of your children. My advice: stay in charge and do what you can to arrive at an agreement with the other parent. Your children's interests will be much better served if you can work together rather than battling it out in court. Remember, most court orders are very restrictive in what they can offer. The legal process is designed to be time limited, not a long-term solution. Yet when you have children, separation and divorce is a lifelong process. As life changes, so will the needs of your children. Rather than put your money and energy into developing an agreement that will be obsolete in a matter of months, consider looking at a bigger picture.

The decisions you make over the coming months have the potential to affect your children's lives for years to come. Not only will your decisions be important, but how you approach your decision-making relationship with the other parent is also crucial. Like many parents, you may feel incredibly unprepared and ill-equipped for managing what lies ahead. Thinking beyond the next few months, let alone the next few years, quite possibly feels overwhelming. Plus you have to figure out how you and your ex are going to make decisions together while you are establishing lives apart.

When it comes to negotiating a parenting schedule, most good lawyers will usually recommend that you get support from professionals outside of the legal process (mediator, family specialist, counsellor or psychotherapist). Often an experienced professional can:

- Offer objective guidance
- Defuse conflict between parents
- Help you stay focused on your children's needs
- Offer additional information and insight about children's needs, long-term consequences, and improving communication between households
- Help you generate creative solutions that benefit your children

Understand that even among professionals there are a wide variety of opinions regarding what's in children's best interest. Some advocate that young children need one primary home, whereas others strongly campaign for a more equal distribution in time between households. To get additional information on how to choose a professional see Chapter 27.

From my perspective no two families are the same, and every situation is unique. Right or wrong, I encourage parents to base decisions on their children's individual needs and avoid a rigid methodology. At the end of the day, what is most advantageous for children is having happy, well-adjusted parents who can provide a stable, predictable life that shields them from unnecessary tension and upset. For some children that may mean having one parent who spends more time providing day-to-day care, while the other parent devotes time to children on weekends and one night during the week. For another family, what works may be parents who live a street away and alternate weeks.

Your kids; your call. Ask yourself: do you really want to hand decisions over to a system of courts and lawyers that has no vested interest in your children's future? If not, then it's essential you find some way to make decisions together.

FINDING COMMON GROUND, DEVELOPING A GUIDING PRINCIPLE

As mentioned before, parents who are able to put aside their differences and work towards putting children first ultimately manage the process more successfully for themselves and for their children.

Of course, doing that is easier said than done. Keeping your emotions in check requires more than a good dose of commitment, it also takes perspective. To gain that perspective, I frequently encourage parents to create what I call a *guiding principle*. Essentially, a guiding principle is a simple one-sentence statement that expresses your highest values as a parent. It is child-focused and articulates your personal vision for parenting your children after you separate. You and your ex can create a statement that reflects your mutual aspirations or you can develop one on your own. More than a statement, a guiding principle is also a tool you can use to help you stay more connected to your values than your emotions when things get rocky or overwhelming.

Examples of a joint guiding principle are:

- Despite how we feel about each other, our children will receive all the love and support we have to offer.
- Our children will grow up with a strong sense of family in both homes.
- We are both committed to raising children who are happy and successful.
- Although our marriage has ended, our children will grow up with two supportive, loving parents who work together.

Examples of a personal guiding principle are:

- I am committed to my children's emotional well-being and success in life.

FIVE QUESTIONS TO ASK YOURSELF BEFORE DEVELOPING A PARENTING PLAN

1. What would an ideal outcome look like for you? For your children?
2. Right now, what are your top three priorities?
3. Five years from now, when you look back on all of this, what would help you feel proud about how you handled this situation for your children?
4. If you took the other parent's action out of the equation, what could you do to make this situation better for your children?
5. What are your strengths and weaknesses as a parent? What are your ex's strengths and weaknesses? How can you use those strengths to benefit your children?

- I will manage my parenting relationship with integrity, regardless of the other parent's actions.
- I will honour the love I have for my children more than the anger or hurt I feel.
- I support my children's right to have an active, healthy and loving relationship with each of their parents.

Think about writing your guiding principle on a note card or a piece of paper. You can either carry it with you or put it somewhere you will see it often. Use it as a way to visually remind yourself of what matters most. Whether you are facing a difficult decision, stuck at a crossroads or locked in an impasse with the other parent, reflect back on your statement and ask yourself if your current course of action is supporting your priorities. If not, then consider what you need to do or change to honour your values.

FACTORS TO CONSIDER AND QUESTIONS TO ASK WHEN CREATING A PARENTING PLAN
What was your children's life like before you separated?

- How involved was each parent in your children's day-to-day care (who took them to school, helped with homework, put them to bed at night)?
- When are your children used to seeing each parent? How have they typically spent time with each parent in the past?
- Are there special activities your children are involved in? Will they be able to maintain those activities? If so, how?
- Now that you are separating, how will each of you realistically be able to fulfil the same needs (will one parent have to work longer hours or go back to work)?

Age and gender of each child

- How old are your children?
- What are the special needs of each child (infants need hands-on care; older children need consistent contact)?
- Consider each child's personality and gender.
- Do your children have or need a stronger connection to one parent at this time (teenage boys need to be actively involved with their father; young girls may identify more with their mother)?
- Are there certain interests or activities that you share with your children? How can each of you be supportive of that (one parent may coach a child's team, whereas another participates actively in school events)?
- How will you accommodate the needs of each child to have quality one-on-one time with both parents?

Meeting the daily needs of the children

- Do both of you work? If so, what are your schedules?
- If one parent stays at home or maintains a home-based business, how will that affect the parenting arrangements?
- Do either of you have jobs that require travel or on-call duties?
- Do either of you frequently have last-minute work-related changes in your schedule? If so, how will you communicate that to one another? How will you make arrangements for the children if one parent is unavailable?
- Do children go to school or nursery? Who is best able to manage parenting responsibilities in the mornings?
- What are the after-school arrangements? Who is best able to handle that parenting responsibility?
- How will homework be handled?

- How will you exchange information about the children's daily needs, homework assignments and special events?
- What plan do you have for managing items between households?
- What will each household be able to provide (bedrooms, personal items, clothes, toys)?

Financial realites of each household

- What do you want your children's quality of life to be like in each household?
- What are the financial realities of each home?
- How will finances need to be adjusted so that children will have what they need with each parent?

Be aware that when determining the level of financial support given and received between households, the current child support system focuses upon the number of overnight stays children have with each parent in the year. This may mean that one overnight stay in the year could have a significant impact on the level of financial support a parent either pays or receives.

In some situations agreeing on finances may stand in the way of creating arrangements that will work best for your children. Consider cross-checking your agreement with your lawyer or a child support calculator to make sure you understand the implications of your decisions. Regardless of which position you are in, do your best to balance financial realities with the needs of your children.

Areas of special consideration

- Do any of the children have special conditions or medical needs?
- How will medical appointments be handled?

- What if a child is sick?
- How will decisions about education be made?
- How will other important decisions be dealt with?
- What are the arrangements for shared expenses (extra-curricular activities, field trips, school supplies, sports, medical needs)?
- How will you arrange special events and holidays? Which events or holiday rituals and traditions are most important to your children? How will you support them?
- How will you handle gifts on birthdays and special occasions for children? What if a child wants to take her gift to the other home?
- How will you help your children handle special occasions for the parents (Mother's Day, Father's Day, birthdays)?
- What kind of contact will your children have with each of you during the summer or during extended periods of time?
- How will you manage holidays or special trips? What is your arrangement about sharing information regarding trips with the children?

How you relate to each other (level of tension, stress, conflict)

- How well do you manage disagreements with one another?
- How will you manage them now?
- What is your plan if you cannot agree on an important issue?
- How will you avoid litigation in the future?
- What guidelines have you established for communicating with one another?
- What will be your primary mode of communication (phone calls, scheduled meetings in a neutral location, texting, email)?

Proximity of households

- Are your two homes in close proximity to each other or a considerable distance apart?
- How will transportation between households be arranged?
- What are the arrangements regarding pick-ups and drop-offs?
- If there is significant distance between the homes, how will you keep each other involved in children's day-to-day lives?

Contact when the children are not with you

- How will you handle telephone calls with children?
- How will you handle extended periods of time in each household?
- What kind of contact will the children need from the other parent when they are with you?
- How will you support each other if the children are having difficulty transitioning between homes (a child doesn't want to go with the other parent or asks not to leave the parent he is with)?

Structure and rules

- What kind of values (honesty, respect, learning, responsibility, safety, faith, family) do you want your children to grow up with?
- How will you support those values in each home?
- How will you handle discipline? How will you support each other around this issue?
- What kind of structure do the children need? How will you each support that?

- How will you address differences between your two households?
- What can each of you do to make transitions between homes easier for your children?

New relationships

- As parents, how will you handle new relationships?
- How will you handle them with the children?
- Will you have a mutual agreement about overnight guests?
- If either one of you remarries, how will you handle decision making? Discipline?

TIPS FOR CREATING A SUCCESSFUL PARENTING PLAN

▶ Write it down

The truth is, you have no idea what the future holds, and planning for every circumstance in your children's lives from this point forward is impossible. However, addressing key areas up front will help substantially. Some parents choose to incorporate their parenting agreement with their final orders. Others may sit down together with a mediator or another neutral party to negotiate a plan. Even if your relationship is very friendly, it's best to acknowledge your mutual understanding by creating an agreement you both sign. Right now you are in the beginning stages and most likely many changes will take place over the coming months and years. When those changes occur, there is the potential for emotions to influence both your memory and your judgement. Putting your plan in writing helps makes expectations clear for both of you from the very start and can help minimise future misunderstandings.

▶ Create flexibility

Keep in mind that things don't always go according to plan. Perhaps one of the children gets sick, another gets invited to a last-minute birthday party, or you got stuck in bumper-to-bumper traffic on your way to drop the children off. Things happen. When drawing up your agreement, give some thought to how you will manage unexpected changes, situations when you don't agree, or a possible change in circumstances.

▶ If needed, use a third party

Often parents tell me, 'If I could talk to the other parent, I wouldn't be getting a divorce,' or 'My ex is impossible, there's no way we can work together.' If either is a concern for you, consider using a neutral third party (such as a mediator, counsellor or family lawyer) to help you negotiate a parenting plan. Some parents find they can work together better once the tension from the marriage has been removed. For those who have difficulty moving beyond the emotions, a third party can often guide conversations and help you stay focused on the needs of your children instead of on each other.

▶ When your ex isn't willing

If you simply can't sit down with your ex to discuss parenting issues, consider making copies of the questions listed in the last section and answering them on your own. Although thinking through issues cooperatively would be ideal, you can still prepare yourself for addressing areas of concern. It is also important to note that children can still benefit substantially even if only one parent commits to higher aspirations and works towards minimising the conflict between homes. Although your ex may not be able or willing to negotiate right now, understand that things could still change in the future.

Once you have each had an opportunity to think things through, take time to review your answers and decide on your top priorities. If necessary, address those concerns with your lawyer and talk about how you might be able to address certain issues in your final order.

DIVIDE AND CONQUER STRATEGY

CREATING ONE-ON-ONE TIME WHEN YOU HAVE MORE THAN ONE CHILD
Instead of exchanging all the children from one home to the other, think about sharing time differently. Arrange times with the other parent that allow both of you the opportunity to spend special one-on-one time with each child. Here's an example:

Michael and Rachel have three children, Nettie, Rosie and Billy. Twice a month, usually on Wednesdays, Michael and Rachel make arrangements to divide the children for the evening. One Wednesday Michael will take both the girls for a father-and-daughter night, giving Rachel one-on-one time with Billy. Another evening Rachel may keep Billy and Rosie for the night, giving Michael time with Nettie. This offers children the opportunity to have individual time with each of their parents.

WHAT IS SHARED PARENTING OR SHARED CARE?

In short, courts do not become involved in parenting arrangements just because you decide to divorce. Actually, most parents continue to parent their children from two different homes without any guidance from judges or magistrates. It is only when one parent asks for an order to be made that the court has a say in decisions regarding your children. Overall, it is assumed that most parents should automatically have 'parental responsibility' for their children. This means that each parent has all the rights, duties, powers, responsibilities and authority a parent can have in relation to their child. Further it is assumed that significant decisions should usually be made jointly. Unfortunately when one parent makes unilateral decisions over things such as choice of schools, religion, medical treatment or involvement in counselling/ psychotherapy then the other parent may feel compelled to complain and seek orders from the court. While each court may vary in how these issues are approached, most judges and sheriffs acknowledge the benefits of children spending significant time with each parent. They are also likely to promote joint decision-making between parents and prefer to minimise their role in determining arrangements for children.

In recognising and encouraging the ongoing active involvement of each parent in their children's lives, terms such as *shared residence, shared parenting* and *shared care* have become more commonplace among legal systems. Although the language may sound more even-handed, these terms do not mean that children will spend equal amounts of time in each home. How time is arranged between parents can vary considerably and is often influenced by a number of factors. Even when both parents share in decision-making powers, children may still spend the majority of their time with one parent in one home, while in other parenting situations shared care may involve a more equal distribution in time. In short, children live part-time with Mum and part-time with Dad. To find out more about what types of parenting arrangements might be available to you, consider consulting a local family lawyer or mediator.

WHAT IS EQUAL TIME AND WILL IT WORK FOR YOUR CHILDREN?

Parents frequently ask me about equal time arrangements and how they work. Usually *equal time* or *shared care* arrangements come about because one or both parents are interested in creating an agreement that feels fair. In my experience, the key to how time is shared between households basically comes down to how well you and the other parent can work together. Arranging time with children should not be based on what feels fair to you or the other parent. As insensitive as this may sound, it isn't about you and it isn't about your ex. The focus of parenting arrangements needs to be what works for your children. And while we're on the subject, how time is arranged with children shouldn't be gender-based or about who is the better parent. As parents, you each fill a special and unique role in your children's lives. The strengths you have to offer your children as parents are incredibly valuable. Instead of focusing on the hours and minutes of your children's lives, do what you can to honour those strengths in one another, and create an arrangement that places your children's needs first.

More equal time agreements benefit children when:
- Both parents can openly share information and consistently communicate with each other in a constructive, child-centred manner
- Each parent values the other and is actively supportive of their relationship with children
- The parents live in close proximity to one another
- The parents respect each other's parenting styles and structure
- The parents are in agreement about overarching values (respect, morals, education, etc.) and maintain a similar structure in each household
- Each parent has the ability to establish a positive and functioning household for their children (including the provision of bedrooms, personal items, clothes and toys)
- The parents are capable of resolving disagreements without exposing their children to adult issues and tension

Equal time agreements do not benefit children when:
- The parents have unresolved hostility and animosity towards one another
- The children are exposed to increased tension and upset between Mum and Dad
- One or both parents are unsupportive of the children's relationship with the other parent

- The parents are not capable of sharing information in a constructive manner that keeps their children shielded from adult issues
- The parents live a significant distance from one another, making transport to school or activities a hardship for everyone
- The parents put energy into trying to control one another's households
- The parents have extremely different parenting styles
- The parents cannot agree about overarching values
- The parents do not have a history of successfully resolving differences

NESTING

Nesting, also often referred to as 'bird nesting', is another type of arrangement that may or may not be a reality in your area. Instead of children travelling between households, parents move in and out of the family home. Essentially, nesting involves creating a schedule in which each parent spends a specified period of time with the children. Times are alternated between Mum and Dad, so that only one parent at a time occupies the family home with their kids.

Reviews of this post-divorce parenting model tend to be mixed. For nesting to be a successful arrangement for children there needs to be a high level of cooperation and workability between parents. For many parents in the beginning stages of separation this is usually a tall order. In situations where parents are angry or openly hostile with one another, the consequences of using this model can be disastrous for the children.

If parents can manage this type of situation, it's possible that their children can benefit. However, nesting is typically not a good long-term option because it offers limited flexibility for families to establish separate households and move forward with their lives.

SHARING ONE HOME AFTER YOU HAVE FILED FOR A SEPARATION OR DIVORCE

Although it is ideal for parents to each establish a separate residence once they have made a decision to end their relationship, it isn't always a realistic option. For various reasons, many families may need to live under one roof for a period of time after parents have decided to split up. In these situations parents often struggle with whether they should tell the children. Many parents worry they will create a more confusing situation for children if they tell them the relationship is over yet continue to share a home.

In my experience, once you are certain about your decision to separate it's best to tell your children. More often than not, children know much more than you think. While you may feel like you are concealing your decision, children's emotional radars are often very sensitive to tension between Mum and Dad. By not saying anything to your children you run the risk that they'll misinterpret the upset or stress. Often not knowing can create more anxiety and put children in a position of trying to make sense of it on their own.

> Regardless of which option you choose, how parents relate to one another is one of the most significant predictors in how children adjust to any parenting plan.

If you and your partner are certain about your decision but are not able to transition into separate households, keep the following in mind:

▶ **Make a plan to tell the children**
When talking to children, let them know that your decision is a permanent one. Also tell them that, for the time being, things may not seem very different. In an age-appropriate way, explain your

reasons for staying in one home. For example, you could say something like, 'Before Mum and Dad can have separate homes we need to work out some important things. Once we have figured out how and when things are going to change, we will let you know.'

▶ Act like parents, not a married couple

If you have told your children that your relationship has ended, then you need to stop behaving like a married couple. It is incredibly confusing to children when parents continue to behave in the same ways they always have yet have told children that things are different. While there may be some emotional distance in your relationship, make sure you talk with one another about how you will responsibly manage your relationship from this point forward. The message you want to send to children is that while you are no longer a couple you will always be Mum and Dad.

▶ Minimise tension for your children

If there is a high level of tension between you and the other parent, do your best to handle it in a constructive way. Consider arranging your schedules so you can avoid spending time together without compromising your children's care. If possible, you may want to consider creating a schedule that allows you to each spend individual time with the children (say Tuesdays and Wednesdays are Mum's night and Thursdays and Fridays are Dad's nights). Trying various schedules while you're under one roof may give you the advantage of working out what will be best for your children. It may also help children adapt to spending time with each of you differently before transitioning into two homes.

19.
PARENTING POINTERS FOR ON-DUTY AND OFF-DUTY PARENTS

You never really understand a person until you consider things from his or her point of view.
– Harper Lee

When it comes right down to it, far too many parents look to the legal process to define their post-divorce parenting roles. In the court system the parent who has more day-to-day contact with children is typically viewed as the *resident parent* or *parent with care*, whilst the other parent becomes known as the *non-resident* or *non-custodial* parent. No matter how you slice it, not only does court-based language support an imbalance in your parenting relationship, but it also does a tremendous disservice to your children (see also Chapter 16).

AVOIDING COURT-BASED LANGUAGE

Instead of looking at yourself or the other parent as either resident or non-resident, the parent-with-care or the non-custodial parent, I strongly recommend you consider using words that actually support both of you as an active presence in your children's lives. Instead of using court-based language, consider referring to your respective roles as *on-duty* and *off-duty*. Although it may have a bit of a military ring to it, keep in mind that words are powerful.

What we say affects and reflects not only our attitudes but also our choices and actions. It is also important to remember that words mean different things to different people.

To illustrate the point, look at the words *resident* and *non-resident, parent with care* and *non-custodial*. In the chart below, each column contains some stereotypical words and meanings that separating parents might associate with each of these legal terms.

WAYS PARENTS MIGHT INTERPRET LEGAL TERMS

RESIDENT PARENT/ PARENT WITH CARE	NON-RESIDENT PARENT/ NON-CUSTODIAL PARENT
In charge	Not in charge
Responsible	Irresponsible
More important	Unimportant, not valued
Better parent	Less than parent
Greater influence	No influence
Decision maker	No choice
Winner	Loser
In control	No control

Think about what kind of feelings come up for you when you read these words. How do you think these interpretations might influence your view of the other parent? How do you think they may affect your ex's attitude towards you?

Making a commitment to using language that promotes a two-home concept supports:

- Both parents as an active presence in children's lives
- Both parents as valued and essential

- Parenting roles as interchangeable, not fixed (regardless of how time is spent with children)
- A sense of family and belonging (children and parents sharing a life together)

WORDS TO AVOID AND WORDS TO USE

LEGAL WORDS THAT DIMINISH PARENT–CHILD RELATIONSHIPS	TWO-HOME CONCEPT WORDS THAT SUPPORT PARENT–CHILD RELATIONSHIPS
Visiting rights	Parenting schedule
Contact	Parenting time
Custody	Time with a parent
Access/contact	Time with Mum, time with Dad
Residential or parent with care	On-duty parent
Non-resident or non-custodial parent	Off-duty parent
Residential home	Mum's home, Dad's home

HOW YOU VIEW EACH OTHER'S ROLES

While each parenting situation is unique, the reality for many families is that one parent typically spends more time being on-duty than the other. Sometimes this is due to the demands of a job, the distance between homes, the personality of each parent, the needs of the children, safety issues, legal precedence or simply an established pattern of parenting that carried over from the marriage.

Of course, those divisions in parenting responsibilities don't just exist in families in which parents are separated or divorced. I spend a significant amount of time being an on-duty parent, for example. For the majority of our marriage my husband has had a very demanding job. It's not uncommon for his schedule to change at a moment's notice. As a result I have had to spend a lot of time thinking on my feet and making last-minute changes to my own schedule. I can tell you it hasn't always been a walk in the park for us, and we have both had to make lots of adjustments. I have had to cultivate the art of being extremely organised and flexible. Learning how to make time for myself has also been essential. My husband, on the other hand, has had to make adjustments as well. He has had to develop new ways of staying connected to our children and making the time he is at home count. Although we have an established and agreed structure, while my husband is away on business the children and I have our own way of managing life. Often my husband finds himself having to adjust his expectations and quickly catch up on what he's missed. There have also been times when we have had to switch our roles. When I'm away from home for speaking tours or training, I become the off-duty parent. During those times I'm reminded of what life must be like for him and how hard it is to be away from the children. Likewise, when he's the on-duty parent his appreciation for managing home life is certainly enhanced.

The difference here is that, as a married couple, we have a vested interest in understanding one another's perspective, respecting each other's roles and communicating our needs. When you are divorced, that commitment or vested interest is removed. The vantage point you see each other from changes. Instead of seeing the very best in one another it becomes much easier to see the very worst.

When this happens, the understanding, respect and communication you once had can quickly turn into resentment and mistrust, with little or no communication.

One way I work to help parents avoid this pitfall is by asking them to step into their ex's shoes. Most of us typically see life on the other side of the fence as somewhat greener. Yet it has been my experience that each role (those who have more time and those who don't) has its peaks and valleys.

Parents who have most of the care-taking responsibility often feel incredibly overwhelmed. Here's what they have said about their roles:

- 'Why do I have to be the only disciplinarian – the bad guy who always has to enforce the rules?'
- 'I don't get to have fun with my children. Seems like every bit of time is taken up by homework, activities, getting them ready for school or putting them to bed.'
- 'I never have any time for me.'
- 'I have to be responsible for everything.'
- 'The other parent doesn't appreciate me or what I do.'

Parents who have less time with their children often feel a deep sense of loss. Here are some of their thoughts:

- 'How can I parent my children? Providing any structure or discipline over a weekend is pointless.'
- 'I've become a spectator in my children's lives. I have no influence.'
- 'I'm missing out on my children growing up.'
- 'The other parent gets to be there for all of the important things in their lives.'
- 'I wish I could be more involved.'
- 'The other parent doesn't appreciate what I'm going through.'

ON-DUTY AND OFF-DUTY PARENTING

Changing the way you think about parenting roles also benefits you as a parent. Parenting should be approached as a shared responsibility, a team effort. When you use supportive terms it puts you both on the same team, not at opposite ends of the parenting pitch.

Consider this: In a sports game the goal is to play your best. However, that doesn't mean that every member of the team is on the pitch at the same time. Even when you're not the one in the game, you still support your team. At other times your role may be more active. You're the player who's on the pitch, playing your best.

I would encourage you to think about parenting out of two homes the same way. When you are the on-duty parent you're the one responsible for taking care of the children. Whether it involves managing homework, providing discipline or chauffeuring your kids to a piano lesson, you're in the game. As an off-duty parent you're on the sidelines for the moment but still playing an active role in supporting your children. Maybe it's through calling regularly, attending school activities or showing up at a cricket match to watch your kid hit a six.

Remember, as life changes, so will your children's needs. And as their needs change, so will your roles as on-duty and off-duty parents. Do your best to stay open to the possibility that you each may need to make adjustments down the road.

Successful parenting involves:

- Making the needs of your children your highest priority
- Understanding that how time is arranged isn't about who is the better parent but rather what's best for your children
- Acknowledging one another's strengths as parents

Again, I want to emphasise that a two-home concept is not about fairly dividing up the minutes and hours of your children's lives (be sure to read Chapter 17). Parenting arrangements should be centred on:

- The needs of your children
- Minimising the amount of stress your children experience transitioning between homes

Keep in mind that what's successful for one family may end up being absolutely disastrous for another. Some children may benefit enormously when parents take a more even-handed approach to sharing time and parenting responsibilities. Other children may really struggle with dividing their time equally between households. More than anything, your children will be most affected by how you manage your relationship with one another. Although it can be difficult at times, do your best to maintain a balanced perception of one another and support each other's parenting roles in word and deed.

Despite the type of parenting plan you arrange, each of you will be parenting differently now than you ever have before. Either role will mean change for you and change for your children. To help you navigate those changes I have provided tips and ideas for both on-duty and off-duty parents. Regardless of which role you are currently filling, I recommend reading through both sections. Not only will you gain some insight into the other parent's situation but you may get ideas about how to support your children when they are with your ex.

Guidelines for on-duty parents

▶ Take time for yourself

Although it's a point that has been emphasised throughout this book, it bears repeating. Self-care is the cornerstone of good parenting. This is especially true when you spend the majority of your time being an on-duty parent. While your children may be a significant part of your life, they should not be the centre of your existence. Not only is it a tremendous burden to place on your children but it opens the door to numerous boundary issues and simply sets a bad example for kids.

Make sure you are allowing yourself time to maintain your physical health and do things you enjoy. Think about it. When was the last time you saw a film you wanted to see without your children, spent time involved in a favourite activity or hobby, or took a trip to visit a friend you haven't seen lately?

If your options are limited, think about small ways to keep up your energy. Spend at least 20 minutes every day by yourself doing something that you want to do. For example, maybe you put the children to bed early so you can take a hot bath, or perhaps you leave your desk once a week to take a walk in the park or have lunch with a friend. If you're running short on ideas, check out Chapter 2.

▶ Manage your time wisely

Often the key to good self-care starts with learning how to manage your time differently. Be selective about how you spend your time and avoid stretching yourself too thin. If you find yourself scrambling to get everything done or always running late for appointments, consider looking over the Weekly Time Management Tips below.

WEEKLY TIME MANAGEMENT TIPS

Start managing your time in a way that honours your priorities and offers you the opportunity to focus on what matters most. Your time and energy are valuable commodities and should be treated as such. Creating a schedule for yourself is a gift, not a sentence you have to serve.

1. Make a weekly plan. Schedule one day a week when you can spend 20 to 25 minutes planning the upcoming week. It's best if you can choose the same day every week for planning and put it in your diary.
2. Identify the have-to-do's and list them for the week. These are things you already have scheduled that have to be done during the week (appointments, picking children up after school, work responsibilities, etc.). Put all of these in your diary first. Be sure to estimate how much time you realistically need for each item.
3. Next, identify the need-to-do's and want-to-do's. These are other things you should or would like to get done (go to the gym, balance your bank statement, pay bills, take the kids to the park, go shopping, etc.).

Now review your diary and see where you have pockets of time. Prioritise these items by need to and want to, and schedule the most urgent or necessary items first.

4. When scheduling, think about how you can combine items or tasks to make your day flow better (making several telephone calls in one sitting, running multiple errands, or pairing up a trip to the gym with buying groceries).

Be sure to schedule breaks for yourself, mealtimes, and prep time for scheduled events.

If needed, use visual reminders to help you stay on track (place sticky notes where you will see them, set alarms or timers, make a habit of carrying a notebook or diary with you).

5. Be gentle with yourself when things don't go as planned. Everyone has off days, and unexpected things will happen. If you get off track, use it as an opportunity to reflect on what did not work and start afresh the next day.

▶ Develop a network

In addition to having people in your life who are emotionally supportive, make sure to put time into building a good community network for yourself. For example, you might want to line up a reputable mechanic for when your car breaks down, a baby-sitter you can trust, someone to clean your house and/or a reliable accountant. Seek out people who offer services that can make life a little bit easier when you are feeling overwhelmed.

▶ Make time to enjoy your children daily; quality is important

When parenting on your own, it's easy to become so caught up in the daily grind that you forget to enjoy spending time with your children. Do your best to set aside some time every day when you can give the children your undivided attention and engage them in an easy, low-maintenance activity. Perhaps you take a family walk around the block before supper, play a game of cards or read a book together every night before bed. Make sure, whatever you do, that it's hassle-free and enjoyable for both you and your kids.

▶ Readjust your priorities

Readjusting your priorities can be a real sanity saver. When you find yourself feeling overwhelmed, take a step back and ask yourself, 'What needs my immediate attention and what can wait?' Chances are there's something you can let go of for the moment. For example, let's say you need to pay the bills, mow the lawn and wash multiple loads of laundry. Instead of staying up until midnight to get everything done, consider washing and drying one load, let the grass grow for a few more days and spend your energy on paying the bills. After all, in the grand scheme of things, what will matter most? That you raised healthy, well-adjusted kids or that there were never dirty dishes in your sink?

▶ Use your time away from the children to recharge

When you spend most of your time being an on-duty parent it can feel a little awkward when your children are not with you. Instead of waiting until your children walk through the door, think ahead about things you can do for yourself when your children are with their other parent. Whether it is to take a hot bath, spend time with friends, engage in a hobby or read a good book, make sure you are doing something relaxing that helps you recharge. Do your best to use the time wisely.

Guidelines for off-duty parents

▶ Help children feel physically connected to your home

Provide children with a space for their things, even if it is only a corner in a room. Sometimes having children help place pictures or give input about where things go gives them a sense of belonging. It also lets children know they are not only an important part of your home but are an important part of your life.

▶ Stay away from suitcases

While it's not always economically feasible, when possible purchase second sets of personal items and clothes for children to keep at your home. Lugging a suitcase between homes is not only difficult and uncomfortable but also serves as a constant reminder that time in your home is limited. Children adjust better if they are able to have what they need at both homes instead of carting belongings back and forth.

▶ Avoid treating your child like a guest in your home

Include children in family activities such as doing the laundry, making dinner and cleaning up. You can also create new family rituals or activities that allow you to enjoy time together.

▶ Minimise distractions for children when making a transition between homes

It may be helpful, especially with younger children, to develop some type of routine or ritual for transition times. It could be as simple as taking a walk together before returning to the other parent's home. Children usually have a greater sense of security and feel more in control when they know what to expect.

▶ Try to keep children updated on changes that occur in your home when they are not there

Quite often as adults we pay little attention to how things change in our home on a day-to-day basis. However, changes we may view as small or insignificant can be a really big deal to your children. When children are hit with lots of new changes at one time they may go into sensory overload, or too many changes can contribute to their feeling insecure. Talking about changes beforehand not only helps prepare children but also leaves them feeling more connected to your day-to-day life.

▶ Create memorable events

Although your children may not be with you the majority of the time, work on creating memorable events. Consider making the ordinary *extraordinary*. For many years in our family we had dinner with my bonus children every Wednesday night. As a result we dubbed Wednesdays as *family dinner* night. On those evenings we would have picnics in the park, go out to dinner or cook special foods. In addition to reinforcing the concept of family when we were together, it also created a special memory for all of us.

▶ Be involved in children's activities

It's always sad to see a child who gets to go to football games only every other weekend because his parents aren't together any more, or to learn of children who miss out on a birthday party with friends because it's the other parent's weekend. While it may not always be convenient, do your best to support and be involved in activities or events that are important to your children.

LONG-DISTANCE PARENTING

If there is significant distance between households, review the following tips for maintaining a strong connection to your children.

▶ Home-made movies and photo albums

Send your children a home-made video or a photo album of where you live. Include everyday things like what your home looks like, where you work, places you like to visit or points of interest in your area. Consider narrating the movie or writing a couple of sentences about each picture so the children will be able to relate to what they are seeing. Videos and photo albums can also be a beneficial way to help children get excited and prepared for when they spend longer periods of time with you (that is, holidays or summer). If you have recently moved, it can be a great way to ease children's anxiety about coming to a new home or city.

▶ Virtual visits

Set up a webcam and schedule regular visits with your children. For younger children, you may need to talk with the other parent about arranging mutually convenient times so he or she can help set it up at his or her end. Web visits work especially well with younger children because they offer them the ability to interact with you visually.

▶ Read a story

Create a CD of yourself reading your child's favourite story or book. Don't have a favourite? Visit a local library and ask for suggestions.

▶ Share a book together

Find a book that you think will interest your child and buy two copies. Send one to your child and keep one. Make arrangements for each of you to read the book together and share ideas about the story. To make it more fun you can:

- Make a positive competition to see who can read the most each week or who can finish first
- Agree to read one chapter at a time and talk about what you read
- Ask your child to read to you over the phone or on webcam
- Schedule reading dates when you read to your child over the phone or on webcam

▶ Do a project together

Similar to sharing a book, you can also engage in other activities. Buy two puzzles or two models to put together. Send one to your child and keep one with you. Each of you can work on putting the puzzle or model together. When you talk to each other you can share the progress you've made, or exchange tips.

▶ Text and email

With older children, consider signing up for a texting package with your mobile phone carrier if you don't have it already. Use texting as a way to touch base with your children throughout the day. Send a short 'I love you' or 'I'm thinking about you' note. You can also do the same with email.

▶ Create a share board

Ask the other parent to post either a bulletin board or a white board somewhere in the home where your children can easily access it. When children think of something they want to share with you they can post it on the share board or write notes to remind themselves about things they would like to tell you about. During phone calls you can ask your children what's on their board to share. You may also want to consider making a share board for yourself so you can post interesting things to share with your children.

▶ Plan conversations

If getting your child to talk is about as easy as pulling teeth, put some energy into planning your conversations. For younger children, consider finding some corny riddles or have a who-can-tell-the-worst-joke contest (this works especially well with six- or seven-year-old children).

With pre-teens and teens, consider looking up current events that might be of interest to them. You can use these as conversation starters when your teen doesn't have much to say. Asking open-ended questions also helps considerably. For example, instead of 'How was your day?' think about saying, 'Tell me one thing that happened today that you enjoyed.'

You can also structure talks by creating rituals for your conversations such as starting every conversation off with taking turns sharing the high point and the low point of your day.

20.
FINANCIAL ISSUES: WHAT DO KIDS NEED TO KNOW?

It is good to have money and the things that money can buy, but it's good too, to check up once in a while and make sure you haven't lost the things money can't buy. – George Lorimer

After years of leading workshops for separated and divorced parents, I know nothing wakes up a room like talking about finances. It didn't take long for me to learn it's usually best to steer clear of discussions regarding maintenance, support and support orders. As a matter of fact, if you're looking for information on maintenance you won't find it here. Based on my experience, it's an issue that not only stirs up lots of strong emotions but also never really gets resolved. Usually those who are paying it feel like they are paying too much, and those who are receiving it typically feel like they're not getting enough.

Instead of debating who should be paying what to whom, I ask parents to look at the financial changes related to splitting up from a different perspective – their children's. Although children may not be directly involved in how money is managed, most are keenly aware of our feelings and reactions to things being different. While it's easy to connect with your own feelings about how life is changing financially, it's important to realise that your children have feelings about how financial changes will affect their lives too.

When parents ask me what children should know about money after they separate, usually my answer is very little. Probably the most important thing your children need to know is that Mum and

Dad will continue to take care of them. Providing specific or detailed information about how finances (maintenance, monthly income, court expenses, etc.) are handled between parents tends to overwhelm and often confuse children. Those are adult issues that do not need to be placed on the shoulders of children.

In addition to shielding children from adult details, be mindful that your own feelings about money can directly influence how you approach money issues with your children.

Consider Paula's situation:

When Paula came into my office she was absolutely flustered. Over the past couple of weeks her seven-year-old son, Sammy, had become completely fixated on money. Apparently, Sammy's grandparents had given him a significant amount of money for his birthday. After receiving the gift, Paula took him to the bank so they could put the money into Sammy's savings account. Initially, Sammy was pretty okay with this; however, it didn't last long.

Several days later Sammy requested to go to the bank and get his money out so he could give it to his mum. Paula reassured Sammy that she didn't need his money. Sammy, however, refused to let the matter drop and quickly became insistent about his request. What disturbed Paula most was that she couldn't work out why Sammy had suddenly become so intent on giving her money. She just didn't know what to do.

As Paula and I began talking, the root of the problem became clear. Since Paula's divorce she had been on a rather restrictive budget and had to modify her spending. Even though Paula never said anything directly to Sammy, she was clearly bitter about the situation and blamed Sammy's father for her financial difficulties. As a result, whenever Sammy asked for something Paula's response was, 'We don't have money for that.' When Sammy asked about moving to another flat, Paula replied, 'We'll get a new flat when we have enough money. I can't just buy things like Daddy does.'

Without realising it, Paula had made this her standard answer for Sammy regarding all money-related issues. Although Paula's intention was to defuse the situation with what she thought was a logical explanation: 'You don't buy things when you don't have the money,' Sammy's anxiety had steadily increased. From Sammy's point of view, his mum was in serious financial trouble. As a result he decided to take matters into his own hands by giving his money to Mum.

When Paula thought about the situation she was able to see how her 'We don't have money for that' response was unsettling to Sammy. She also realised that Sammy was probably picking up on some of the resentment she felt towards her ex and the financial strain the divorce had put on her. Once Paula understood Sammy's perspective, she committed to taking a more positive approach to the problem. Rather than giving Sammy an answer that focused on limited finances, she decided to use it as an opportunity to teach him about the value of money. Instead of saying 'no' because they lacked money, Paula explained to Sammy that as a family they would need to make choices about how they spent money. Buying him something every time they went shopping was not a responsible choice. If there was something Sammy really wanted, Paula let him know that they could talk about it, and then make a decision. Paula also made sure she kept a close watch on how she was handling her feelings about her ex and her financial situation.

While you are certainly entitled to have feelings about how divorce has affected you financially, it's important to pay attention to how your children are feeling and thinking about money and divorce. To keep your children's perceptions and stress levels in check, keep the following tips in mind.

WHAT DO CHILDREN NEED TO KNOW ABOUT MONEY AND DIVORCE?

▶ That they are going to be okay

Just like Sammy, kids can often become anxious and worried when big changes like divorce happen. Not only do children have to adjust to things being different between Mum and Dad but they'll also need information about how their quality of life with each parent will change. Younger children are usually more focused on how their immediate lives are going to be affected. ('Will we have to move?', 'Is our family going to make it?', 'Will we be able to afford things?') Older children may really struggle with how divorce is going to affect their future. ('Will I be able to go to university?', 'Should I get a job, so I can help pay for my things?', 'What will I have to give up?')

Whether your children are older or younger, make sure you reassure them that although things are changing the family will be okay.

▶ How life is going to change

While you may be worried that talking about it will make things worse, actually age-appropriate conversations can help children do

---

WHAT CAN YOU TEACH CHILDREN DURING THIS TIME?

- How to make smart decisions about money
- Stretching the value of a pound
- Creative ways to approach challenging times
- Understanding the difference between what you want and what you need
- Valuing quality time as a family over spending money

According to a study conducted in the US, 87 per cent of surveyed parents reported that they thought children were too materialistic. Then the same researchers interviewed children about what they really wanted. Children's top answer? One-on-one time with a parent.

When you are dealing with a lot of changes, it's all too easy to focus on all the things you can't give your children. Don't lose sight of the fact that what matters most to your children isn't what you buy them. It's the time you spend with them.

a better job of managing financial changes. It's okay for children to hear words like *budget*. The truth is, in this day and age any family can experience financial hardships, not just families in which parents have chosen to separate or divorce. When money is limited, talk to your children about how life will be different. For example, children may need to hear that instead of going to the cinema and out to eat on Saturday night you're choosing to rent a DVD and have pizza at home.

Most important, let children know how things will change for now. Keep in mind you can also use this as an opportunity to help your child develop some important values that could benefit them for the rest of their lives.

▶ Assure children that both parents will continue to support them

If you feel resentful or unsettled about money issues with your ex, do your best to set aside your own feelings and concentrate on your children's perspective on the situation. Although it can be difficult, avoid discussing issues such as support or household finances with your children. Exposing children to detailed adult information about finances usually creates more anxiety than it offers answers. Regardless of your children's ages, what children most need is reassurance that both parents will continue to provide for them.

If your children have received information about finances or support from your ex or other family members, do your best to defuse the situation. Let your children know you don't agree with the other parent's choice to share that kind of information. Reinforce that issues regarding money should be addressed between Mum and Dad. Although it can be very tempting, avoid offering children your side of the story about money matters; those kinds of details create an immediate conflict for children. Even though you may feel like you are providing your children with accurate information when there are differing opinions, children are left in a no-win situation. If they believe you, then by default the other parent hasn't told them the truth. And what kid wants to believe their mum or dad is a liar?

Instead, let your children know you're choosing not to discuss money issues with them because you don't want them to feel caught between Mum and Dad. If you completely disagree with how the other parent has represented the situation, then you can say things like, 'I don't agree with Dad's opinion,' 'Mum and I see things differently,' or 'I have a different view about this issue.' Remember, even though older children are capable of understanding the value of money, most find it very stressful when they become involved in financial matters between parents.

▶ Stay mindful of your attitude

Pay attention to what kind of messages you are giving children about money in your household. As Paula learnt the hard way, what we say to children about money makes a difference. Keep in mind that it's not always what you say that kids notice. Often your attitude about how things have changed makes a big impression on children.

To get a better understanding of how your attitude may affect your children, consider the following questions:

- What are your current feelings and attitudes about your financial situation?
- What do you think your children's current perceptions are about your financial situation?
- What kinds of messages are your children getting about money and divorce from you? What about from your ex?

More important:

- What would you like your children's perceptions or values to be?
- How are you giving them messages that support the perceptions and values you want them to have long term?

WHEN THERE ARE SIGNIFICANT FINANCIAL DIFFERENCES BETWEEN HOUSEHOLDS

During a presentation to a group of parents about managing financial differences between households, I had a father in the class confront me. From his point of view, reassuring children and telling them the truth was a direct contradiction.

'Christina,' he said, 'you just told us that one of the things children need to hear when parents divorce is we're going to be okay. But you also said I should be honest with my children. What if the truth is things aren't okay? I live in a horrible flat and my kids can see for themselves that I'm struggling. They know that everything is fine at their mother's house but with me it's a different story. What do I say to them? Should I be dishonest and tell my children that things are fine when they can see they're not? Or do I tell them the truth – that things are really bad – and give them more to be worried about?'

It wasn't hard to see that this dad had a very valid concern. How can you speak honestly with children when your financial situation is very different or even uncertain?

And this dad isn't alone. Many parents feel caught between a rock and a hard place when the financial changes in one household are more significant than the changes in the other home. Unfortunately, this type of situation can be a breeding ground for added tension and conflict for both parents and kids. So what do you do?

▶ Be honest about the situation without overwhelming your children

If your current financial situation is bleak, don't misrepresent the situation or try to hide it from your kids. Keep in mind, however, that there are lots of different ways to speak the truth. The key is to be honest without creating additional worry or anxiety for your children. It's okay to admit that things aren't easy right now. However, it will be more helpful to your children if you present the situation with an attitude of resilience (we'll find a way to make it through this) and not one of a victim (poor me, it's not fair).

First and foremost, let children know that when parents split up lots of things change. Acknowledge that they have probably noticed some of those changes, like how much money Mum and Dad have to spend on things or perhaps different living situations for each parent.

> In the long run, buying presents won't mean nearly as much to your children as being present.

You can also let children know there may be other differences between Mum's and Dad's homes. At times there may be some things that Mum can do for you, and at others there will be things that Dad can do for you. Share with children that you understand some of those changes may be harder than others. If your children ask questions about your current situation that you can't answer, it's all right to admit that you don't know what the future holds. Most important, make sure conversations are age appropriate and that you share information in a way that won't overwhelm children.

▶ Don't make your issues about financial differences a problem for your children

Whether you are in better standing than your ex or worse off, avoid the temptation to comment on the other parent's financial status. Again, it's okay to acknowledge that there are differences between the households. However, be sure you draw the line by not sharing your personal opinions about the other parent's financial status. Whatever has happened between you and your ex, keep your children out of your issues with one another.

▶ Avoid over-extending yourself financially

When there are significant financial differences between households, avoid competing with the other parent. Although it can be tough to stand back and watch the other parent indulge children while you scrimp to make ends meet, don't forget that children will remember you for how you loved them, not what you bought them. While some children will initially have a difficult time adjusting to having less, don't give in to buying children things you can't afford.

If there are things that your children want to do or buy, find ways to be creative. Spend time talking with your children about what they want and help them set a goal. For example, if your teenage daughter feels she simply can't live without a £150 pair of designer shoes, work with her to generate options. Perhaps she could earn the money by taking on a part-time job, wait until Christmas or her birthday, watch for upcoming sales or even research discount stores online. While the circumstances surrounding your financial situation may not be ideal, in the long run teaching children good money management skills can really pay off.

21.
DEALING WITH
A DIFFICULT EX

Hanging onto resentment is letting someone you despise live rent-free in your head. – Ann Landers

If you've chosen to read this chapter, chances are it's with good reason. Difficulties with an ex can come in all shapes and sizes. Suffice to say, the dynamics surrounding these situations are nothing short of complex and varied. Sometimes difficulties with an ex can have subtle overtones, such as consistently being inflexible or passively undermining your authority with children, or they can be more extreme or blatant, such as using physical intimidation, making verbal threats, badmouthing and name-calling in front of children. Usually the degree and intensity depend on the circumstances surrounding your situation.

Here are some factors that may influence the level of conflict:

- Circumstances surrounding the separation or divorce (issues of infidelity, financial stress, suddenness of divorce or separation)
- Personality of each parent (issues of controlling the relationship, managing anger)
- Reaction of each parent to the conflict (tendency to withdraw or give up, tendency to fight back)
- Emotional state of each parent (acceptance, denial, depression, anger)
- Influence of extended family members (significant family members take sides, encourage hostility)

- Prior history or pattern of behaving (level of conflict before the divorce)
- Level of involvement in litigation (managing or coping with the legal process)
- Emotional stability of one or both parents (history of mental illness or emotional problems)

Regardless of the circumstances, dealing with a difficult ex-spouse can easily feel as if you were serving a life sentence with no end in sight. However, before you completely abandon all hope, it may help to know that in the beginning stages it's very common for separating parents to experience a certain amount of tension and conflict.

This initial discord experienced by many families can take a lot of different forms, such as:

- General badmouthing
- Frequent breakdowns in communication
- Difficulty agreeing on what's really best for children
- Problems negotiating changes
- Exchanging angry emails or letters
- Bringing up unresolved issues from the relationship
- Threatening to either enforce court orders or instigate further litigation

While it may be hard to see a light at the end of the tunnel, for the majority of families the friction and stress experienced between parents early on eventually dies down. With the passing of time emotions usually become less intense, and many parents find they're able to move beyond their differences or at least find ways to contain the conflict. For others, the ability to parent co-operatively may ebb and flow. Some issues may be enormously challenging to resolve, while others may be relatively easy to navigate. Once parents move beyond this turbulent period, most reach a point at which they can steer clear of the emotional bloodshed.

In general, for a large number of families the dust settles and life calms down.

HIGH-CONFLICT SITUATIONS

There are a small percentage of families (approximately 8 to 12 per cent) for which the hurt and anger never truly get resolved. In these situations there is a high and/or sustained level of conflict between parents that transcends the customary tension most separating couples experience. Typically these high-conflict situations involve one or both parents actively engaging in a series of destructive behaviours aimed at controlling, criticising, wounding or getting even with one another. It goes above and beyond the occasional falling out or difference of opinion. In many cases the conflict is deep-rooted and generated by unresolved hurt and intense bitterness or anger towards the other parent.

Over the years I have found that families dealing with high-conflict situations more or less fall into two categories:

- Both partners are committed to a *he said, she said* type of battle.
- One parent is invested in maintaining the conflict.

When both parents are committed to the conflict

Parents who engage in ongoing *he said, she said* battles usually wage war on each other through endless amounts of arguing and fighting in and out of court. As each one is adamant that the other is the problem, these parents mistakenly get sucked into believing that they are helpless and at the mercy of the other parent. In their minds the only way to make things better is for the other parent to stop being difficult. Often they remain clueless and are not able to take responsibility for their part in the conflict or recognise how they are contributing to the problem. Instead of shielding children from the fighting, the parents end up putting a tremendous amount of energy into trying to control the other. Very quick to point out the ex's flaws, these high-conflict parents are frequently oblivious to how their individual actions are destroying their children.

To illustrate, let's take a look at Patricia and Ed.

After spending more than a year involved in a volatile custody dispute over their two young daughters, the court recommended Patricia and Ed engage in mediation to work on improving their parenting relationship. Individually they each appeared to be reasonable and rational, with a desire to do what was best for their children. Both informed the mediator that they felt incredibly disregarded by the other. According to Patricia, Ed didn't respect her judgement as a mother. She felt the girls were too young to stay overnight at his house and that the current situation he had created was very stressful for the children. From her perspective, Ed wanted to have the girls overnight only so he would appear to be involved in their lives. Ed, on the other hand, felt the girls would be fine with him overnight and that the issue was more about Patricia not wanting to give up control. He firmly believed Patricia was using litigation to gain the upper hand so she could continue to make his life miserable. Although each said they had a sincere interest in developing a cooperative relationship, neither believed the other parent was capable of doing so. Interestingly enough, the one thing Patricia and Ed shared was their unwavering belief that working together as parents was just not possible.

When both parents were finally placed in the same room for a session together, it didn't take long for the gloves to come off. Patricia and Ed started the session by randomly hurling insults at one another, which quickly escalated into a full-fledged screaming match. They each repeatedly questioned the other one's motives and refused to budge an inch from their individual positions. At one point in the session they even argued over who would leave the mediator's office first. Each was suspicious that the other was trying to have a private conversation with the mediator so they could persuade him to be on their side.

Given the way Patricia and Ed behaved in front of the mediator, one can only imagine how they carried on in front of their young children. Both were so consumed by their hatred for each other that they weren't even mildly aware of how their ongoing battles with one another were affecting their daughters. Evidently since they no longer passionately loved each other, Patricia and Ed put everything they had into passionately hating each other. Unfortunately, intervention was too little too late for this family. Unable to work out their differences, Patricia and Ed ultimately ended up back in court.

Much like Patricia and Ed, when both parents are more committed to the conflict than to their children, what follows is a pattern of acting and reacting that keeps the conflict going. As parents become entrenched in their views of one another, the conflict continues to escalate and nothing gets better for the children.

Characteristics of conflictual parents:
- Not respecting or valuing the other parent's opinion
- A strong need to be the only decision maker regarding the children's needs
- Inability to tolerate opinions that are different from their own
- Unable to separate the needs of the children from their own needs
- Cannot move on, consistently bringing up past relationship issues
- Have a strong need for things to be fair
- View oneself as a martyr (the one who has sacrificed everything for the children) or a victim (feels persecuted by the other parent or the system)
- Seek retribution for being wronged
- Unwilling to compromise unless one directly benefits from the situation
- Verbally aggressive (swearing, name-calling, shouting) or physically aggressive

- Refuse to take responsibility for any problems and instead consistently blame the other parent
- Openly share negative comments about the other parent with children or provide them with adult information
- Attempt to interfere with the children's time in the other home either overtly or subtly
- Track the hours and minutes of one's time with children; highly sensitive to being cheated or short-changed; insist on make-up time when scheduling changes are needed

An uncooperative parent is not someone who:
- Has a different opinion than you
- Approaches parenting in a different way from you
- Maintains different rules or structure than you

When one parent is invested in the conflict

It's been said that it takes two to tango. That is to say, if you are dealing with a difficult or uncooperative ex-spouse then it stands to reason you must be difficult too. I don't tend to subscribe to this type of thinking. Over the years I have worked with a considerable number of parents for whom the scales definitely tipped in one direction more than the other. Truth be told, situations exist in which one parent has a much greater role and investment in maintaining the conflict. Typically these conflictual parents haven't been able to emotionally come to terms with their feelings about the past or the end of the relationship.

Take Isobel, for example.

By all accounts, Isobel had done everything she could think of to make things right for her three children. However, at the end of the day she felt completely hopeless that things would ever change with her former husband, Donald. Over the past four years she had gone through three lawyers and numerous court hearings and still had not been able to finalise her divorce. Any and every issue that cropped up about their divorce seemed to warrant another letter from either her lawyer or Donald's lawyer. She felt as if her life were being sucked up by endless amounts of litigation, all of which was slowly destroying her financially. The legal issues, however, weren't what concerned her most. It was the constant conflict. Every time she turned around it felt like she was facing a new problem with Donald. If he wasn't making degrading statements about her in front of the children, he was giving them information that contradicted absolutely everything she said. Often the children would come back from his house angry, confused and ready to test her authority.

Eventually the conflict started taking its toll on their middle son, Euan. Isobel started receiving calls daily from school due to Euan's deteriorating behaviour. Normally a bright and easygoing kid, Euan had become increasingly disrespectful with teachers and disruptive in the classroom. Despite Isobel's best efforts, Donald consistently refused any attempts she made to talk with him about the situation. There were days when Isobel just wanted to give up, but she knew if she did her children would pay the price.

To counterbalance Donald's disruptive nature, Isobel worked diligently to provide the children with a stable and predictable home life. Since returns from Donald's house were especially challenging, Isobel made sure she was consistent in how she handled the children's behaviour. She set appropriate limits and discipline with the children when needed. Instead of trying to defend herself against Donald's contradictions, she stayed focused on how confusing it must be for the children to hear different things from each parent. To keep her on track, Isobel got parenting support through a local organisation, which provided her with a place to gain insight in handling Euan's school problems. Although it was hard, Isobel began to feel like she was in control of her life once more.

WHEN YOUR EX DOESN'T THINK THEY'RE PART OF THE PROBLEM

While it may feel very personal and intentional when you are on the receiving end of your ex's bad behaviour, keep in mind that the decision to be conflictual isn't always conscious or deliberate. In some cases other factors may play a significant role in the ongoing hostility, such as unresolved issues from the past, previous family dynamics, emotional instability or mental health issues (for more information, see Chapter 22).

On the contrary, some high-conflict parents sincerely view themselves as reasonable and may very well view you as the problem parent. You may also find that the relationship and level of tension fluctuates, depending on the mood or emotional state of the conflictual parent. Frequently, when a conflictual parent feels threatened by an issue or action the level of conflict increases accordingly. But when he or she feels more secure and stable your ex may actually be capable of engaging in parenting issues very appropriately. This yo-yo effect often leaves the non-conflictual parent very frustrated, as he or she never knows what to expect. Likewise, it also creates a considerable amount of confusion for children because the parenting relationship between Mum and Dad never stabilises. Regardless, conflictual parents often remain oblivious to the damage they are inflicting on children as they unconsciously manage their resentment and hurt in destructive ways; less conflictual parents, on the other hand, feel trapped and helpless to make the situation better.

Consider Charlie's situation:

Charlie had been divorced for several years. Initially his relationship with his ex-wife, Gwen, was fraught with frequent disagreements and heated arguments. Over time Charlie realised that his reactions to Gwen's angry outbursts were probably not helpful. As a result Charlie tried to avoid escalating situations with Gwen and put effort into handling discussions in a business-like manner. Regret-

tably, things continued to fluctuate. Although Gwen's hostility was not as intense towards Charlie, she consistently did what she could to undermine his relationship with their five-year-old daughter, Amber. She was often rigid about arrangements involving pick-ups and drops-offs, yet frequently scheduled activities for Amber that conflicted with Charlie's time. Charlie was also rarely able to attend Amber's school events because Gwen took the stance that it wasn't her job to keep him informed. The way she saw it, if Amber wanted her father there then she would tell him about it. As a result, with the exception of medical bills and notifications about additional expenses, most of Charlie's information about important events in Amber's life came from Amber.

Despite Charlie's ongoing attempts to parent cooperatively, Gwen consistently excluded him from important parenting decisions, sending a subtle yet clear message that she was the only real parent Amber had. On multiple occasions Gwen would instruct Amber to discuss parenting issues with Charlie, justifying it as something that was between Amber and her father. Yet in the same breath Gwen would criticise Charlie for discussing adult matters with Amber rather than addressing concerns directly with her. According to Gwen, Charlie frequently had trouble keeping Amber out of the middle.

If you asked Gwen if she engaged in shared parenting she would without a doubt say she viewed herself as a very accommodating and flexible parent. After all, she certainly never kept Amber from spending time with her father. However, Charlie's relationship with Amber was his responsibility, not hers. It wasn't Gwen's fault that Charlie had made the choice not to be more involved in Amber's life.

While the conflict with Gwen continued to shift, Charlie focused his energy on maintaining a strong relationship with Amber. He used his time with her to engage in family activities that offered them quality time together. Charlie also made it a habit to call Amber regularly to check in and started visiting Amber's school website for news posted about upcoming events. Since Charlie couldn't change the fact that Gwen refused to consult him on important matters, he did his best not to react when something caught him off guard. If he significantly disagreed with a choice Gwen made, Charlie would share with Amber that he had a different opinion when the topic came up. Although not always successful, Charlie did his best not to criticise Gwen when he had discussions with Amber. While his parenting relationship with Gwen was far from ideal, in the end Charlie managed to have a loving relationship with his daughter.

DEALING WITH AN UNCOOPERATIVE EX: TAKING HIGHER GROUND

Even when you've put your best foot forward, there may be times when the other parent simply isn't going to play by the same rules. **While you can't stop the other parent from being conflictual, do what you can to prevent your children from experiencing additional tension.** When you adopt an eye-for-an-eye philosophy with your ex, your children are the ones who pay the price. When you simply cannot resolve differences or the other parent is committed to being conflictual, be the bigger person. Understand that at times that may mean biting your tongue or swallowing your pride. Giving up the need for a fair or just resolution is certainly much easier to talk about than it is to live day in and day out. Remember, it takes an even greater degree of commitment to make concessions when you feel you're the one standing on moral high ground.

Keep in mind, however, that turning the other cheek or being the bigger person doesn't mean you need to become your ex's doormat. When dealing with a difficult ex, appropriate boundaries and self-respect are a must. What it does mean, however, is that you pick your battles carefully and do your best to protect your children from the fall-out. To put it another way, use your children as a gauge for determining how you manage your relationship with your ex.

When things get tough, ask yourself:

- How will my choice about this situation affect my children?

- How will it benefit them now? In the future?
- How will it hurt them now? In the future?

FIRST STEP IN MANAGING THE CONFLICT

One of the first steps in effectively managing difficulties with your ex may actually be the hardest. It involves assessing your role in the conflict. Yes, you may be in a situation like Charlie or Isobel in which the other parent is clearly and justifiably difficult. Believe it or not, even though you may not be invested in sustaining the conflict, the way you respond to it could be making things worse for yourself and your kids. Honestly evaluating how your reaction may be contributing to or influencing the situation is vital.

Let's look at Simon's situation:

Simon's ex, Maria, was always stirring the pot. Even though they had been divorced for some time and both remarried, Maria had never really got over their divorce. From Simon's perspective Maria was constantly looking for ways to pick a fight and get back at him. Whenever an issue came up regarding their son, Alan, Maria would either leave Simon a series of angry voicemail messages or send him accusatory emails.

Maria also made it a regular habit to involve others in their disputes. Once she convinced Alan's school principal that Simon was creating problems for them and upsetting Alan. To maintain her control, Maria persuaded Alan's head teacher not to allow Simon on school grounds unless she was contacted first. At home, Maria continued her campaign by insisting Alan call his stepfather 'Dad' since he was the only one who had ever really been a father to him. To add insult to injury, Maria instructed Alan to call Simon by his first name.

Early on, Simon typically responded to Maria's attacks by immediately defending himself. Usually he would call her as soon as he got her voicemails, reply instantly to her emails or directly confront her face to face. Even when Maria was at her worst, in the end Simon would manage to control his anger and try to work things out. Once Maria calmed down, she and Simon would shift into talking about the old days or make casual conversation. Just when Simon thought that they had finally turned a corner, Maria would start things up again. Simon felt caught in a web of endless divorce drama. What Simon failed to realise was he was giving Maria even more incentive to create problems.

How was Simon making things worse?

Every time Maria incited a problem Simon responded immediately. When they argued, Maria temporarily had Simon's undivided attention. If Simon replied to one of her angry emails, Maria had an open line of communication and the ability to keep her connection to him alive. Although the interactions were highly charged, for Maria there were definitely benefits. This type of interaction is often referred to as *maintaining negative intimacy*. Since Maria no longer had a loving relationship with Simon, she channelled her energy into keeping the conflict alive as a way of staying attached.

How did Simon effectively handle the situation?

Once Simon was able to see the pattern of interaction that had developed, he was able to alter the way he responded to Maria. With the exception of emergencies and time-sensitive issues, Simon stopped responding immediately to Maria's angry emails and messages. If the issue required a response, Simon would stay focused on what Allen needed and avoid rehashing personal issues from the marriage. When Maria tried to engage Simon in a fight, he would let her know that he was not interested in arguing. If Maria persisted, he would end their conversation and revisit the issue later. Whenever possible, Simon also tried to prepare for his conversations with Maria so he could stay calm instead of adding fuel to the fire. (For more advice on dealing with highly charged situations like this, see Chapter 23.)

WAYS NON-CONFLICTUAL PARENTS INADVERTENTLY MAKE THINGS WORSE

- Trying to prove to children you are the victim
- Putting energy into convincing your children that the conflictual parent is at fault and you are the one who is blameless
- Giving too much energy to the conflict
- Allowing the conflict to take over your life and drain you versus setting appropriate boundaries for yourself and ex
- Abandoning the situation
- Deciding to cut your losses and withdraw from your children's lives
- Over-responding
- Getting caught in the trap of responding to every situation and crisis the conflictual parent creates
- Taking out your frustration with the other parent on the children
- Asking children to explain or justify a parent's conflictual behaviour (ranting about the other parent to children)
- Allowing the situation to affect your attitude and interactions with the children
- Becoming so consumed by the conflict that you feel hopeless or depressed, no longer able to truly enjoy your relationship with your children

TIPS FOR DEALING WITH A DIFFICULT EX

▶ **Don't let the situation take over your life**

Perhaps the most challenging aspect of dealing with a difficult ex is there are no easy answers or sure-fire cures. Sometimes the best you can do is take a deep breath, manage your reaction and think through your response. Whenever possible, put the situation or issue into perspective by looking at the bigger picture. (Six months from now what difference will this make?) **More than anything,**

don't allow your ex's behaviour to become the focal point of your life. When things are difficult, do your best to limit the amount of emotional energy and time you give to the conflict.

▶ Maintain your integrity

Just because the other parent isn't focused on the needs of your children doesn't mean you have to reciprocate. **Don't get caught in the trap of thinking that you are helpless.** While you may not have control over the other parent's actions, you do have control over how you respond and how you process the situation with your children.

▶ Avoid matching the other parent's anger

When the other parent's temper flares, do your best to stay level-headed. Don't rise to the occasion and match his or her anger. If past issues get dredged up, redirect the conversation back to the issue at hand – the children. Let your ex know that you don't have an interest in fighting and, if he or she continues, you will end the conversation. If your ex refuses to let go of the issue or argument, then calmly hang up the phone or walk away from the discussion.

> If tensions are running high and you expect a situation to be confrontational, think through how you want to handle the situation ahead of time. For conversations that involve sensitive subjects, consider writing down your points beforehand and making a plan for how you will manage things if your ex becomes challenging.

▶ Exercise control over communications with your ex

If your ex is prone to creating crisis situations, keep in mind you don't have to be at his or her beck and call. If an issue comes up, avoid a knee-jerk reaction. Aside from an emergency, very few situations require an immediate response. If an issue is not time sensitive, consider delaying your response and giving yourself time to consider how you want to respond. When things are especially conflictual, seek out ways to minimise unnecessary communication (face-to-face contact, personal calls or emails) and deal only with what's necessary.

▶ Document your interactions when necessary

Dealing with ongoing conflict effectively is not only emotionally exhausting but it can be a real challenge to keep the facts straight. Difficult exes are notorious for changing the rules of the game, bringing up past issues or allowing one incident to bleed over into another. While I don't recommend you write a novel about how your ex has done you wrong, you may want to consider keeping a small notebook handy to document what happened when. To maintain your emotional energy, record information as if you were reporting the news. Keep entries brief, and stick to the facts. By writing things down you may also begin to see a pattern in your ex's behaviour, which in the long run could provide important clues on how to manage your parenting relationship. In addition, for more serious situations, such as interfering with a parenting schedule or alienating behaviour, it will help to have a record of the other parent's actions.

▶ Use litigation as a last resort, not a first option

Sometimes you don't have a choice and may need to use the legal system to address significant issues, such as ongoing interference with your parenting time or the safety of children. Even though children may not be directly involved in the process, keep in mind that they are greatly affected when parents attempt to resolve issues through the court system. More often than not, children experience higher levels of anxiety, have greater awareness of parent problems and re-engage with feelings of loss.

When a serious issue comes up that you cannot resolve with the other parent on your own, think about using other alternatives, such as mediation, whenever possible (for more on mediation, see Chapter 5).

▶ Shield children from disputes with the other parent

If your ex involves your children in a dispute, you may need to engage in damage control. Don't make the situation worse for your children by offering a counter-argument, trying to explain how you see the situation or trying to convince your children that you are being victimised. No matter how well intentioned you might be, you are ultimately putting your children in the middle of a no-win situation.

A better approach is to defuse the situation by letting children know you are sorry that the other parent has decided to involve them. It's okay to let your children know you don't agree with the other parent or that you have a different opinion. Most important, children need to know they are not responsible for solving or fixing the problem, and you don't want them caught in the middle of a disagreement between Mum and Dad. While it can be very tempting, avoid providing children with intimate details or adult information to counteract what the other parent has said.

When children repeatedly get exposed to parental conflicts they often feel trapped. Make sure your children know they do not have to take sides or work out who is right and who is wrong. If the situation has been particularly upsetting for your children, do your best to support their feelings.

22.
LESS-THAN-IDEAL SITUATIONS

The ultimate measure of a person is not where he or she stands in moments of comfort and convenience, but where he or she stands at times of challenge and controversy. – Martin Luther King Jr (adapted)

Janice had been married to Ben for over 12 years. Although he had always drunk more than most, Janice consistently turned a blind eye. When the children asked about their father's drinking, Janice downplayed the situation. She frequently minimised Dad's inappropriate behaviour by telling the children that, even though living with Daddy was tough, you don't give up on family. While all the children were aware of Dad's drinking problem, Janice never talked about it. Unfortunately Ben's drinking steadily got worse, and he eventually became violent. Janice finally realised she no longer had a choice. To keep her children safe, she had to leave Ben.

Now sitting in one of my parenting workshops, Janice was feeling very conflicted. For the past two hours she had listened to how important it is to support the other parent's relationship. She also understood that no matter how angry she was at the children's father or his addiction, badmouthing him was only going to hurt the kids. She looked at me with tears in her eyes. 'What do I do now?' she asked. 'My kids hate me for leaving their daddy. From their point of view, I left when he needed us most. How do I tell my children I had to leave without running their father into the ground?'

I realise that a considerable amount of what I offer separated and divorced parents may at times feel like pie-in-the-sky kind of thinking. This is especially true if you are a parent, like Janice, who is dealing with what I refer to as a less-than-ideal situation. During one of my presentations I was talking about these situations when a woman in the back of the room raised her hand and said to me, 'Yes, but Christina, don't you think anybody who has ever gone through a separation feels like their situation is less than ideal?' Okay, point taken, there isn't much about the process of separation and divorce that feels ideal. My intent here isn't to trivialise the difficulties that surround splitting up. I do, however, want to point out that there are families in which the divorce is only one of many issues parents must carefully navigate.

Situations that fall into the less-than-ideal category involve one or more of the following issues:

- Alcoholism
- Substance abuse
- Physical, emotional or sexual abuse of a child
- Domestic violence
- Mental health
- Parental neglect or abandonment
- Emotional instability of a parent
- Alienation of a child by a parent
- Involvement in excessive litigation
- Problems with rage or excessive displays of intense bitterness

In the wake of separation you may find yourself facing a range of issues that will influence how you support your children during this time. When a parent has engaged in destructive or inappropriate behaviours (such as abuse, domestic violence, alcoholism or drug use), addressing only the issues related to your divorce or separation is not enough. The dynamics surrounding less-than-ideal situations and how they will affect your children's adjustment must also be taken into consideration.

While I am a relentless advocate of children having a relationship with both parents, I will also tell you that children's safety trumps everything. To be clear, **any circumstance that places your children at risk must be managed in a way that protects and preserves your children's safety**. In those types of situations the concepts involved in shared parenting will need to be modified or approached in a different manner. While children deserve the right to maintain a loving relationship with both Mum and Dad, the physical and emotional well-being of your children must always be the top priority.

Having said that, I also want to emphasise that it's just as important to realise that a difference in parenting styles or values doesn't justify labelling the other parent as unfit, unsafe or a risk to children. A parent who allows young children to watch a PG-rated film is very different from a parent who downs several pints and then decides to drive with the children in the car. One situation involves a difference in parenting styles and values; the other clearly places children in substantial danger. Yes, differences in parenting values should be addressed, but not all situations warrant the same response. As a parent, it's important for you to honestly evaluate the risk to your children's safety before taking action. If you are unsure about how to best handle a situation, consider consulting an objective outside source, such as a family lawyer, organisation or counsellor with specialised skills regarding your area of concern. For example, if the other parent has a history of abusing prescription drugs you may want to speak with a professional who has a background and experience in dealing with addictions for information on how to develop a safety plan for your children.

STAYING SAFE: DEALING WITH DOMESTIC VIOLENCE, ADDICTIONS AND DIVORCE

There are times when almost every parent in a difficult situation considers sticking things out, hopeful that the other parent will eventually change or the problems will go away. When this happens, the non-offending parent places both himself or herself and the children at enormous risk. Even when things improve for a period of time, significant change can occur only if the offending parent has acknowledged the problem and is actively seeking professional help. If you are a non-offending parent, you need to be resolute in advocating for the safety of your children.

Less-than-ideal situations that endanger the safety and well-being of children almost always require legal intervention. In principle the judicial system seeks to protect children; however, in reality there are often limits to what courts can do. In divorce cases, information regarding abuse, neglect, addictions or domestic violence may be viewed in a variety of ways. Because divorce cases traditionally tend to focus on exposing the absolute worst qualities of each parent, serious issues may be viewed with a sceptical eye or an over-reactive one. Accusations regarding dangerous, inappropriate or abusive behaviour of a parent must often be substantiated with the court, and in the meantime action towards safeguarding children may be delayed.

Be sure to let your lawyer know immediately if the other parent has

- Threatened you or your children
- Hurt you or the children physically or sexually
- Attempted to control or isolate you
- Behaved in a way that is emotionally abusive
- Engaged in behaviours that place children at risk (driving while intoxicated, exposing children to unsafe people, leaving young children unsupervised for significant periods of time)
- A history of inappropriate drug or alcohol use

Your lawyer will be able to best advise you about how to protect yourself and your children. In some cases a non-molestation order or other actions may need to be taken to legally prohibit an abusive parent from coming to your home or approaching your children. Family lawyers can also recommend options for contact between your children and the other parent that do not expose either you or the children to further risks.

If you believe you or your children are at risk or under the threat of abuse, there are several organisations that offer excellent information on the web about actions to take before and after you decide to leave your abusive spouse (see Resources at the back of the book). Most suggest you document any abuse, inform your family and your lawyer about the abuse and your plans to leave. Other advice includes notifying your place of work and co-workers, your children's school and the police.

HOW TO HELP CHILDREN MANAGE LESS-THAN-IDEAL SITUATIONS

When children are exposed to serious situations, especially those involving domestic violence, abuse or addiction, knowing how to respond can be a real struggle. Like Janice, you may feel at a complete loss when it comes to explaining the circumstances of your situation to your children. While your top priority should always be to protect your children, keep in mind that doesn't mean you avoid talking about it.

Sometimes in an effort to shield children, parents may:

- Minimise the seriousness of the abuse or violence
- Pretend the problem doesn't exist
- Change the subject when children raise the issue
- Avoid conversations about the problem or the other parent
- Make up excuses to justify or explain away the other parent's actions

It is extremely important that you support your children emotionally in difficult situations that involve inappropriate or dangerous behaviours of a parent. Often children involved in these types of situations have ambivalent feelings about the other parent. Some may feel deeply responsible for a parent's behaviour, whereas others may feel quite conflicted and worry about betraying one or both parents. Of course, how children are able to handle difficult situations is often influenced by many different factors. One of the most significant aspects, however, is how parents talk with children and help them understand the situation.

TALKING TO YOUR CHILDREN ABOUT LESS-THAN-IDEAL SITUATIONS

Although the details and circumstances vary from situation to situation, it cannot be emphasised enough how incredibly important it is to talk openly yet appropriately to children about less-than-ideal situations. Keep in mind, talking openly does not give you a free pass to completely trash the other parent, share adult information or disclose intimate details about the problem. What it does mean is that, as a parent, you create a safe space for children to acknowledge what has happened. By doing so you provide children with the ability to emotionally disengage from adult problems or issues without feeling responsible or guilty for a parent's choices and actions.

The following offers some insight on how to approach conversations about difficult situations.

▶ **Acknowledge what has happened and allow children to talk**
Some parents mistakenly believe that talking with children about a serious situation such as domestic violence, abuse or addiction will either overwhelm or scare children. Actually, not talking about the situation leaves children defenceless and often feeling more afraid because they do not understand what has happened or why. Talk with your children openly and honestly, offering them age-appropriate explanations and information. Children usually feel a

great sense of relief when they have received permission from a parent to talk about the situation. Children also need to know that they can talk about their feelings and ask questions without being fearful of making things worse or getting in trouble. If you are unsure what to say to your children, seek professional support or guidance from a trained counsellor or therapist who has experience working with circumstances that match your issue. For additional sources of information, see the Resources section.

▶ Educate your children about the problem

Along with supporting children's feelings, it is vital that you educate them about the problem. Educating children helps them:

- Understand the situation is not something they can influence or control
- Identify dysfunctional behaviour
- Increase the likelihood that they will not repeat the behaviour in their own lives
- Build skills versus feeling afraid
- Feel empowered instead of helpless

In addition, you can help your children learn how to stay safe by teaching them personal protection skills, such as:

- How to recognise and/or avoid unsafe situations
- When and how to call for emergency help
- How to develop a safety plan
- How to find and approach a safe adult when there is a crisis
- How to feel confident instead of scared
- How to develop good judgement when interacting with others

▶ Talk about the problem, not the person

While it may be challenging at times, avoid making statements that criticise or condemn the other parent. Note the difference between saying, 'You can't see Mum right now because she's a nasty drunk who needs help' (attacking the person) and saying, 'Mum has a drinking problem, and when she drinks too much she can't make safe choices. Until Mum makes a decision to stop drinking you may have to spend time with her in a different way' (addressing the problem).

Furthermore, children need to be reassured that their safety takes priority over everything else. While they may feel sad or upset about the choices their other parent is making, let them know the destructive behaviour is not appropriate. Help your child understand the dynamics of the issue, abuse or addiction in a way he or she can comprehend. If needed, use age-appropriate resources for children such as books or educational pamphlets (see the Resources section for suggestions).

▶ Allow children to have positive feelings about the other parent

Although it may be very difficult for you to see any redeeming qualities in the offending or abusing parent, remember that your children will most likely not feel the same way. Even when a parent has engaged in destructive or inappropriate behaviours, children frequently still want to maintain some type of positive connection and have a strong wish for things to be different. Don't forget that children view themselves as half Mum and half Dad. Although your ex may have made some bad choices, your child will still need your support in having a balanced view of his or her parent.

▶ Reinforce that what has happened is not their fault

Many children in difficult situations feel guilty or responsible for what has happened in the family. Make sure your children know the situation is not their fault and that they cannot change their other parent's behaviour. Remember, you may have to have several conversations with your children to accomplish this. It is also helpful to let children know that no matter how much they may hope or wish, the other parent is the only one who can change the situation.

▶ Inform your children about how life will change for now

When domestic violence, abuse or addiction issues are involved, contact between parents and children may need to be suspended or supervised. If this occurs, talk with your children in an age-appropriate way. Let them know in clear terms when and how they will see their other parent. If contact is not possible, be sure to support your child's feelings. It is normal for a child to have mixed feelings about not seeing the other parent. While they may truly appreciate being in a safer situation, they may also have difficulty letting go of the wish that everything could be okay. It's also possible that your children may be angry with you for not letting them see the other parent. Reassure your children that it's okay to feel upset, and that your only goal is to make sure they are safe.

▶ Provide children with a stable and consistent environment

Children who have lived with domestic violence or addiction experience very chaotic and unpredictable lives. Although going through the process of divorce can bring even more changes to a family, do what you can to create a consistent, predictable and peaceful home environment for your children. Children can actually make a successful adjustment and heal from the past with the support of one consistent, loving, stable parent in their lives.

▶ Seek support for both yourself and your children

Healing for families who have dealt with these issues takes time. Be sure that you are accessing support for yourself as well as for your children. While reaching out to others can be hard to do, it is an important part of making life better for your family. Organisations and resources that can help with domestic abuse and addiction issues are listed in the Resources section in the back of the book.

23.
ALIENATION: WHAT IS IT AND HOW TO RESPOND

I can move mountains but not clouds.
– Divorced parent dealing with alienation

When a parent becomes dedicated to turning a child against their other parent it is often referred to as parent alienation or parent alienation syndrome, also known as PAS. While awareness of this post-separation dynamic has increased over the past several years, parent alienation has been, and still is, a hotbed of controversy in many professional circles and legal systems all over the world. For some, parent alienation is viewed as nothing more than a courtroom tactic used by abusive parents to gain access to children, whereas others see parent alienation as a very real issue that warrants professional recognition as a diagnosable disorder. Others have made it a political issue, advocating changes in the legal system. Unfortunately, the broad range of opinions that exists about parent alienation often makes it a complicated and challenging phenomenon to identify and treat. Even experienced professionals frequently struggle with defining what exactly constitutes parent alienation and where to draw the line. Sadly, the debate rages on, and as it does the very system designed to protect children's rights to a relationship with both parents has become rather inept at doing so.

From my perspective, parent alienation is not a black-and-white issue. Rather it is a dynamic that exists on a continuum, ranging from subtle to severe. Regardless of how you classify it (syndrome or not), regardless of what you call it, it is a very real issue for many families. Regrettably, due to a myriad factors, early detection and intervention for parents dealing with this issue tend to be the exception rather than the rule.

Why is early detection of parent alienation difficult?

- Divorce and separation are, by nature, conflictual processes in which emotionally charged reactions by a parent (even when inappropriate) are expected and often minimised.
- Lack of knowledge and clarity about parent alienation exists among court systems and professionals.
- Courts and legal professionals are not trained or equipped to provide early detection.
- Alienation is often not given merit until it has reached a critical stage.
- In many cases, alienating parents are able to use the legal system to their advantage and create what seems to be justifiable distance between the parent and the child.
- Parents typically lack information and often don't understand the implications of the other parent's behaviour until alienation is well established.

Rather than get mired down in the debate over what parent alienation is or isn't, the focus of this chapter is to offer you information. A parent dealing with alienation once said to me, 'I can move mountains, but not clouds.' To me the statement is a powerful reminder of how difficult it is to put shape or form to parent alienation. It is also equally difficult for parents to know how to respond, especially when there are so many differing opinions. Most parents feel unprepared and caught off guard by the rejection of their children. Many of the parents I have worked with are shocked at how quickly the loving relationship they once had with their children has become a faded memory or, in some instances, completely forgotten. Often they have spent extensive amounts of time, money and energy only to end up confused, frustrated and hopeless. More than anything, most are looking for answers and help. At what point do a parent's actions become alienation versus just inappropriate? How can you defend yourself against something that others don't see or perhaps aren't willing to acknowledge? How do you know if alienation is really occurring or if it's a phase you should let your children work through?

I could have written an entire book on just this topic alone. Luckily there are already several excellent resources that provide invaluable information about how to recognise, manage and respond to alienation (see the Resources section at the back of the book). This chapter will provide you with not only an increased level of awareness but the ability to detect possible alienating behaviours and respond effectively.

WHAT IS PARENT ALIENATION?

Parent alienation, most often seen in situations involving separation or divorce, occurs when a child is influenced by one parent (often called the *alienator*) to completely reject their other parent (often known as the *target*). While there are varying opinions regarding the age at which children are most susceptible, this type of manipulation can occur in children at almost any age. In severe cases, parent alienation results in the child's complete rejection of the target parent. Typically, the reasons for the child's rejection are frivolous or unjustified. A participant in one of my training sessions once talked about working with a child who refused to spend time with her father because he made her eat chicken. More serious cases of alienation may involve a child alleging abuse or making unfounded accusations about the target parent. Some of these accusations are loosely based on events that happened, whereas others may be a complete fabrication designed to create distance between the target parent and the child.

Several years ago I worked with Jeremy, an eight-year-old who had not spent time with his father for over a year. Eventually his father was able to get the court involved, and contact between the two was restored. Sadly, the court order did not deter Jeremy's mum from pressuring him to reject his father. Consequently this child lived in a state of constant anxiety as he tried to balance his overwhelming desire to have a relationship with his father and yet remain loyal to his mother. During one of our sessions Jeremy stated he should not be forced to see his father any more because he had disciplined him for breaking a biscuit barrel. When approached about the incident, the father was completely dumb-founded by the accusation. The reported weekend from the father's perspective had been incredibly positive, and Jeremy had seemed to really enjoy himself. According to Dad, not only had the incident never happened but there wasn't even a biscuit barrel in his house.

Regrettably for many parents, the accusations are much more severe than breaking a biscuit barrel. When an alienating parent feels threatened, quite often accusations regarding physical or sexual abuse are alleged against the target parent. In these circum-stances child protection services typically become involved, and for a period of time contact may be suspended or supervised.

When dealing with parent alienation, it is incredibly important to understand the enormous pressure children are put under. This dynamic literally places children in a situation where they must view one parent as all bad and one parent as all good. It leaves absolutely no space for a child to love both parents. Given that children view themselves as half Mum and half Dad, the end result is that children are forced both emotionally and psychologically to deny or reject a part of themselves.

Although a target parent may sense that the behaviour of the alienating parent is inappropriate, most are ill-prepared to handle their children's rejection. Many parents describe having a formerly loving and close relationship with their children only to be completely flattened by the fact that their children no longer want to have any contact with them. In acute cases children join the alienating parent's hate campaign and actively engage in degrading the target parent without remorse or guilt. Children who have been successfully alienated essentially assume the beliefs and perspectives of the alienating parent as their own. They adamantly believe their rejection of the target parent is an independent choice they have made.

HOW DO YOU KNOW IF YOUR CHILD IS ALIENATED?

In his book *Divorce Poison*, US psychologist Dr Richard Warshak cautions parents to evaluate certain factors surrounding children's refusal or rejection before assuming alienation is present or responding as if it existed. To clarify the point, he states that one of the most significant defining characteristics is that 'alienated children relate to one parent, but not the other, in a *consistently negative manner*'.

If your children are distancing themselves from you, bear in mind that it doesn't mean parent alienation is necessarily taking place. In some situations parents may alienate themselves from children by engaging in behaviours that are harmful, abusive, destructive or hurtful. A child who can offer a reasonable explanation for his or her choice, such as physical abuse or domestic violence, is not a child who is being influenced by alienation. Also, there may be circumstances in which a parent's reaction to the divorce, children or the other parent has strained the parent–child relationship. For example, suppose a parent had difficulty controlling his anger in the past. Perhaps a majority of his frustration was directed at the child. If he remains overly critical or verbally abusive towards the child, then the child may independently make a choice to detach from that parent.

CHARACTERISTICS OF PARENT ALIENATION SYNDROME (PAS)

When PAS is present children will:

- Express and demonstrate an unwavering hatred or contempt for the target parent without guilt or remorse
- Base hatred on unjustified or frivolous reasons versus personal experience
- Refuse any contact with the target parent
- View the alienator as the good and honest parent and the target as the untrustworthy and bad parent
- Mimic accusations and opinions of the alienating parent, yet insist they have formulated ideas about the target parent on their own
- Reject extended family members or others associated with the target parent

When PAS is not present, children will:

- Freely acknowledge positive and negative characteristics about each parent
- Maintain good memories or occasionally enjoy time spent with the target parent
- Express only temporary or situational hatred or contempt towards the target parent
- Agree to spend periods of time with the target parent (even when it's not frequent or consistent)
- Continue their relationship with extended family members, despite difficulties with the target parent
- Have justified reasons for rejection based on personal experiences with the parent (abusive, harmful or hurtful behaviours)

HOSTILE AGGRESSIVE PARENTING

Another dynamic closely related to parent alienation is hostile aggressive parenting (HAP). Instead of focusing on the symptoms and behaviours of the child, hostile aggressive parenting concentrates on the actions and behaviours of the alienating parent. Whereas HAP has the potential to develop into parent alienation syndrome, it does not always lead to the child's rejection of the target parent. It does, however, greatly interfere with a child's ability to maintain a strong, healthy relationship with one of his or her parents.

So, for example, suppose a father said to his child, 'Your mother is a liar, and you should hate her. She can't be trusted. Just look at how she has ruined your life.' Instead of joining with the father's anger, the child manages to separate herself from the father's feelings and realises that the feelings she has for her mother are different.

Hostile aggressive parenting most often occurs in high-conflict situations in which one parent has remained connected to past hurts, and the emotional pain regarding the separation or divorce still runs deep. As a result the alienating parent attempts to use the children as a way to manipulate, control or seek revenge on the target parent. Hostile aggressive parents are usually incapable of acknowledging the needs of their children and frequently view children as belonging exclusively to them (*my* children versus *our* children). Another distinguishing feature of HAP is that it acknowledges the influence of other significant adults in a child's life. HAP can also be used to identify inappropriate behaviours and negative influences of grandparents, step-parents, extended family members or the partner of an alienating parent.

Although there is significant debate within the court system and among professionals regarding how parent alienation and hostile aggressive parenting should be handled, it is imperative that parents understand the dynamics of these high-conflict situations. While PAS and HAP are not present in every situation, the best intervention you can invest in is prevention. Knowing what to look for, paired with strategies for safeguarding your relationship with children, can make a tremendous difference in how vulnerable your children are to the influence of alienation. Regardless of the other parent's actions, I encourage you to do your best to engage in positive shared parenting behaviours early on.

MISCONCEPTIONS ABOUT ALIENATION

▶ It either is or isn't

Parent alienation consists of a range of insidious behaviours. Mild alienation involves consistent derogatory remarks, making negative comparisons between a parent and the child, subtly placing children in situations in which they are asked to take sides, and leading children to believe that time spent with the other parent isn't valuable or necessary. Severe alienation includes blatantly interfering with contact, rewarding a child's rejection of the other parent, making abuse allegations, and insisting that the other parent is bad, evil or someone to be feared.

If you suspect that your relationship with your child is at risk, seek the advice and support of a qualified professional. Be sure to find someone who has both training and experience in dealing with parent alienation. In the absence of professional support, put effort into educating yourself by reading books and possibly connecting with other parents in your area or online (see the Resources section for a list of suggestions). If you are already in a situation in which your child is refusing contact and you feel alienation is present, talk to your lawyer about possible options for restoring contact.

▶ If children do not want to see you, then the other parent must be guilty of alienation

When a child distances himself from a parent, that doesn't necessarily mean parent alienation is taking place. In some situations a parent may alienate themselves from a child by engaging in harmful, abusive, destructive or hurtful behaviours. When a parent does not take responsibility for his or her inappropriate behaviour, children may independently make the choice to distance themselves. Before jumping to the conclusion that the other parent is responsible for the situation, first consider other possibilities. If your child does not want to spend time with you, think through how you may be contributing to the problem.

▶ If your children do not want to see you, you should respect their wishes

While forcing your children to spend time with you is not recommended, neither is taking a passive stance. If your child says she does not want to spend time with you, don't try to rationalise the situation or talk her out of her reluctance. Rather, do your best to be supportive and talk with your child about why she is unwilling to see you. Her answers may provide you with some important insight.

It's okay to let your child know you think spending time together is important and that you're disappointed. Instead of taking a passive stance, offer possible alternatives, like spending an afternoon together instead of the entire weekend. Maintain your focus on continued positive contact with your child. Shorter consistent periods of time that enhance your relationship are better than no time at all. Eventually you can work on gradually increasing the amount of time you and your child spend together.

▶ Alienating behaviours of a parent always result in rejection by children

Actually, there are some circumstances in which parents can take steps to actively protect their relationship with children and minimise the impact of alienation. Often timing and intervention make a significant difference. The sooner a potential target parent is able to recognise and actively respond to alienation tactics, the less likely children are to be influenced by the insidious and destructive nature of PAS.

What makes a difference? Here are some factors that affect a child's ability to resist alienation, including some questions to ask yourself.

- **The intensity of the alienation**
  How aggressive is the campaign? Does the child have any reprieve from the alienating parent? How much support does the alienating parent have to affirm their perspective such as step-parents, new partners or extended family members who support the alienation?
- **The target parent's previous relationship with the child**
  What was your relationship with the child before the separation or divorce? How involved were you in your children's lives before the separation? Was your relationship emotionally close or distant?
- **The characteristics and personality of the child**
  Do your children possess a high level of resilience? Is their confidence strong enough to resist the negative views or statements of the offending parent?
- **Your response to the alienation**
  Have you contributed to the alienation by being unresponsive, withdrawing from your children's lives or engaging in a counterattack on the alienating parent?

▶ **If children do not reject a parent, then alienation is not occurring**
In an article about how to detect PAS, researchers J. Michael Bone and Michael Walsh coined the term *attempted PAS,* which refers to situations in which the dynamics and characteristics of alienation are present but children have not adopted the alienating parent's perceptions. Although alienation may not appear to be successful, it is important to realise that the effects are still very toxic to children; therefore the relationship between the target parent and the child still requires protection.

▶ **You should keep silent about the alienation and not discuss it with your children**

Although trying to convince children you are being victimised by the other parent won't be helpful to them, neither is keeping quiet. When children are repeatedly exposed to alienation there may be times when it is appropriate for you to provide them with an *alternative perception of reality*. In short, this does not mean you should bash the other parent or overwhelm children with adult information about the situation. Rather it involves engaging in a conversation with children that focuses on the problem or conflict, not the person. Author and PAS expert Richard Warshak debunks the 'silence is golden' myth and suggests that sometimes it may be appropriate to offer children constructive criticism. Constructive criticism is not about vindicating yourself or giving yourself licence to condemn the alienating parent. When you engage in a counterattack your actions are just as damaging as the alienator's.

Constructive criticism involves:

- Helping children gain an understanding of a parent's conflictual, irrational or confusing behaviour
- Providing children with a more balanced perspective of the conflict and each parent
- Giving children the ability to disengage from adult feelings (for example, 'Your feelings don't have to be the same as Mum's or Dad's.')

When an alienating parent is poisoning your children's minds you may need to help them gain a more objective perception of the situation. However, before engaging in a conversation with your children about the other parent it's important to honestly evaluate your intentions. Ask yourself:

- Is this information my children need to know?
- How will sharing this information help my children?

- How could it potentially hurt them?
- How would I address this issue if I were still married to my ex?

▶ Key messages for children regarding alienation

Support children in seeing the conflict with the other parent from a more neutral perspective. In so doing, you can also reinforce important concepts for children, such as:

- When parents separate, children should never have to take sides.
- You should never feel like you have to choose one parent over the other.
- Your feelings don't have to be the same as Mum's or Dad's. Usually when divorce happens children have different feelings than their parents.
- If Mum or Dad are upset with each other that doesn't mean you have to be angry with one of us. It is important for you to have loving relationships with each parent.

WHAT CAN PARENTS DO?

▶ Understand the dynamics of the problem

More often than not, parents do not understand the dynamics of alienation until it is too late or the situation has become severe. If you feel that the other parent is making attempts to sabotage your relationship, raise your level of awareness and understanding about parent alienation. There are several excellent resources regarding alienation and hostile aggressive parenting (see the Resources section at the back of the book).

COMMON ALIENATING BEHAVIOURS

Be mindful that this list is not a diagnostic tool, and one stand-alone behaviour does not constitute parent alienation syndrome or hostile aggressive parenting. Both happen over a period of time and involve an ongoing campaign that pressures children to reject one parent. If you have concerns about your relationship with your children, educate yourself about the dynamics of alienation and work on developing a network of support.

- Directly interferes with the target parent's scheduled time by:
  - Frequently changing the schedule or scheduling events for children without consulting the target parent
  - Taking children places so they are not available for scheduled handovers or insisting on unrealistic times for exchanging children
  - Offering irrational reasons why children cannot spend time with the target parent
- Engages in name-calling or makes derogatory statements about the target parent or significant family members in front of the children
- Makes verbal threats
- May attempt to physically or emotionally intimidate the target parent
- Refuses to acknowledge or talk to the target parent
- Expresses extreme distrust of the target parent to the child
- Has a strong need to protect the child from the other parent and seeks to prove the target parent does not have the ability to care for the child
- Unable to separate the child's needs and feelings from his or her own or to shield children from his or her own emotional pain or anger ('What I feel is what you feel.')
- Unable to separate the child's divorce experience from his or her own ('She left us.' 'He lied to us.')
- May accuse the target parent of abuse, neglect or inappropriate parenting

- Provides children with inaccurate information about the target parent and his or her household
- Refuses to follow court orders
- Tells children his or her household is the only real home they have
- Insists children call target parent by his or her first name instead of Mum or Dad
- Withholds significant information about the children
- Blames the children for refusing to spend time with the target parent ('What am I supposed to do? I can't help it if they don't want to see their dad.')
- Excludes the other parent from important decisions regarding the children
- Asks the children to hide information or keep secrets from the target parent
- Uses the children to gain information about the target parent and his or her home
- Refers to the children as 'my' children, not 'our' children
- Seeks out professionals (counsellors, mediators, doctors, lawyers) to support his or her perspective and views about the other parent. Anyone who disagrees with the alienator becomes the enemy and is vilified
- May actively interfere with telephone contact when the child is in his or her home (won't answer or return phone calls, distracts children when they are speaking with the target parent, listens in, does not give children privacy for calls)
- Reinforces negative concepts or ideas about the target parent to the children while ignoring positive qualities
- Creates ambivalence for children when they are going to spend time with the target parent by saying things like:
  'I'm sorry you have to go. I hope you're not too scared when you are there.'
  'Remember, if you need me to come and get you, all you have to do is call me.'

'I don't know what I'm going to do without you. Don't forget I will be thinking about you every minute you're gone.'

'I wish you could go to the beach with me, but it's not my weekend. I wish Mum wasn't being so mean.'

- Cannot take responsibility for how their actions affect the children and instead places blame on the other parent ('The children are under a great deal of stress because she is making things so difficult.')
- Frequently uses litigation as a means of controlling the target parent
- Cannot disengage from a negative perspective of the target parent and does not integrate new information. They believe the target parent has an ulterior motive for any positive behaviour
- May treat children as peers
- Will refer to the target parent in the third person, or by an impersonal name ('That woman, Ms Smith.')

▶ Maintain contact with children

Do what you can to maintain regular, consistent contact with your child. The primary mode of operation for alienating parents is, *You are either for me or against me.* Children learn early on that if they do not side with the alienator they risk rejection. Having seen how the alienator has dealt with the target parent is a clear and ever-present reminder of this. When a parent withdraws from a child's life, or does not maintain consistent contact, children are defenceless against the alienation. Not only does it reinforce the alienator's perspective, it also does not give children the opportunity to have an *alternative perception of reality*. When spending time with your children, put energy into making it conflict free and positive. This is clearly an opportunity where your actions will speak louder than your words.

▶ Don't take the rejection or rude behaviours of your children personally

While your children may be giving you every indication that they don't want you involved, they still need you. Even if it is not openly acknowledged, knowing that you care and are available can be incredibly valuable to children who are dealing with the pressure inflicted by an alienating parent. Although it may seem like a small consolation, it may help to know that most alienated children feel more secure in their relationship with the target parent because he or she does not put them in a position where they are forced to choose.

▶ Get support

Parent alienation is a complex and emotionally demanding challenge to face. The journey to repair your relationship with your child can be long and often requires an enormous amount of patience and persistence. Seek out support to help you manage the stress and emotional drain that parents frequently experience when rejected by a child.

▶ Don't over-expose your children to professionals

When a target parent begins to realise the extent of the damage, he or she may try to seek help for the children. While therapy and counselling can be enormously helpful for kids in these types of situations, it is rarely effective. Most alienating parents are not comfortable with counselling or therapy unless they feel the professional involved supports their view of the target parent. Placing children in counselling often intensifies the pressure and anxiety they experience. More often than not, the alienating parent will become relentless in either sabotaging the sessions or significantly influencing what children say to professionals.

In some circumstances the alienating parent may respond to treatment by taking the children to his or her own expert. Bear in mind that not all professionals are experienced or knowledgeable about parent alienation. A well-meaning professional can sometimes do more harm than good, and unknowingly support the alienation.

▶ If necessary, evaluate options with your lawyer

When alienation is present it almost always requires some level of legal intervention. In situations where the alienation is mild or in the early stages, a letter from your solicitor may be enough to get things back on track. For more severe cases, bringing the matter before the court may be your best or only option for restoring contact. Again, the responsiveness of legal professionals and court systems tends to vary greatly. Before engaging in further litigation consider discussing the realities of your situation with your lawyer. While there are family lawyers who are educated and knowledgeable about PAS, many still are not. Make sure the lawyer you are working with understands the dynamics of alienation. If not, consider providing your lawyer with additional information.

▶ The best intervention is always prevention

Regardless of the other parent's actions, stay committed to using positive shared parenting behaviours. Remember, the most important factors in protecting your relationship with your children are:

- Maintaining consistent positive contact
- Nurturing a strong emotional and psychological connection
- Not applying additional pressure on the children to take sides

▶ Don't give up hope

When dealing with high-conflict situations, it can sometimes be hard to see how your actions are making a difference. In some parent–child relationships it may take years before you will see the results of your choices and efforts. Never make the mistake of thinking you do not matter to your children – you do.

SOMETHING TO THINK ABOUT

Almost all parents at some point during the separation process let their emotions get the best of them and they slip up. Whether intentional or unintentional, it is important that you recognise the implications of your own behaviour. No matter how justified you may feel, do not make statements or engage in actions that undermine the positive image or affection your children have for the other parent.

If you have made a mistake, seek to correct the situation immediately by acknowledging it, apologising to your children and making a commitment not to repeat the behaviour. Be mindful that alienation of any kind not only damages children's image of themselves but may also eventually damage their image of you.

24.
HOW TO HELP CHILDREN DEAL WITH FEELINGS AND BE A GOOD LISTENER

The first duty of love is to listen. – Paul Tillich

Out of the blue one day while my husband was at work my then six-year-old bonus son came into the room and asked, 'Christina, if Daddy dies will you take care of me?' Although it wasn't a standard run-of-the-mill question, I was preoccupied with cleaning up something and only half listening to what had been said. Without much thought I quickly responded by offering him reassurance: 'Sweetie, there's no need to worry. Daddy's very healthy, and I'm sure he'll be around for a very long time.' I assumed he had recently seen some programme on television and, like many children, was processing it by relating to his own life.

It immediately became apparent that my quick dismissal of his concern wasn't going to do the trick. Again with a fair amount of seriousness in his voice he said, 'Yes, but Christina, if Daddy dies are you going to take care of me?' This time I stopped what I was doing and looked at him. Obviously he wasn't going to let me off the hook. Not entirely sure what this line of questioning was all about, I tried again. 'Well,' I said, 'if something happened to Daddy you and your sister would still live with your mum, and she would take care of you just like she does now.'

'Yes,' he replied, 'but what about when I'm here in this house? If something happens to Daddy, will you take care of me?' Evidently I still wasn't getting it.

After several minutes of trying to calm his fears with what I deemed reasonable and appropriate explanations, he still persisted. It was clear from his determination that I still hadn't answered the question. So I decided to take a different approach. 'Hhmmm, I can tell this is a pretty important question to you,' I said.

'Yes,' he quickly replied with an impatient look in his eyes.

'So it sounds like you're wondering if I would still love and care for you if Daddy wasn't around.'

He nodded his head to confirm my suspicions. 'So will you take care of me?' he asked.

'Yes, sweetie,' I replied. 'If something happened to Daddy, I would be here to take care of you.'

'Okay,' he said. Seeming both relieved and content, he skipped out of the room to go and play.

Truly listening is hard, especially when you are a parent. Much like the conversation with my bonus son, sometimes it's easy to miss what's really going on with our children. For him the issue wasn't his dad's health or what the contingency plan was if one of his parents wasn't available. It didn't have anything to do with his mum or picking one home over the other. For the moment he was just trying to work out who was going to be a permanent fixture in his life.

When you separate it's expected that there will be lots of different issues that come up for your children. Some of them will be obvious ones, such as: Where am I going to live? When will I see each of my parents? Why did this have to happen? Yet there will also be lots of other feelings and issues that your children may have that aren't so obvious or straightforward. Keep in mind that your perceptions of how life is changing are probably going to be very different from the way your children see the world right now. At times it may be really tough for you to recognise what's brewing underneath the surface. This is one of the many reasons that being a good listener is vital during this time in your children's lives. Listening is not just about hearing what is being said, it's understanding what's behind the words.

WHY IS LISTENING SO HARD?

To compound the issue, when your kids are having a difficult time or are dealing with a painful experience, it's very natural as a parent to want to fix it, make it better or take away the hurt. I have found in my work with separating and divorced parents that this is particularly true. No matter how old your children are, it is absolutely gut-wrenching to see your children hurt or upset. However, when your children are facing difficult life challenges, such as divorce, one of the most meaningful things you can do is just listen. While it may not seem like you are doing very much as a parent, supporting your children's feelings is enormously helpful.

When you listen to your children, it helps them:

- Develop a more meaningful connection to you
- Learn how to identify their feelings
- Accept how they feel without judgement or shame
- Feel comfortable about expressing their feelings
- Build a sense of self-competency, the belief that they can handle hard or difficult situations

Your children don't need you to fix the problem; they need you to understand it.

In theory it sounds pretty simple: they talk, we listen. However, listening isn't a passive process. It's actually an active one that requires engaging with and responding to your children in a different way. Part of improving your skills in the listening department comes with recognising the factors that affect your ability to genuinely listen to your children.

Qualities of being a good listener

▶ Managing your own judgements and perceptions about the situation or issue

It can be incredibly difficult to suspend your own judgements or perceptions when your children say or do things that you have strong feelings about. It can be especially tempting to react when the issue involves the other parent or household. If your children say something that strikes a chord, do what you can to distance yourself from your immediate response and stay focused on them. If you are finding it too difficult, give yourself time out to process what is going on and how you are feeling about the situation. After you have had an opportunity to think things over, readdress the issue with your children.

Again, how you manage your feelings plays a significant role in how you support your children. Make sure you have access to other healthy, trusted adults to use as a sounding board when things get tough.

▶ Accepting that you may not know how your children are feeling

How your children are feeling isn't always evident. What you as a parent are seeing on the outside may not always match up with what your children are feeling on the inside. Sometimes children may manage situations or feelings in ways that are more comfortable or familiar to them. For example, your 13-year-old may handle embarrassment by acting angry and lashing out, whereas your eight-year-old may deal with sadness by pretending what has happened is really no big deal. Avoid making assumptions. Even if you think you have a pretty good idea of what's going on, spend time checking things out.

▶ Moving beyond your own discomfort

There may come a time when your children will say things you don't really want to hear. Perhaps they raise an issue you feel uncomfortable with, bring up a sensitive matter about the divorce that you're not prepared to address, or say something hateful out of anger. When you find yourself headed into rough waters, remember that your job is to listen, not to defend your position or talk your children out of their feelings. When a difficult issue surfaces it's okay to tell your children that you need time to think about what has been said. If you really feel like you are in over your head, seek the support of a trusted friend or perhaps an experienced professional to sort things out. Once you've worked out how you want to handle things, set aside time to follow up with your children.

▶ Letting go of the need to solve the problem rather than understand it

As parents, we often have a strong drive to fix or resolve problems for our children. If they're hurting, we want to make it better. If they're upset, we want to fix it. When they're in pain, we want to comfort and shield them. When you jump into resolving before understanding, you deprive your children of a valuable learning experience. Although it is tough to watch your child struggle, building a sense of self-competency (a belief that you can handle tough and challenging situations) is an important skill. If children are never given the opportunity to struggle, they are also never given the opportunity to grow.

QUESTIONS TO USE WITH CHILDREN

BEFORE RESPONDING, CLARIFY THE EVENT	GAIN AN UNDERSTANDING OF YOUR CHILD'S FEELINGS OR PERCEPTIONS
What happened?	How did that make you feel?
Where did it happen?	What were you thinking when this happened?
When did it happen?	Then what happened?

How did you feel when... ?

Can you tell me more about what happened?

What happened right before you became upset?

What happened right after?

What was most difficult, sad or upsetting?

On a scale of 1 to 10, how upset (angry, sad, are you feeling?

What did that mean to you?

UNDERSTAND CHILD'S REACTION

Can you help me understand how you handled the problem?

What did you do when you were feeling upset (angry, sad)?

How did you show your feelings?

How did the person (parent, friend) respond?

On a scale of 1 to 10 how hard did you hit (loud did you yell)?

How did handling things this way help?

How did it hurt?

HELP CHILD WEIGH OPTIONS FOR MANAGING THE PROBLEM

Can you help me understand what you want?

What do you want?

What would feel helpful to you?

How do you want to handle this problem?

What would feel like a good solution for you?

How would you like things to be different?

What else could you do?

How would that help or hurt the situation?

TIPS FOR BEING A BETTER LISTENER

▶ Be an approachable parent

When parents separate, children may be reluctant to share how they feel or talk when they are feeling troubled. It's not uncommon for children to worry about making an already difficult situation worse between Mum and Dad or possibly even hurting a parent's feelings. Although it may seem obvious to you that it's okay for your children to talk about how they feel, keep in mind that they may need your reassurance. Make sure you are an approachable parent by letting your children know that what they are thinking and feeling is important to you. Reinforce that it's okay to ask questions or talk about problems without worrying how it will affect Mum or Dad.

▶ Give children your full attention when they are talking to you

Let's face it, for most parents in today's world dropping what you're doing to have a heart-to-heart chat with your kids is a tall order. Although it's not always convenient or easy, it's important to let children know you are physically and mentally present when they are talking to you. When children need to talk, remove yourself from momentary distractions (turn off the TV, stop putting away the shopping, don't read email). Let children know they have your full attention by sitting down and making eye-to-eye contact with them.

Keep in mind that taking time to listen in the moment doesn't necessarily have to be a lengthy process. When children have your full attention you may find you get to the root of the problem more quickly. Giving children your undivided time and attention also sends a clear message that what they are feeling and thinking matters and has value. It also sets the bar for how you expect them to listen to you.

If your children raise an issue or are asking to speak to you when you can't stop what you are doing, let your child know what they have to say is very important to you. Explain to them that right now is not a time when you can give them your full attention. Then arrange a time with your children when you can talk without interruption. Remember, however, that it's best to ask children to wait minutes not hours, otherwise you may miss your opportunity.

▶ Listen to your child while resisting the temptation to talk, give advice or lecture

Listening is hard and rarely comes naturally. When the temptation to talk is strong, do your best to curb the impulse by asking open-ended questions. An open-ended question is one that can't be answered with yes or no. Here are some examples:

- Instead of 'Did you have a good time with Mum today?' try 'What did you enjoy about your day with Mum?'
- Instead of 'Do you feel angry with Dad for not showing up?' try 'How do you feel about Dad not showing up?'
- Instead of 'Are you feeling sad about Mum and Dad getting a divorce?' try 'Can you tell me what you feel most sad about?'

Keep in mind that listening doesn't involve correcting; it involves connecting. Avoid lecturing, giving advice or talking to children about what they should or shouldn't be doing. This approach usually adds to children's frustration and ends up pushing them further away.

▶ If emotions are strong, do your best to stay calm and level-headed

When emotions are running high for your children, do your best to maintain your composure. Although it may be difficult, staying calm puts you in a much better position to deal with what's going on. Don't forget that your tone and volume play a part in how children respond to you. We've all heard the saying, 'It's not what you say, it's how you say it.' This couldn't be truer with children, especially angry ones. If you match your child's level of emotion by increasing your own tone and volume, expect things to get out of hand very quickly.

It can take a great deal of restraint not to come totally unglued when your child looks you straight in the eye and tells you, 'You're really stupid,' or 'I hate you!' However, when you stay calm and level-headed children will be more apt to settle down and deal with their feelings more appropriately.

▶ Seek to understand your child's feelings and perspective

One way you can convey understanding is by focusing on what your children are feeling and putting that feeling into words for them. You can make statements such as, 'I can understand why you would feel that way,' 'It sounds like you are ...' and 'That must have been really difficult when ...' Remember, just because you understand how your children feel doesn't mean you have to agree with their perception or opinion. It only means you understand.

▶ Take action

When children are dealing with a difficult situation or issue they need to talk to someone who is supportive and understanding. Again, remember that taking action doesn't mean you fix the problem or give advice. Children benefit more when we support them in creating their own solutions. Once you feel you understand your children's perspective, then you can make a decision about how to respond. Sometimes all your child may need is reassurance and a hug. At other times you may take a more active role by helping them brainstorm possible solutions or thinking through options.

IF YOU HAVE A CHILD WHO DOESN'T WANT TO TALK

When children don't talk, parents often struggle with how to interpret the silence: Should I be worried? Am I missing something? Does my child need professional help? Keep in mind that some children simply aren't good at putting their feelings into words. When you consider the stress many children feel about what's happening in the family, it's easy to see that it might be hugely uncomfortable to say out loud what they're feeling inside.

There are lots of different reasons why children may resist talking about how they feel. Some children avoid talking about the divorce because it makes it feel too real, while others may be worried about making things worse between Mum and Dad. Regardless of the reasons, if your child doesn't want to talk or resists discussions about divorce, don't force the issue. Perhaps one of the best things you can do is let her know you realise this is hard for her. Tell her you understand she might not want to talk about it right now. You can also reinforce that you are willing to be available by letting your child know that when she is ready to talk you'll be ready to listen.

If you sense that your child wants to talk but may be having trouble taking the first step, consider taking what I call a back-door approach. Sitting down to have a heart-to-heart conversation with Mum or Dad usually makes any self-respecting kid a little nervous. I have found in my work with children that some of the best conversations occur when children are engaged in doing something else. To help put your child at ease, think about arranging some one-on-one time where you can get him involved in a low-key activity. Maybe you decide to kick around a football, take a drive in the country, have a quiet walk in the park or sit down to colour in a picture. Often when children are occupied by another activity their anxiety decreases, leaving open to discussing how they feel.

Age-appropriate books or resources can be another way to initiate discussions with children. Frequently children will have an easier time talking about something that happened to a character in a book than what is happening in their own lives. Most children feel very alone when they are dealing with a difficult situation or problem. Using books or other resources not only normalises some of those feelings but may also help them find the words to describe what's going on.

If all else fails, let children know you understand it may not always be easy to talk with Mum or Dad, especially about the divorce. Help them identify at least three other safe adults they can share their feelings with (coach, clergy, teacher, school counsellor, grandparent).

SOMETHING TO THINK ABOUT

- What do you usually do when your children are having a tough time?
- How comfortable are you with just listening to what they have to say?
- Do you respond the same way every time, or are there certain feelings or issues that are more difficult for you to hear?
- What's one thing you could do this week that would make you a better listener for your children?

25.
HOW TO HANDLE THINGS WHEN YOUR CHILD IS ANGRY

While we try to teach our children all about life,
our children teach us what life is all about.
– Anonymous

Joe had always been a pretty easygoing kid. However, once he worked out his parents weren't getting back together everything changed. He seemed determined to do whatever he could to challenge his mother's authority. He frequently talked backed, disobeyed the rules and threw temper tantrums when he didn't get his way. Amanda, Joe's mum, felt like her house had turned into a war zone. Everything with Joe had become a battle, from doing homework to getting ready for bed.

Amanda tried to talk with Malcolm, Joe's father, about the problem. From Malcolm's perspective Amanda was the one to blame, not Joe. Malcolm felt that Joe was a well-behaved kid when he had the right kind of discipline. Malcolm told Amanda he never had problems with Joe because Joe knew Malcolm wouldn't put up with it. If Amanda would just put her foot down she wouldn't have these problems.

Amanda was infuriated. What did Malcolm know about discipline? He didn't have to be the bad guy day in and day out. Whenever Joe was at Malcolm's house for the weekend it was all fun and games. Malcolm never had to struggle over homework, get Joe up in the morning or make Joe go to bed by eight o'clock. All they did at Malcolm's house was go to the cinema, play games and eat junk food.

Sound familiar? Both Malcolm and Amanda fell into the trap of getting so focused on what the other wasn't doing that they missed the boat and couldn't see what was happening with Joe. So what did they miss?

CHILDREN'S SENSE OF SECURITY AND HOW THEY EXPRESS ANGER

In order for children to share their anger and upset with a parent, they need to feel safe. Children need to know that, no matter what, Mum and Dad will always be there. Children who feel safe know that even if they get upset, feel frustrated or throw a horrific fit their parents' love will endure. When parents split up, that sense of security gets shaken for kids. Children are left wondering, 'If Mum and Dad can stop loving each other, what would it take for them to stop loving me?' Of course, the idea of losing a parent's love and acceptance is devastating to children, and they will do almost anything to avoid it, even if it means hiding how they really feel.

In some situations, children's sense of security may be greater with one parent than the other. In many divorce arrangements one parent tends to stay in the family home and function as the primary household for children. If children spend more time in one household than the other, they may feel safer with that parent. However, because of their unspoken worry ('Will my mum or dad stop loving me?'), children may not feel as safe expressing their anger with the off-duty parent.

To make this clearer, let's take another look at Malcolm and Amanda's situation. Suppose we accept the idea that children need to feel safe to express their anger and upset. It stands to reason that Joe probably feels emotionally safer with Amanda. Because life has changed least with her, Joe feels confident that Mum isn't going anywhere. Even if she sends him to his room 100 times, Joe knows that at the end of the day Mum will still love him.

Okay, now let's consider what's going on with Malcolm. Before the divorce Joe saw his dad every day. Now Joe has limited time with Malcolm, and that time with Dad has become very precious. Like lots of kids, Joe doesn't want to do anything that will jeopardise or mess up his time with Dad. The belief that Dad will love him no matter what may not be as strong for Joe. If Joe is worried about losing his connection to Dad, it makes sense that he may hide his anger and upset. Joe won't rock the boat.

What could Malcolm and Amanda do differently?

- Keep the focus on Joe.
- Reassure Joe that it is normal to feel angry.
- Make sure Joe knows that, no matter how he feels, Dad will always love him.

It would probably also help Joe if Malcolm and Amanda used a two-home concept. Instead of making Dad's house a fun place to visit, it would be more helpful to Joe to feel that he also had a home with Dad. When children are treated like visitors in a parent's home they usually end up feeling less secure.

In Joe's situation, feeling connected to both households would not only help him feel safer about sharing his feelings with Dad but it would also decrease his anxiety about losing Dad. Amanda may find she has less acting up to deal with and more support from Malcolm because he will feel included as an active parent.

DIFFERENT WAYS CHILDREN MANAGE THEIR ANGER
Young children

As we covered in the developmental chapters (Part II), younger children will typically express their feelings by acting them out. When toddlers become angry they may exhibit those feelings through a variety of behaviours (such as throwing temper tantrums, biting, hitting or kicking). Even though your little one is going through a difficult time, remember she still needs structure and consistent discipline when she behaves inappropriately.

While school-age children have the ability to communicate their feelings with words, expect at times to see some misdirected behaviour. Although they may be able to identify the feeling, they still need your help in working out how to manage it. Support your school-age children by developing a list of acceptable and safe ways to express anger in your home.

Here are some suggestions for safe ways young children can express their anger:

- Punch a pillow
- Exercise (do sit-ups or push-ups until they are not angry any more)
- Pound feelings out using an empty plastic bottle
- Draw or colour out their feelings ('Colour how mad you're feeling,' 'Draw a picture of why you're feeling angry.')
- Talk with someone (make a list of three safe people your children can talk to when they are angry or upset)
- Take time to cool off
- Count their anger out
- Take several deep breaths

Pre-adolescents and teens

Although older, when it comes to managing anger tweens and teens can frequently behave like toddlers. Instead of talking things out they may choose to act on their feelings. Of course, the way a teen expresses their feelings and the way a toddler does so are very different. Older children have the ability to channel their feelings into serious risk-taking behaviours like drinking too much, driving dangerously, becoming overly cynical, becoming more sexual, testing your authority or harbouring thoughts of self-harm. Like younger children, they will need both love and limits during this time.

Healthy ways for older children to manage anger include the following:

- Write or draw in a diary about their feelings
- Write a letter
- Exercise (run at the track, play sports, use a punch bag, work out)
- Walk away from the situation and give themselves time to cool off
- Talk to a friend or someone they trust
- Deep breathing
- Meditation, or give themselves time to think about how they want to handle a situation
- Prayer

CREATING CONSEQUENCES

Be careful of responding to your children's inappropriate behaviour in the heat of the moment. If needed, give yourself time to cool off or think things through before disciplining or setting a consequence.

- Avoid giving unreasonable or extremely long punishments. Instead keep consequences obtainable and manageable (no telly tonight versus no telly for a month).
- Don't create situations that end up punishing you (taking away the car so you now have to chauffeur your teen versus limiting the use of the car).
- Take away activities or privileges that are not constructive (television time, use of computer, mobile phones, videos games) versus those that positively contribute to your child's life (piano lessons, football practice, scouting or team sports).

Silent anger

Often silent anger is the scariest kind of anger for a parent to handle. You may sense your child's anger, but rather than openly express it your child chooses to withdraw, close down or emotionally shut you out. When anger is not expressed, kept silent and turned inward it can easily develop into a more serious form of depression. You may hear your child say things like, 'Nothing matters any more,' or 'Maybe if I wasn't around it would make everyone's life easier.' Be sure to take statements like this very seriously. Suicide is one of the leading causes of death in young people. While your child may not have the clear intention of permanently hurting himself or ending his life, he is clearly letting you know he needs your help. In these circumstances it is best to seek professional help immediately (see Chapter 27).

SIX STEPS TO HELPING CHILDREN HANDLE ANGER

▶ Make time to talk about the problem

Schedule a time to talk with your children about the situation. Make sure it is during a time when neither you nor they are feeling upset. Let your children know you understand this is a difficult time for them. Consider apologising for the hurt and pain your decision has caused and give them a chance to share how they feel. While it may be hard, make an effort not to be defensive (see also Chapter 24).

▶ Acknowledge feelings while setting limits

Explain to your children that, while it is okay to feel angry, how they are handling their anger is a problem. Clearly identify which behaviours are not acceptable ways to express they are upset (for example, hitting, being disrespectful, breaking things). Let your children know what will happen if they choose an inappropriate way of handling their anger. Make sure the consequence is both age appropriate and enforceable. For example, with younger children you might say: 'When you are disrespectful, you will have to go to your room.' For older children you might consider withdrawing a privilege such as taking away a mobile phone or restricting computer time, television viewing or video games playing.

▶ Create options

When children get angry they often get caught in a double bind. This means that when they get angry you do a good job of telling them what they can't do, but you don't tell them what they can do. Consider changing the way you correct behaviour.

SUGGESTED PHRASES FOR CHANGING THE WAY YOU CORRECT CHILDREN

NEGATIVE REQUEST (TELLS CHILDREN WHAT NOT TO DO)	ACTION-ORIENTED REQUEST (TELLS CHILDREN HOW TO BEHAVE)
Don't hit	Please keep your hands to yourself
Don't run	Please walk inside the house
Don't talk back	Please listen without being disrespectful
Don't ignore me	I need you to look at me and give me your full attention
Don't interrupt me	Please wait for your turn to talk
Don't call names	Please talk to each other without using insulting names

Just as you need healthy ways of dealing with your anger, so do your children. After you have reinforced that feeling angry is normal, work with your child to come up with three to five healthy, appropriate ways he can express his anger in your home. Some good choices are:

- Exercising
- Hitting or screaming into a pillow
- Keeping a journal or diary
- Drawing or colouring feelings
- Stepping away from the situation
- Taking time to cool off
- Talking to someone he or she trusts
- Taking a walk
- Deep breathing or counting to calm down

Once you have come up with some ideas, write them down and post them somewhere your child can see them daily. For younger children, you may want to draw or cut out pictures of what they can do when they are feeling upset. You can also take pictures of children engaging in the appropriate activity and post photos with their list. Anything that visually helps children see themselves making different choices increases the likelihood that they will be able to put those behaviours into action.

▶ Practise the skill

Be sure your children understand what they need to do and how to do it. If you tell them that they can take time to cool off, explain what that means (going outside for a walk, not leaving the house without telling anyone where you are going). If they need to take a deep breath, then show your child what a deep breath looks like. Demonstrating and practising these skills are especially important for younger children. Expect that your children may mess up sometimes and revert back to what they did before. Just because you've practised doesn't mean they will get it right the first couple of times. When they make a mistake, offer a reminder and keep practising with them. Also, remember children usually do as we do, not as we say. If you want your children to handle their anger in a healthy way, you need to practise what you preach.

▶ Stay consistent

Once you have worked out a plan regarding what your kids need to do, make sure you stick to it. Change takes time. Realise your children will probably need reminding about what to do when feelings are strong. If your children start to get angry and revert to old behaviour, give them a warning. Remind them that there will be consequences if they choose to handle their anger in this way. Redirect them by suggesting they make a different choice. If they do not, you need to enforce the consequence immediately in a calm and controlled manner.

▶ Follow up

Mark a date in your diary to remind yourself to check in with your children. Give them a chance to talk about how they are doing. A central part of creating positive changes in children's behaviour involves helping them feel good about who they are. While it is important to let them know what they need to work on, put effort into catching your children being good. Be sure to compliment them when they make positive choices about handling anger and upset.

POINTS ABOUT ANGER FOR PARENTS

▶ Normalise it

Let children know it's okay to be angry. They need to know that it is normal to feel upset or mad about what has happened in the family. It can also be reassuring for them to know that their feelings about the divorce don't have to be the same as Mum's or Dad's. For example, just because Mum and Dad are upset with one another doesn't mean they have to be angry with one or both of their parents. To sum up, children need to hear they have every right to feel any way they want. Remember your job is not to fix, explain or talk them out of how they feel. Instead it's your job to be supportive and understanding.

▶ Don't take it personally

It is really tough to hear words like 'I hate you,' or 'I don't want to live with you any more,' and yet it is one way your children may express their hurt and pain. When children say hurtful or mean things, don't take it personally. Realise they are feeling angry and may not know how else to express it. Although it doesn't feel great when your children are angry with you, be grateful that they feel safe enough with you to express their anger.

▶ Manage your own reaction

To support your children through this stage, it is imperative that you are able to handle your own feelings of anger in a healthy way. Even though it may be hard not to react, you need to show through your words and your actions that you can handle your child's anger. When things get heated, calmly but firmly address the situation.

If your children say something hateful out of anger, don't immediately discipline, unless the situation is out of control (for example a child is threatening to harm you or another family member, becoming verbally or physically aggressive or is threatening self-harm). Identify the feeling by saying something like:

- 'I can tell you are very angry with me right now.'
- 'So what is it that you hate the most?'
- 'I want to understand how you are feeling. Can you tell me what you are angry about?'

Be sure to give your children an opportunity to express how they feel as long as they are not behaving in a dangerous or offensive way. Once they have had an opportunity to calm down, remind them that there are okay ways and not okay ways to be angry.

26.
WHAT TO DO WHEN YOUR CHILD IS SAD

Making the decision to have a child is momentous. It is to decide forever to have your heart go walking around outside your body. – Elizabeth Stone

Rebecca could see it on her 10-year-old daughter's face when she walked in the door. Something was up. Louise sank into the couch and avoided looking at her mum. When Rebecca asked, 'How was your day, darling?' Louise muttered, 'All right, I guess,' as she continued to look down at the floor.

Rebecca felt helpless; she hated seeing Louise upset. Ever since her father, Vince, left, Louise had been really sad. To make matters worse, Vince had moved five hours away to take a new job and get a fresh start. Over the past few months he and Louise had hardly talked. Before Rebecca asked Vince for a divorce, he and Louise had been inseparable. Now it seemed like Louise cried all the time. Rebecca looked at Louise again. She just didn't have it in her to see Louise hurt. 'Hey, sweetie, I have your favourite cake in the kitchen. Want a snack?'

'No, thanks,' replied Louise.

Rebecca tried another approach. 'Guess what? That new film you've been wanting to see came out today. Why don't we go and see it tonight after you finish your homework? We could even go to your favourite pizza place for supper.'

When Louise looked up there were huge tears in her eyes. 'That's all right. I think I just want to go to my room for a while.'

Rebecca felt so guilty. This was all her fault; she should have never asked Vince to leave. 'Oh, poppet, you know I hate to see you cry. Why

don't you go and lie down for a while? I'm sure things will be better tomorrow.'

After Louise went upstairs Rebecca noticed some papers on the couch. On top of the stack was a school notice reminding parents about the Father's Day event next week. Rebecca's heart sank. How was she ever going to make this up to Louise?

It doesn't really matter how old your children are or how long you have been a parent. It's never easy to see your children hurt. When your children are sad, usually you feel sad too. It's even more difficult when the guilt kicks in and you feel you're to blame. I worked with a father once who felt tremendously guilty about not being able to make his marriage work. For him the hardest part was accepting that the divorce would be his children's first heartbreak. Lots of parents struggle with guilt. It's actually very natural to feel a strong sense of responsibility for your children's upset and hurt. However, like Rebecca in this scenario, if you become more focused on shielding your children from feeling the sadness they'll never work out how to handle it.

So how could Rebecca have supported Louise's feelings while keeping her own guilt in check?

Let's look at this scenario again.

Rebecca could see it on her 10-year-old daughter's face when she walked in the door. Something was up. Louise sank into the couch and avoided looking at her mum. When Rebecca asked, 'How was your day, poppet?' Louise muttered, 'All right, I guess,' as she continued to look down at the floor.

Even though Rebecca hated seeing Louise upset, she knew she couldn't fix it for her. Rebecca walked over and sat down on the couch next to Louise.

'Looks like you've had a tough day,' Rebecca said.

Tears streamed down Louise's face as she nodded her head.

'Can you tell me what you're feeing so sad about?' asked Rebecca. Louise was quiet for a few minutes and then handed Rebecca a leaflet

from school about the Father's Day event. 'I guess this leaflet made you start thinking about how sad you are that Dad's not here. You must really miss him.'

'I just wish he hadn't moved so far away. I feel like I'll never see him again. I hardly even talk to him any more.' Louise continued to cry.

Rebecca put her arm around Louise. 'I'm sorry this is so hard for you.'

'All the other kids will have their dads at school, and I will be the only one without a father. Why can't he just come back and live with us again?' said Louise.

'It must be really difficult to have Dad so far away. You wish things could go back to the way they were before. Sounds like you're also a little worried about being the only kid without your dad there,' replied Rebecca.

'Yeah, I really wish he were here. The school thing isn't such a big deal. It just made me think about Dad,' Louise said as she dried her eyes.

'So what would you like to do about missing Dad?' asked Rebecca.

'I think I would like to call him,' said Louise.

Although logic may tell us sadness is necessary, usually our gut instinct tells us something very different. Even when guilt isn't a factor, as parents there's a strong pull to want to jump in, make it better, take away the sadness or shield our children from the pain. However, by doing so we really aren't helping our children. When you sidestep the sadness you deprive children of building what I call a sense of *self-competency*. Essentially, self-competency can be summed up as a belief in one's ability to handle hard, difficult or uncomfortable situations. When it comes right down to it, divorce will not be the only tough or challenging time your children will ever experience. Most likely they will encounter lots of challenges in life – challenges that you won't be able to fix or change. While it may not feel like you are doing much, one of the best ways you can help your children deal with adversity is to listen. Your children need to know it's okay to feel sad. At the same time they also need your help finding healthy and constructive ways of dealing with it.

When children feel sad they need to:

- Understand it's normal to feel sad about how the family has changed
- Be able to express their sadness without shame or worry
- See parents coping with their sadness in healthy and constructive ways
- Identify positive ways to manage sadness or depression

In the first scenario Mum missed a huge opportunity to help her daughter develop a valuable skill. Yet in the second scenario, when Mum was able to focus on how her daughter was feeling, things took a very different turn for both of them. By acknowledging her child's feelings instead of glossing them over, she was able to understand more quickly why her daughter was upset. As a result the child didn't withdraw from her mother or keep her sadness to herself. Once Rebecca understood how her daughter was feeling she was able to help her think about how to manage her sadness.

Keep in mind that listening to your children talk about their sadness isn't going to be easy. Hearing what your children have to say without trying to fix it or make it better takes practice. Despite your best efforts, you may have a child who doesn't talk. If your child chooses to clam up and not say a word, it doesn't mean you have done anything wrong. Some children may need a little space to think things through first. Others may not be immediately comfortable sharing their feelings. Most important, don't give up. Remember, it may take a couple of attempts before your children feel ready to talk. For more tips on how to handle a child who doesn't talk, see Chapter 24.

WAYS PARENTS AVOID ACKNOWLEDGING CHILDREN'S SADNESS	A MORE HELPFUL WAY TO RESPOND
DISMISSING THE FEELING 'Oh, you're just tired. Why don't you get some sleep? That'll make you feel better.'	'Can you help me understand why you are feeling so upset?'
MAKING IT BETTER 'Hey, we don't need to sit around the house and be sad just because Mum didn't show up. Why don't we go out to eat and see a film?'	'You feel really disappointed that Mum didn't pick you up today. It upsets you when she doesn't show up, doesn't it?'
REMOVING THE PROBLEM 'If Dad's phone calls make you feel sad then maybe he should stop calling you every night.'	'You really miss Dad. When you talk to him it reminds you of how sad you are that he's not here.'
EXPLAINING THE FEELING AWAY 'Come on, don't be a baby, you're too big to cry about this.'	'It's okay to cry when you're feeling sad. Sometimes I feel sad too.'
IGNORING IT 'Everything will be better tomorrow.'	'I'm sorry this has been so hard for you.'
DENYING OR SHAMING THE FEELING 'Come on, don't be a baby, you're too big to cry about this.'	'It's okay to cry when you're feeling sad. Sometimes I feel sad too.'
CHANGING THE SUBJECT 'Yes, I know that was upsetting for you. But wouldn't you rather talk about something happy like what we're going to do this weekend?'	'Sometimes it's not easy to see you upset but I want you to know how you're feeling is important to me. I don't always know what to say but I will do my best to listen when you need to talk.'

DEPRESSION AND CHILDREN: HOW TO RECOGNISE IT

Generally anger and sadness are two of the most predominant feelings children struggle with when parents part. They are also two of the most dangerous stages for children and parents to get stuck in. Although you may think of them as very distinct and separate emotions, there's not always a clear delineation between them. It's possible that there will be times when the sadness is masked by anger. While on the surface you may see an angry child, the underlying emotion could be a deep sense of helplessness and loss. On the flip side, some children may deal with their anger by withdrawing and shutting themselves off from you, which is known as *silent anger* (see Chapter 25). This is when a child chooses to cope with his anger by pulling away from others and letting the anger fester. Be aware that when anger becomes repressed it can easily transform into depression.

Although you understand that feeling sad is a normal part of separation and divorce, it doesn't necessarily make it easier to gauge. When children are depressed many parents wonder at what point they should become concerned. Overall, what's most important about managing the sadness at any stage is keeping it in perspective. If your child's sadness seems to be constant, growing stronger or significantly interfering with his day-to-day life, professional intervention may be necessary.

When to be concerned

- Child displays multiple depressive symptoms (two or more)
- Symptoms are consistent (occurring for most of the day, nearly every day for several weeks or an extended period of time)
- Child expresses a desire to disappear, no longer be alive, or has a preoccupation with death

- An overwhelming sense of hopelessness exists, and the child is unable to experience anything as positive, is primarily focused on the past and cannot see things ever getting better

Signs of depression for children

- Problems in school (significant drop in grades, easily distracted, lack of motivation or interest)
- Extreme change in personality or behaviour (from a happy-go-lucky kid to a quiet and withdrawn child)
- Overly pessimistic, can't see the good in anything
- Doesn't seem to care
- Physical symptoms (stomach aches, body pains)
- Has trouble focusing or staying on task
- May become withdrawn or separate from friends and family
- Is irritable, short tempered or moody
- Loss of interest in things that used to be important
- Cries excessively or frequently becomes easily upset
- Has trouble sleeping at night
- Seems tired, fatigued, sleeps all the time
- Loss of appetite or sudden weight loss
- Weight gain, seeks out comfort foods when upset or sad
- Expresses the wish not to exist or talks about how things would be easier if he or she weren't around

For the majority of children the intense sadness they feel related to divorce is often temporary. Usually with time the strength of the sadness and upset lessens. Children are able to reconcile their sense of loss and find ways to adjust to their new lives. Be mindful, however, that as life moves forward it's possible for children to re-experience certain stages. Sometimes significant changes, transitions or new situations can awaken old hurts or feelings of sadness for your children.

WARNING SIGNS: THINGS CHILDREN MIGHT DO OR SAY WHEN DEPRESSED

A depressed child may:

- Make statements like, 'My life sucks. No matter what I do, nothing will ever get better,' 'I wish I could just disappear forever,' or 'Everything would be so much better if I wasn't around.'
- Frequently talk about death
- Become preoccupied with death or what would happen if they died
- Idealise the idea of death or view it as a way to make a statement ('If I died then I bet everyone would feel really sorry for what they've done to me.')
- Express a desire to 'not exist any more'
- Write stories, poems or draw pictures about dying or death
- Post statements, stories or poems online (Facebook, chat rooms, blog posts or MySpace) about death or going away for ever
- May give away possessions or things of significance to family members or friends
- Consistently isolate themselves from family, friends and activities they once cared about

When children says things like 'I wish I had never been born'

Any statement made by a child that indicates a wish to die, disappear or no longer exist needs to be taken very seriously. Don't wait for your child to act on these feelings. Seek help immediately. Although your child may not have the intention of permanently hurting himself or herself, when children are depressed they often act impulsively and lack good decision-making skills. When children make statements about taking themselves out of the picture, they are sending you a clear message: they need your help. Be sure to read Chapter 27.

WHEN YOU FEEL SAD TOO

While it's vital to help your children find safe and constructive ways to cope with depression, it's just as critical for you to deal with your own sadness in a healthy and responsible way. Parents often ask me if they should keep their feelings hidden from their children. Most worry that sharing their upset and hurt will only make things worse for their children. Actually, when you are responsibly handling your feelings, sharing your sadness with children can be enormously healing. One of the biggest reasons goes back to the idea that children often don't do as we say but rather they do as we do. Remember you are one of the most influential features in your children's lives. When children see you deal with your feelings in a healthy and constructive way, the chances are they will follow in your footsteps. Sharing your feelings also reinforces in a very powerful way that it's okay to talk about how you feel and gives children permission to express those feelings.

Be mindful that sharing your sadness does not mean you bare your soul to your children. Children (regardless of their ages) should never be a primary source of emotional support for parents. Make sure you have healthy adults in your life who can be emotionally supportive so children don't end up feeling responsible for you.

SOMETHING TO THINK ABOUT

- How comfortable are you with your children being sad?
- What kind of messages did you get about being sad when you were a child?
- What's one thing you could do to be more supportive of your children when they are feeling sad or upset?

Sharing your feelings of sadness with children:
- Reinforces that it's okay to be sad
- Lets children know you are capable of handling sadness
- Models safe and appropriate ways to deal with sadness

HEALTHY WAYS TO EXPRESS SADNESS
For younger children
- Draw or colour the sadness
- Have a good cry
- Read a book or story about divorce
- Talk to Mum, Dad or another safe adult
- Write a story about feeling sad
- Talk about happier times when things felt better, and remember not every day will be sad

For older children
- Draw a picture or write a poem about how you feel
- Keep a diary about your feelings
- Talk to a friend, family member or trusted adult
- Cry
- Talk about a time when things felt better and how you might be able to make changes in the future
- Find a book or story about divorce to read and then talk about it
- Listen to your favourite music or something that feels soothing
- Take a walk outside
- Do something relaxing by yourself that gives you a chance to think about how you feel (going for a walk, riding a bike, taking a hot bath or shower, reading a book)

27.
WHEN TO GET HELP FOR CHILDREN

When written in Chinese the word 'crisis' is composed of two characters – one represents danger and the other represents opportunity.
– John F. Kennedy

Knowing when to seek professional help for children can sometimes be a tough call. When your five-year-old ends up sleeping in your bed every night, you may be wondering if it's a normal reaction or a sign of poor adjustment? Should you be concerned that your teen hardly speaks to you and spends most of his waking hours away from home? If your eight-year-old goes from being a perfect student to a kid with less-than-stellar marks, is that cause for concern? Maybe yes and maybe no.

In my experience, **most children don't need professional intervention to successfully deal with separation and divorce**. Many times when parents have access to helpful information and support, they can create the kind of positive changes children need to move forward. However, there are exceptions to every rule. While there are lots of different factors parents should consider, when in doubt my suggestion is to trust your gut instinct. You know your children better than anyone else. If something is concerning you about your children, it's probably a wise choice to pay attention to that feeling.

While trusting your instincts is a good first step, knowing what to do about them is another matter entirely. Looking for help when your family is in crisis can often be just as frustrating as the issue you are dealing with. Because this is a rather broad topic I have designed this chapter to be a little more straightforward than the rest of the book. Keep in mind that the information included is not meant to be a diagnostic tool or to replace a thorough evaluation by a qualified professional. While it cannot possibly cover the specifics of every situation, I hope it will provide you with enough information to help you determine the best course of action for you and your children.

> Keep in mind that psychotherapy and counselling are processes that primarily addresses mental and emotional disorders. Separation and divorce are not disorders but rather significant transitions. When children are having problems dealing with family change, they tend to gain more from support that is focused on offering information, developing coping skills and sharing feelings.

ASSESSING YOUR CONCERNS

Not all problems are created equal. Before deciding how to respond it's probably best to consider assessing the seriousness of the situation. If you have a child who is having issues adjusting, ask yourself the following questions:

- Is this behaviour or problem significantly interfering with my child's day-to-day functioning?
- How is the behaviour or problem affecting our family?
- Is the behaviour getting worse?
- Does the behaviour or problem put my child or others at risk?
- With information and support is this a behaviour I may be able to influence?

After reviewing these questions, think through your answers. If the issue seems to be seriously affecting your child's daily functioning, greatly impacting on your family life, becoming more serious or is placing your child at risk, seeking help sooner rather than later is advisable. When a child's behaviour or issue is manageable but concerning, it may be beneficial for you to first consult a professional to discuss your concerns. You can also seek support from local organisations that offer parenting support. (For suggestions check the Resources section in the back of the book.)

SITUATIONS THAT WARRANT AN IMMEDIATE RESPONSE

Although there are no cut-and-dried answers for every situation, there are some circumstances that clearly warrant a more direct and immediate response. If your child is engaging in any type of dangerous behaviour that puts her or others at risk, do not wait to take action.

While every situation is unique, this section presents some issues that require parents to respond without delay.

▶ Thoughts of self-harm

It cannot be emphasised enough that any statement made by a child that indicates a wish to die, hurt oneself or cease to exist must be taken very seriously. Although it may seem difficult to believe that your child would ever want to hurt himself, those kinds of statements should always be viewed as sincere. When emotionally distraught, children are much more likely to make rash and impulsive decisions. Any expression that suggests they wish to disappear or make it all go away is a clear sign that they need your help. Keep in mind that younger children are also capable of having these kinds of thoughts, not just teenagers. For more on things children might say when depressed or suicidal see Chapter 26.

▶ Unmanageable or dangerous behaviour

When pre-teens and teens become emotionally distressed they may handle those feelings by acting in dangerous ways. While some risk taking and experimentation during adolescence is normal, experimenting with drugs, drinking and driving, inappropriate sexual behaviour, using razors or sharp objects to cut their bodies, or pushing limits either at home or at school are not behaviours you should minimise.

▶ Physical aggression

Although anger is a normal part of coping with divorce, expressing it physically with others is not. Be mindful that when physical aggression goes unaddressed it can escalate and become out of control very quickly. If your child is behaving in an aggressive manner towards you or others, it is imperative that you address this issue as soon as possible. Examples of inappropriate aggression can range from showing a general lack of respect for authority, making verbal threats and physically intimidating others, to pushing, shoving or hitting. Often schools or school counsellors can help you locate resources within your area.

▶ Significant changes in your child's behaviour towards you

If your child has become rejecting, is refusing to have contact with you, displays unjustified anger or is making statements like, 'I never want to see you again,' or 'You are a liar and I can't trust you,' your ongoing relationship with her could be in jeopardy. In some cases these types of behaviour are the early warning signs of parent alienation. Although there are many reasons why a child might resist spending time with a parent, make sure you know what to look for. More detailed information on how to detect alienation can be found in Chapter 23.

Other signs your child may need help are:

- Drastic or extreme changes in behaviour
- Increasing or persistent problems with sadness or depression
- Difficulty with day-to-day functioning
- Overwhelming sense of hopelessness

STEPS FOR SEEKING HELP

Evaluate your family's resources, the availability of support in your area and the time it will take to access help.

NHS

In England: For parents using the NHS (National Health Service), your first port of call should be to make an appointment with your GP to discuss your concerns. If additional support is warranted your GP can refer you to an area professional or organisation.

In Scotland: Parents have the ability to engage services without a referral from a GP. Research local not-for-profit organisations such as Relationships Scotland to find out what types of services and supports are available.

Be aware that waiting lists can be long and that services may not be available immediately.

PRIVATE MEDICAL INSURANCE

If you have the benefit of private medical insurance, check with your provider regarding your plan options. Often insurance providers will have a listing of qualified professionals to choose from. Make sure you understand the scope of your benefits, if a referral is needed, and clarify any questions you have about up-front costs, reimbursement procedures or out-of-pocket costs for services.

SELF PAY

If you have the financial means available or need to access help more quickly, you may want to consider going the private route. When possible seek recommendations from people or sources you trust (such as friends, family members, schools or local organisations). In setting up a first appointment, be sure to ask about the billing procedure and the cost of initial and subsequent sessions. Some psychotherapists or counsellors may offer 'sliding scale' payment options. This means that services are provided at a reduced rate for individuals or families who meet certain criteria.

WHERE TO FIND HELP

Unless you have a psychology degree or some past experience with mental health professionals, knowing where to begin can be a bit daunting. You might be wondering what type of professional you need to see, how you will know if he or she is qualified or even able to help. It can become even more confusing when you find yourself faced with the task of deciphering a myriad of initials and abbreviations behind each professional's name.

Fortunately there are several well-respected membership organisations that offer national registries of individual practitioners throughout the UK. Members of these organisations commit to maintaining a high level of standards, ongoing training and ethical behaviour. To gain a better understanding of various types of credentialling, certification and differences between professions visit the public pages for the following organisations:

- British Association for Counselling (BACP) bacp.co.uk
- Untied Kingdom Council for Psychotherapy (UKCP) psychotherapy.org.uk
- British Psychological Society (BPS) bps.org.uk

I often tell parents, 'Psychotherapists and counsellors are a lot like shoes. Just because they look good doesn't mean they're a fit.' No matter how skilled a professional may be, not every psychotherapist is going to be someone you or your children will work with well. It may also help to know that in general there is a considerable amount of overlap between various professionals and disciplines. While you should always seek an individual who is qualified, a professional's educational background or the type of psychotherapy he or she practises has very little to do with how effective he or she may be working with your family. The success of treatment has more to do with your level of comfort and the relationship you are able to establish with your psychotherapist or counsellor. Make sure you find someone you and your children feel comfortable with and have confidence in.

WHAT ARE COACHES?

Professional coaches are not currently regulated at national level, although reputable coaches typically adhere to a code of ethics and the requirements outlined by the International Coaching Federation (ICF, coachfederation.org). In addition to specialised training in the area of coaching, most coaches have education and experience in other areas of practice. Coaches do not engage clients in psychotherapy or counselling and do not provide diagnoses or evaluations. Rather, coaches work in partnership with individuals to identify core strengths and gain the necessary clarity and skills to improve the quality of their lives. As with other professions, coaches often have specialised areas of expertise. Just as you would with any other professional, be sure to ask about a coach's experience, background and level of education.

Getting referrals

Instead of searching for the one who is right for you, I would recommend getting at least two referrals. Consider asking people whose judgement you trust (family, friends or colleagues) for recommendations. It may also be a good idea to speak to a school counsellor, talk to your child's GP, contact a clergy member or check out a local counselling agency.

If you contact a therapist or counselling agency that is unable to help you, be sure to ask them if they have any recommendations. Often local professionals are familiar with other experienced individuals in similar areas of practice.

INITIAL APPOINTMENTS

Once you have located a professional, if possible, make an initial appointment for yourself before introducing your children. First appointments are designed to:

- Provide you with an opportunity to assess whether a professional is a fit for your family
- Give you the chance to ask questions
- Gain a better understanding of a professional's practice and policies
- Offer you feedback regarding your issue or problem
- Help you make a more informed choice

Questions to ask a potential psychotherapist or counsellor

- What is your background and training?
- Are you accredited, and by what organisation?
- How long have you been working with children? How much experience do you have working with children who are in my children's age range?
- What percentage of your practice deals with separation and divorce?
- What is your general treatment philosophy?
- If my family were to work with you what would be the focus of treatment? What type of intervention would you initially recommend for my children (short-term or long-term therapy; individual, family, or parent–child sessions; age-appropriate group therapy).
- What is your policy about confidentiality and communication with parents?
- When parents are separated or divorced, how do you engage with the other parent?
- What is your rate per session? Do you have cancellation and rescheduling fees, and payment options?

During your first meeting

- Share your concerns and get feedback.
- Ask for the counsellor's initial treatment recommendations.

Evaluating your first appointment

After interviewing a potential professional, spend some time reviewing your needs and what each possible candidate has to offer. In making your decision ask yourself the following questions:

- How confident do I feel about each professional's level of experience and credentials?
- Did each adequately answer my questions and concerns?
- Which one is a person my children would feel comfortable with?
- How comfortable did I feel with each professional during our meeting?
- How did I feel afterwards?
- Do the practical aspects of the services offered meet my needs (availability of appointments, location of office, fees)?

POSSIBLE STUMBLING BLOCKS
When your child doesn't want to go to counselling

I think it's safe to say that most children aren't exactly thrilled to go to psychotherapy or counselling. From your child's perspective, he didn't do anything wrong, which leaves him wondering why he's the one who has to talk to some stranger about how he feels. While some resistance from children is expected, forcing them to go to therapy isn't always the best idea.

If your child is reluctant to engage in one-to-one sessions, there are some other options you may want to explore.

▶ You attend psychotherapy first

It's been my experience that when divorce occurs most parents are capable of providing children with the support they need to make a successful adjustment. Certainly that's not to say that in some circumstances professional help isn't important or valuable. Clearly there are times when children can benefit substantially from having someone other than Mum or Dad to help them sort things out. However, from my perspective, before involving a reluctant child in counselling, parents may be wise to invest some time in working with a professional on their own. In the event that psychotherapy becomes necessary for your children, by engaging with a professional first you will be in a better position to prepare them for what to expect.

▶ Check out age-appropriate groups for children dealing with divorce

Most children feel very isolated when parents separate, and often think they are the only ones in the world who feel the way they do. Sometimes children can significantly benefit from participating in groups with other children who are dealing with divorce. In some areas not-for-profit organisations, such as Relate and Relationships Scotland, may have age-appropriate programmes available. Overall, groups are most effective when they offer children informational support that is focused on helping them understand their feelings about how their family has changed. Such groups tend to be a good fit for children between the ages of 6 and 12 years.

▶ Use books, DVDs and other home-based resources

If you have a child who is struggling but not interested in talking, consider looking for age-appropriate resources such as books, DVDs and interactive workbooks. Often reading a story or watching a programme that deals with the topic of divorce can help children understand they are not alone. Also, for many children relating to a character or story is much easier than having a face-to-face discussion about their own lives. (See the Resources section at the back of the book for recommendations.)

When parents divorce, children need to:
- Understand they are not responsible for what has happened in the family
- Know their feelings are normal and accepted
- Have stability and structure
- Identify constructive ways to express their feelings
- Receive the continued love and support of both parents
- Be protected from adult issues and parental conflict

When the other parent doesn't think there's a problem or won't support getting help

As mentioned in earlier chapters, it's not uncommon for one parent to be more aware than the other of a problem situation with children. In some divorce situations children may have a greater level of comfort or security with one parent than the other. Often the parent who has more day-to-day contact with the children is the one who sees more of the upset, hurt and anger, and the parent who has less time may be under the impression that everything's fine. When this happens, you may have a difficult time convincing your ex that professional support is necessary. You may hear things like: 'You're just making a big deal out of nothing,' 'The children are fine when they're with me; maybe you're the problem,' or 'You're just playing mind games. There's nothing wrong.'

Although you may feel like throttling the other parent, keep in mind your ex may not be seeing the same issues in his or her home that you see in yours. When children have limited time with a parent they may worry about the permanence of their relationship. For that reason they may be afraid to show their anger and upset. Also, when time with a parent is limited, children may view it as a precious commodity and be reluctant to do anything that might mess things up.

Even when your ex isn't seeing things in the same way, it's still important to try to get his or her support before involving your child with professionals. When one parent is not supportive of counselling or psychotherapy, that parent can easily undermine any relationship your child establishes with a professional.

Here are some tips, if the other parent doesn't see a need for professional help.

▶ Encourage your ex to get an objective opinion

If possible, arrange for the other parent to get information from another source other than you. For example, if your child is having problems at school, invite the other parent to speak with the child's teacher or attend a parent–teacher conference.

▶ Don't try to talk the other parent out of his or her perception

In the short run you may get more mileage out of agreeing to disagree. Instead of trying to get your ex to see things the way you do, let your ex know you understand that he or she has a different opinion. Rather than asking the other parent to support treatment, focus on getting his or her support for an evaluation.

▶ Share information regardless

Even though your ex may be throwing up walls when it comes to getting professional help for your children, keep the other parent in the loop. If for no other reason, it takes your children out of the role of informant. When possible, provide your ex with background information about the professional along with contact information *before* scheduling an initial session. If your ex's objection is that you are doing the choosing, then ask him or her to suggest some names as well. It may also be a good idea to propose that he or she speak with the professional you are considering. This will give the other parent an opportunity to address any concerns he or she might have. Whether your ex participates or not, you have done your part by offering information and making a sincere attempt to involve him or her in the process.

If you just can't agree, propose a meeting with a mediator or an objective third party to work things out. In extreme cases you may need to involve the family court. However, litigation should be used as a last resort to access help, not a first option.

When divorce is not managed well or there are situations involving specialised circumstances (domestic abuse, family violence, high conflict, addiction), serious issues for children can develop. In these types of situations you may need to seek a professional who has experience working with children around these dynamics.

28.
WHEN CHILDREN HEAR BAD THINGS ABOUT ONE OF THEIR PARENTS

Every word we say to our children, good or bad, positive or negative, shapes their future. Choose wisely. – Christina McGhee

Several years ago I came across a story of a young boy whose parents were going through a particularly nasty divorce. Despite their differences, his parents had somehow managed the foresight to seek out professional help and find their son a counsellor. During one of the sessions the counsellor asked the young boy to draw a picture of himself as a tree. After putting considerable effort into the picture, he finally showed it to the counsellor. On the page, as requested, was a picture of a tree. What puzzled the counsellor was the way in which he had drawn it. The boy had carefully drawn a thick black line from top to bottom down the centre of the page. On one side of the line was a tall, lush-looking tree with lots of green leaves and blooming flowers on it. However, on the other side of the line the tree had been coloured in various shades of black. It looked barren, withered and lifeless. When asked about the picture the boy said, 'This half is the part of me that is like my mum, and the other side of the tree is the part of me that is like my dad.'

Without a doubt, children see themselves as half Mum and half Dad. Not only does it form the basis of how they define who they are but it also plays a significant part in their self-esteem. Be mindful that children usually interpret the bad things they hear about one of their parents as something bad or negative about themselves. When parents are engaged in a loving relationship, kids typically gets lots of positive feedback regarding their likeness to Mum or Dad. We say things like, 'Oh look, you have your father's charm,' or 'You're so witty, just like your mum.' Unfortunately when parents split up, often what children hear from Mum and Dad about each other takes a new turn.

WHAT IS BADMOUTHING AND HOW DOES IT AFFECT CHILDREN?

Simply put, when you say or do something that discredits or diminishes your child's positive image of the other parent (regardless of how justified you feel your perception is), that's badmouthing. Whether a subtle comment made in passing or a direct insult made towards the other parent, the outcome for your children is the same. The impact of negative words is powerful. Many parents don't realise that badmouthing is a form of negative verbal interaction, and badmouthing the other parent packs just as much punch as directly insulting your children. When children are overexposed to negative verbal exchanges between parents, it often results in the development of negative self-talk. More to the point, children are more likely to develop a critic inside their heads. For example, let's say little Molly got a B in her maths test. Instead of telling herself, 'Hey I got a B, that's pretty good,' or 'Well, a B's not so bad, bet next time I can get an A,' Molly's negative self-talk kicks in with, 'How stupid! What kind of idiot gets a B in an easy test like that? I'm crap at maths.'

Children who engage in negative self-talk are more likely to be depressed, feel anxious and have low self-esteem. You may think what you say about your ex doesn't matter; however, even when negative statements are clearly aimed at the other parent your children still feel the effect.

Ways parents engage in badmouthing

- Name-calling or using foul language ('What a bitch', 'He's a worthless bastard')
- Directly making degrading statements to or about the other parent in front of children ('Your father is a liar. He never tells the truth', 'Your mum's a psycho')
- Statements that judge, criticise or diminish the other parent's worth ('What do you mean your father lets you have sweeties for breakfast? He's so irresponsible. He has no idea how to be a parent')
- Making negative comparisons between the other parent and your child ('Charlene, go and change your clothes. That outfit makes you look trashy. It looks just like something your mother would wear. She never had any taste')
- Derogatory comments about something the other parent does ('Let me guess. Your mother taught you how to fold clothes. I always hated the way she folded my clothes. Here, let me show you the right way to do it')
- Venting to a child about something the other parent did to indirectly criticise them ('You won't believe what your father just did. I was trying to talk to him about this weekend so we could go camping, and he was completely unreasonable. He wouldn't even consider changing the schedule. He's so stubborn. Said it wasn't convenient for him. I don't want to put you in the middle by saying something negative about your dad. I just don't know how he could do that to you')
- Making inside jokes or subtle negative statements about the other parent ('So did your mum try to cook a turkey for Christmas dinner again this year? Bet that bird was tasty! I swear that woman could burn water').

When a relationship breaks down it's normal for parents to harbour some strong feelings about each other. It doesn't come as any great shock that the mixture of hurt and anger about past issues leaves most of us less motivated to see the very best in each other. Sometimes when I talk about badmouthing, some parents feel a little defensive. To be clear, I'm not suggesting that the feelings you have towards your ex aren't valid. Nor am I encouraging you to deny or ignore how you feel. You certainly have every right to feel any way you want about your ex. There is, however, a line to be drawn. It is imperative that you shield your children from your negative feelings about the other parent. Feel free to call your ex every name in the book. You can ring up a friend and vent your spleen about how unfair the situation is or scream you head off about what a loser your ex turned out to be. You are well within your rights to do all that and more, as long as your children never hear a word of it.

The bottom line is that children deserve to have an unrestricted loving relationship with both of their parents, whether they live in one home or two. Children should also be able to feel good about the people their parents are, no matter how Mum and Dad feel about each other. Do your best to honour that by keeping what you say about the other parent in check. In short, make sure that the love you have for your children outweighs any anger and hurt you feel towards your ex (see also Chapter 16).

WHAT CAN YOU DO IF YOU ARE THE ONE DOING THE BADMOUTHING?

Badmouthing is a slippery slope. Most of the parents I've worked with truly want to do right by their children. While they understand that they shouldn't say bad things about their ex, often their anger gets the best of them. Other parents genuinely don't realise how powerful their words truly are or how damaging those seemingly casual comments can be. One of the best ways to minimise badmouthing is to start paying attention to what you say about the other parent and how your say it. Here are some tips to help you keep control over what you say.

HOW TO PUT BADMOUTHING INTO PERSPECTIVE

STEP 1

On a sheet of paper, write down three statements that describe your ex. They can be things you have said or would like to say to your ex-spouse. For the purpose of this exercise there are no restrictions; you can say anything you want about your ex. No holds barred. Start each comment with your ex's first name.

For example:

1. John, you are an irresponsible, self-absorbed git, who has never cared about anybody but yourself.
2. John, you are absolutely worthless. You never follow through with anything.
3. John, you are an insecure control freak who just uses people to get what you want.

1. _____
   _____
2. _____
   _____
3. _____
   _____

STEP 2

Rewrite your three statements about your ex word for word, but this time, instead of starting the sentence with your ex's name, substitute your children's names.

1. _____
   _____
2. _____
   _____
3. _____
   _____

- How did it feel to replace your ex's name with your children's names?
- How do you think it would feel if your children heard you say these things out loud about them?
- What's one thing you could do differently to protect your children from negative statements in the future?

▶ Make sure you are managing your feelings in a constructive way

When you're feeling overly resentful or angry with your ex, it can be very tempting to share what's on your mind with children. To avoid falling in that trap, find some healthy way to blow off some stream. Vent to a trusted friend or family member; take a walk; or perhaps go into another room, take a deep breath and remind yourself how much you love your children.

▶ Let go of things that feel unjust, unfair or hurtful

The process of uncoupling almost always leaves some scars, whether it's harbouring an old hurt, feeling that you've been treated unfairly, or being angry about how your ex has handled a situation. Although forgiveness may not be in the cards, **for your own sake find some way to make peace with the past,** whatever it may be. Hanging on to old hurts will only hold you back from living the life you want.

Resentment is like drinking poison and waiting for the other person to die. – Malachy McCourt

▶ Have a plan

Most unintentional badmouthing occurs in the heat of the moment. Perhaps your children unknowingly raise a sensitive or unresolved issue that leaves you on the verge of blowing a fuse. To stop yourself diving head first into your anger, think through how you can handle those moments when your desire to say something nasty or negative about the other parent is strong. A plan might include recognising the behaviour, stepping away from the situation, or giving yourself a phrase to repeat when you are feeling overwhelmed (such as 'My children don't deserve to hear this,' or 'I will honour the love I have for my children more than my anger').

If you have participated in badmouthing, don't beat yourself up. Just commit to making a change in the way you talk about your ex in front of the children. If you have said something you shouldn't have or now realise you should have handled your feelings differently, come clean with your kids and admit your mistake. Apologise for the inappropriate things you said, and let your children know you are going to do your best not to badmouth in the future. Then do your best not to repeat the behaviour. You can also ask your children to help you stay accountable. Give your children permission to let you know if you say anything that makes them feel uncomfortable or if it seems like you are putting the other parent down.

WHAT IF THE OTHER PARENT IS BADMOUTHING YOU?

Perhaps one of the most frustrating aspects of divorce is that there are so many things you can't control or change. And badmouthing is definitely one of those areas that fall completely out of your control. Although you may realise the importance of not slamming the other parent, it's quite possible your ex may see things differently. Most of the parents I work with feel very conflicted about how to handle badmouthing from the other side. Usually the responses vary from fighting fire with fire to keeping quiet and saying nothing at all.

Managing badmouthing is a bit like walking a tightrope. It requires a combination of practice, balance and skill. Like many things discussed in this book, it's also easier said than done.

Making sure your children are shielded as much as possible while offering them skills to deal with the negative things they are hearing takes work.

Trish had been separated from her ex, Tony, for only four months. Right away things got rocky. Every time her boys came back from spending time with their dad they were angry, confused and usually armed with new information about the upcoming court case. Tony would regularly sit down with their 13-year-old son, Sean, to have what he called man-to-man talks. During conversations with Sean, Tony would blame the divorce on Trish, telling Sean things like, 'Your mum is trying to rob me blind and take everything I've worked for away from me,' and 'Don't listen to anything she says. She's just trying to fill your head with lies.' Tony even went so far as to ask Sean to be his lookout and report back to him things that were happening in Trish's home.

Unfortunately the badmouthing got to the point that Sean started confronting his mum. Because Trish didn't want to make things worse for her sons, she often avoided saying anything at all and would punish Sean for talking back. When Trish discovered that the boys were sneaking things out of her home and taking them to Tony, she knew things had to change.

With support, Trish learnt that keeping quiet when the boys repeated Dad's derogatory statements wasn't making the situation better. Instead, Trish made a plan to speak to the boys about some of the things Dad had been saying. She let them know how very sorry she was that Dad was choosing to say mean things about her. She reinforced that it must be very difficult for them and they probably felt very confused about who they should believe. Trish further explained that it was not their job to work out who was right and who was wrong. More than anything, she wanted them to have a good relationship with both Mum and Dad. She made sure both boys understood she did not agree with Dad's decision to talk about court matters but was also careful not to make any negative comments about Tony. She set firm boundaries with the boys about respectful behaviour, which included taking things from one house to the other without permission. Although it took some time, the longer Trish remained consistent, the more things began to smooth out. When the boys talked about the negative things Dad said she focused on how they felt instead of ignoring the conversation altogether. As the boys became more comfortable talking about the situation, she was able to discuss with them different ways to handle the things that Dad would say.

What to do when children are exposed to badmouthing

▶ Don't retaliate or try to set the record straight

When children are given information that is untrue, distorted or simply an outright lie, it can be incredibly difficult not to share your version of the truth. Keep in mind that while you may feel that you are being genuinely honest with your children, your ex will have a different perspective. When you counter or contradict the other parent, your children are still caught in a no-win situation between two people they love.

Certainly that doesn't mean you have to roll over when your children are repeating things the other parent has said that you view as untrue or extremely one-sided. It's okay to tell children things like:

- 'I don't agree with what Dad has said.'
- 'Mum and I have different opinions about what has happened.'
- 'When parents split up, they usually don't see things the same way. You don't ever have to decide who's right or who's wrong.'
- 'This is an issue that Mum and Dad need to work out. I am sorry that you got involved in this.'

▶ Stay focused on your children's feelings

When children are given contradictory or negative information about a parent, they usually feel confused and trapped. While children may not believe the badmouthing, they may respond by keeping quiet, afraid to disagree or worried that they may anger a parent. When children talk about badmouthing, do your best to focus on their feelings. Consider saying things like:

- 'How do you feel about what Mum said?'
- 'What do you think about the things Dad is saying about me?'
- 'I'm sorry you had to hear that.'

▶ Help your children process what they have heard

In addition to helping your children cope with their emotions, they also need to be able to disengage from adult feelings. Essentially, this means that children understand the feelings they have about divorce can be separate and different from their parents' feelings and perceptions. This is also a good time to reaffirm for children that they are not responsible for the problems between Mum and Dad. Here are some possible things to say:

- 'Sounds like Mum was feeling really angry. Sometimes when divorce happens, adults get angry and say things to hurt each other.'
- 'When parents split up they often feel angry and hurt. Please understand your feelings don't have to be the same as Dad's. Just because he is upset with me doesn't mean you have to be upset with me.'
- 'While I can understand why Mum feels upset, I don't agree with how she is handling her feelings.'

Help children learn how to cope with the problem

Once your children have had a chance to talk about how they feel, it can be helpful to discuss different ways they can handle the badmouthing. This section offers some ideas.

▶ Speaking out against the badmouthing

When badmouthing is mild or when children feel safe enough to express themselves to a parent, you can teach them to say things like, 'Please stop talking about someone I love,' or 'It really upsets me when you say mean things about Dad.'

▶ Vow of silence

For situations in which children feel intimidated, you can talk with them about taking a vow of silence. This involves giving children permission to love their other parent when they are listening to the badmouthing. For example, you could say, 'I know it must be very hard to tell Mum how you feel when she says mean things about me. It's okay for you to keep the love you have for me and know in your heart that I'm a good person.'

Other subtle ways children can feel empowered is by giving them permission to leave the room or by letting them know they can choose to ignore the mean things they hear. Older children can be taught to dismiss the badmouthing as the adult's problem, not theirs.

▶ When appropriate, offer a different perception of reality

If the badmouthing is increasing or becoming more intense, you may need to take a more direct approach and offer your children another perception of reality. Again, make sure when you're sharing information that your intent is to give children information that is constructive, not destructive. This means addressing the problem or situation without launching a counterattack.

If excessive badmouthing goes unaddressed it can develop into a more serious situation, such as parent alienation. If you feel your relationship with your children is being compromised or is in jeopardy it may help to review the information in Chapter 23.

Badmouthing doesn't always occur just between Mum and Dad. When a relationship ends, extended family members have strong feelings too. Although it's not always a conscious choice, many family members feel compelled to take sides and share their opinions and feelings with children. This is often a common problem with grandparents.

If your parents are the ones doing the bashing, set appropriate boundaries. Let them know that while they have a right to be angry about what has happened, when they trash the other parent they are hurting your children. When it's your ex in-laws who are jumping on the bandwagon, first try to address the issues with your ex. If your ex isn't supportive, use the tips listed earlier in this chapter to deal with the situation.

WHEN BADMOUTHING BACKFIRES

Keep in mind that, regardless of who is doing the badmouthing, it can backfire. Remember when an adult badmouths you in front of your children they're not damaging your relationship, they are damaging their own. Many children grow to resent the ongoing negative commentary about their mum or dad. At some point they may even choose to distance themselves from the adult who is bashing the other parent.

It's also important to remember that children are incredibly insightful. In my years of working with children I have learnt that they are often far more perceptive than we give them credit for. Confident children with a good sense of self can easily tell what's true about a parent and what's not. They are usually very quick to size up situations.

Take Leonora's case, for example. While sitting at the dinner table one night her five-year-old daughter looked up at her and said, 'Mummy, Gran says you're really ugly.' Caught a little off guard by the statement Leonora replied, 'I wonder why Gran would say that?' Without missing a beat her youngster quickly replied, 'I think it's because she doesn't like you, Mummy.' How insightful is that?

PART FOUR

Moving on from Divorce

29.
GOING FROM WE TO ME
BEING SINGLE AND REDEFINING YOUR FAMILY

The most profound relationship we'll ever have is the one with ourselves. – Shirley MacLaine

Following divorce, all families redefine and evolve in different ways. Often we associate this redefinition with new relationships, second marriages and blended families. Although a significant number of parents choose to recouple, not all parents do. Despite the ever-growing number of single-parent families that exist, solo parenting still tends to be viewed as not the norm. While there may be lots of pressure in our society to couple up, it's important for single parents not to view themselves as less than. Without a doubt, single parenting will present certain challenges that two-parent homes don't have to deal with. Yet that doesn't mean you can't be successful at building opportunities for your children to flourish and thrive.

Regardless of whether you choose to stay single indefinitely or you're leaving your options open, here are a few tips on making the most of parenting on your own.

BEGINNING STAGES: ADJUSTING TO BEING SINGLE

▶ Take things slowly
Sometimes following a big transition such as divorce the inclination to make everything different all at once can be very strong.

While it may seem appealing to jump on the fast track to redesigning your life, keep in mind there are some advantages to taking a more thoughtful approach. Avoid making rash or sudden decisions, especially about significant matters. Take time to think through your options and how the decisions you make today will affect you and your children in the long term. When necessary, seek out additional information and support so you can make informed choices about things like finances, where you will live or a possible career change.

▶ Get to know yourself again

Between your existence as somebody's husband or wife and somebody's mother or father, it's easy to wake up one day and wonder what happened. Where's that person you used to be? Over the years, lots of parents gradually slip into a pattern of allowing their own interests and hobbies, likes and dislikes to take a back seat to the needs of their marriage and children. Although it may not feel like the best of circumstances, you have the opportunity to use your break-up as a catalyst for reinventing and rediscovering you.

Consider the following:

- What's something you haven't done in years that you used to really enjoy?
- Were there things in your relationship that you compromised on that you want to be part of your life now?
- What in your life are you ready to let go of?
- What kind of music do you enjoy?
- If someone asked you to name five of your favourite places to eat, would you be able to list them?
- What goals, plans or dreams would you like to be a part of your future?
- What's most important to you right now?
- What priorities do you want your life to reflect?
- When's the last time you did something fun without your children?

▶ Find ways to boost your self-esteem

Ending a partnership can often take a huge chunk out of your self-esteem. Right now you may be questioning lots of different aspects about your past as well as your former relationship. During this time, avoid comparing yourself to other people and instead put energy into feeling good about who you are. Consider the following ideas:

- Take up a hobby
- Make a list of your positive qualities and put it where you will see it
- Surround yourself with positive people
- Update your wardrobe
- Join a gym
- Try something new
- Get involved in something you love (volunteer, go back to college or take up a new hobby)

▶ Don't try to fill the emptiness with a new relationship

While you don't need to wait years on end before you start dating again, you also don't need to rush it. It's very natural to feel lonely or a sense of emptiness as your relationship comes to a close. When you are feeling vulnerable, the lure of jumping into a new relationship can be very tempting. While you may think finding a new partner will make you feel better, the chances are it's only a temporary fix. In truth, second relationships don't tend to fare well when you haven't resolved old hurts. It's been said that before you can find the right person you need to be the right person.

Do yourself a favour and focus on feeling whole again before moving into a new relationship.

▶ Seek new ways to express your independence

Ironically, one of the silver linings of being a single parent is that you often have more flexibility. Instead of having to navigate issues on a day-to-day basis with another adult, you can make decisions that feel right for you. While there are certainly more demands on your time, you may discover you have more energy to focus on your children. Often in a relationship you can become distracted with attending to the needs or interests of a spouse. Not to mention when tension in the marriage is high, your capacity to parent your children often becomes diminished.

In relationships you also typically make concessions and compromises. Suppose your spouse was a meat and potatoes man and you enjoy exotic foods. Maybe to keep peace you never really cooked the way you wanted. Now that you're on your own, perhaps it's time to learn a new skill, allow yourself to enjoy decorating your home the way you want, or start cooking those exotic meals.

▶ Broaden your circle of friends and create a support network for yourself

As you move forward with your life, you may find that some of the friends you had when you were married simply start disappearing into the woodwork. Sometimes it's because they feel conflicted and don't want to take sides. At other times it may be due to the fact that you now have less in common. Or, as silly as it might sound, some friends may worry that divorce is somehow contagious.

If you seem to be lacking in the friends department, make a point of broadening your social network. Think about interests you have or activities you would like to try that might offer you the opportunity to meet new people. Keep in mind you don't have to make a commitment to regular meetings or groups. Even if it's a one-time event, seek out opportunities to meet new people who share a common interest.

▶ Spend quality time with your kids

When you are in the process of adjusting to single parenthood, it's natural to get caught up in the daily grind and throw yourself into autopilot. Between cooking dinner, washing clothes, paying bills and making sure the homework gets done, enjoying time with your children can get lost in the shuffle. Although the daily family schedule may be packed, do what you can to carve out quality time with your kids. A good place to start might be setting aside 30 minutes each evening to read a book together or play a game. You can also declare one night a week family night, when you intentionally turn off the phones and spend the evening playing with your kids.

TIPS FOR SUCCESSFUL SINGLE PARENTING

▶ Focus on what's most important

You are only one person, and there is only so much you can realistically get done on any given day. Avoid beating yourself up for never getting enough done. Make time to think through what your top priorities are as a parent and a person – for example, is it to always have a spotless house or to raise balanced children? Do you want to work yourself to the brink of exhaustion or be a happy, well-adjusted person? Then evaluate how you can honour those priorities on a daily basis.

▶ Learn to say no

The urge to make sure your children don't go without can be strong for single parents. Yet consistently over-indulging or spoiling your children isn't a good option either. What matters most to children is having time with you. Seek out activities that offer the opportunity for quality time with your children instead of trying to indulge their every whim.

▶ Make sure you get me-time

By whatever means necessary, make sure you're getting some time for yourself on a regular basis. If finding a spot in your schedule for me-time seems impossible, explore creative options like trading baby-sitting hours with another single parent or putting everyone to bed 30 minutes early so you can have some quiet time to yourself.

▶ Avoid making your children the centre of your universe

No matter how much you love your children, don't allow your world to completely revolve around them. Good parenting is all about balance. Therefore make sure you are living life with your kids, not for your kids.

▶ Maintain a strong sense of family

Probably as a family you had some special rituals and routines. Now that you are parenting on your own, think about creative ways you can create new or revised family traditions. Perhaps it's pancakes every Sunday morning when your kids are with you, or maybe it's scheduling an annual spring camping trip.

▶ Make eating dinner together a priority

For some this may sound like a no-brainer. However, when you're parenting alone it can be enticing to avoid the dinner table and let everyone eat wherever their plate happens to fall. Those with younger children may quickly fall into the habit of catching up on chores (unloading the dishwasher, reading the post, catching up on phone calls, etc.) while their children eat. Parents with older children may find it easier to just let kids park themselves in front of the telly or head to their room with plate in hand. Even though life may be busy, make a point to eat together as a family at the dinner table at least a couple of times a week.

Families who eat together:

- Demonstrate better communication skills
- Have enhanced parent–child relationships
- Typically promote healthier eating habits in children
- Have teens who are less likely to smoke, use drugs or abuse alcohol
- Promote better academic achievement in children

▶ Be sure to provide love and limits

When you are parenting on your own, providing your children with love is easy. However, maintaining a consistent structure may be a steeper hill to climb. Let's face it, sometimes it's just easier to give in than enforce the letter of the law. Other times guilt may get the better of you. You may feel bad about what your children are going through, so you think, why make things harder? Surely cutting them a little slack couldn't hurt? The truth is, children need to be reassured that life will go on whether they are in two homes or one. Providing children with a consistent environment that includes love and limits gives them a better foundation for dealing with change.

30.
DATING, NEW RELATIONSHIPS AND KIDS

When you first started dating the big question was always, 'Will Mum and Dad like them?' With post-divorce dating you no longer care about what your parents think. It's the kids you've got to worry about. – Anonymous

When should you start dating again? In all honesty, you are the only one who can truly know when you're ready to start dating. The average estimated range of adjustment for most families tends to fall somewhere between one and three years. And no, that does not mean you need to wait a couple of years before you start thinking about dating. But you do need to be aware that the time-frame for making that initial adjustment is different for everyone. For some, the breakdown of the couple relationship begins long before the legal process is initiated. As a relationship starts to deteriorate, it's not unusual for one or both parents to emotionally disengage from the marriage. This may lead to dealing with feelings of loss sooner rather than later. When this happens, some parents may feel emotionally ready to enter a new relationship not long after their divorce has been finalised. For others, however, the process of emotional separation may be very different. In situations in which the separation was especially difficult or sudden, it may take a longer time to reach a place of acceptance. For those parents, the idea of dating or new relationships may be much further down the road.

Whether you initiated your separation or not, it's very natural to feel a sense of incompleteness when your relationship ends. If you're like most, over the years you've probably placed a lot of value on your identity as a husband or wife, mother or father. Before moving into the dating world again, make sure you have given yourself time to heal and feel whole again.

Essential aspects of moving forward involve the following:

- Making peace with what has happened in your marriage or partnership
- Taking responsibility for your part in the relationship not being successful
- Identifying what didn't work and what you want to be different in future relationships
- Re-establishing your identity as an individual

Remember, however, that just because you're ready to move on doesn't mean your children are ready to see you with someone new. For your children, seeing you enter the dating world means accepting the reality that their family has permanently changed. Most children have a difficult time letting go of the hope that some day their parents will get back together. A new relationship brings the impossibility of that wish into sharp view.

Be aware that, depending on the dynamics of your divorce and the age of your children, your kids could have a wide variety of reactions. Some children may be willing to accept someone new, whereas others may be more difficult to win over. Working out how to honour your needs while managing your children's adjustment is a balancing act.

WHEN TO INTRODUCE YOUR CHILDREN TO SOMEONE YOU ARE DATING

When you first meet someone special, it can feel incredibly exhilarating. During those first several months of dating, the chances are you have a totally new outlook as your life becomes filled with romance and possibility. And it's only natural that when something good happens in your life you want your children to be a part of that happiness.

However, as a general rule of thumb, regardless of your children's ages, it's usually best to wait until a relationship has moved beyond casual dating before involving your children. Even when your someone new seems absolutely wonderful, it's important to remember that what may feel best for you may not be best for your children. Just because you're ready to spend every waking moment with this person doesn't necessarily mean your children should. Here are things to think about.

▶ Children need time to adjust

It's important to remember your children's time frame for moving forward may be very different from your own. Make sure your children have had an adequate amount of time to adjust before introducing them to new relationships. While there aren't any hard-and-fast rules about how much time is enough, pay attention to how your children are handling change in general (see also Chapter 7).

▶ Dating is a process of getting to know each other

When it comes to children's safety, it's always best to err on the side of caution. In the early stages of dating it's very difficult to know whether someone will be a safe or appropriate person for your children to be around. After all, most dates don't come complete with background checks, references and written summaries outlining their personal values and moral character. How do you know if he or she even likes kids? The bottom line is: take time to get to know new adults before exposing them to your kids.

▶ Children need to be protected from additional losses

As you well know, although you may initially really like the person you are dating, things don't always work out. When parents prematurely involve children in their dating relationships they may be setting their children up for more heartache. Look at it this way: Let's say while you were dating, your children got to know your new 'Totally Perfect for You' and really liked that person. From your child's perspective, they may be seeing your date as a permanent fixture in their lives. However, when perfect ends up being not so perfect, you may not be the only one left picking up the pieces. In your children's mind they have just lost someone they really liked. This, of course, leads to yet another loss and may even cause old hurts to resurface.

Keep in mind, when children are continually exposed to casual relationships and experience multiple losses there may come a time when they just stop attaching. When you finally do meet someone you want to be involved with long term, children may be hesitant to accept the relationship.

Although there are no absolutes, it's not uncommon for young children to form quick attachments to an adult their parent is dating. Young children are generally more accepting and often intrigued with the idea of meeting new people. From their perspective, they've just been given the opportunity to make a new friend. Young children are also usually significantly influenced by what their parents think and feel. So if you are of the opinion that this new person is pretty wonderful, it stands to reason that they should think so too.

Older children, however, are rarely won over easily. You may find your older children are much less receptive to the idea of you having a new relationship. Don't be surprised if your pre-teen's or teen's attitude takes a cynical turn. It's not uncommon for teens to become defensive and angry when you start dating. You may even find that your teen is more than willing to go out of his or her way to make you and your somebody new completely miserable. Take heart, it isn't that your children don't want to see you happy. Chances are they're just not ready to accept that life is changing, especially since those changes are happening whether they like it or not.

HOW TO HANDLE YOUR DATING LIFE WITH CHILDREN

KEEP FIRST MEETINGS KID FRIENDLY

Once your relationship has moved beyond casual dating and you feel this person may be an important feature in your life, it's time to think about introducing your children. Be sure to keep first meetings kid friendly and casual. Consider going to the park, out to dinner, catching a film and a pizza, or perhaps spending the afternoon at the zoo.

AVOID PUTTING PRESSURE ON CHILDREN

Don't expect your children to instantly love or even like the person you are dating. Your children will probably have a wide range of feelings about seeing you with someone other than their other parent. Most important, give your children space to get to know this new person on their own terms.

BALANCE YOUR TIME

While it's natural to want to spend time with both your children and your new girlfriend or boyfriend, make sure you are still scheduling one-to-one time with your kids. Although you may be totally up for spending all of your time with the new love of your life, don't expect your children to feel the same way. Do your best to balance your need for adult time with your children's need for time with just you.

▶ If you're ready but your kids aren't

If you're ready but your kids aren't, it's perfectly okay to let them know you are spending time with other adults. Be prepared for the third degree; often children will want details about how you are spending your time away from them. If children ask direct questions about your dating life, it's best to answer their questions honestly and openly. Let them know dating is about getting to know someone and that for now you are simply enjoying time with this person. Reassure your children that if someone does become special to you they will be the first to know.

Don't say we're just friends. Sometimes parents think they can slowly introduce children to someone they are dating by telling children that he or she is just a special friend. While it may seem like a good way to transition children into accepting your new relationship, it is also a good way to compromise your credibility. Be aware that when your children discover this new person is not really a friend but someone you are dating, they may feel you've been dishonest with them. It may also leave your children wondering what else you haven't been truthful about.

WHEN THE OTHER PARENT INTRODUCES YOUR CHILD TO SOMEONE HE OR SHE IS DATING

So let's say that you have been playing by the rules and have kept your dating life separate from your children, but your ex has decided to play by a different set of rules. I frequently get asked by parents, 'How can I stop my ex from introducing a new boyfriend or girlfriend to the children?' To put it bluntly: you can't.

When children are introduced to a new adult by the other parent, it can elicit a variety of reactions from both children and the ex. Sometimes the best you can do is take a deep breath, step back and focus on what your children need. In all likelihood your children will have mixed feelings about meeting another adult, particularly if they sense you're not okay with it. Although it may not be easy, work to control your feelings about the situation. When children talk about Mum's or Dad's new relationship, do your best to be positive and supportive. Pay attention to what your children say. If they seem uneasy or worried about betraying you, reassure them that when they are with their other parent you want them to have a good time.

If your ex is intent on introducing the children to every person he or she dates, again there's probably very little you can do about it. Do your best to make sure your children are safe and continue to help them process their feelings about their time with the other parent. Although you may feel like your words will fall on deaf ears, you may want to attempt a conversation with your ex about the issue. Instead of trying to change the other parent's mind, it may help to take a softer approach. Let your ex know that you can appreciate his or her situation but that the children still need occasional one-to-one time with them. It may even help to discuss ways you could be supportive of that. For example, if your ex has a scheduling issue (her weekends with the kids are the only weekends she can see her boyfriend), perhaps you could offer to be flexible about the schedule.

31.
BEFORE YOU SAY 'I DO' AGAIN
SECOND MARRIAGES, BEING A BONUS PARENT AND BLENDED FAMILIES

The bond that links your true family is not one of blood but of joy and respect in each other's lives. Rarely do members of one family grow up under the same roof. – Richard Bach

It seems logical to assume that, if we learn from our mistakes, you would definitely stand a better chance of being successful the second time around. Maybe the first time you just married the wrong person. Now that you've found the right person, things should be fine. Right? Actually, no. Surprising as it may seem, second marriages are at greater risk of ending in divorce than are first marriages. Sorry to be the one to break the bad news. Current statistics reflect that approximately 4 out of 10 first marriages result in divorce, whereas the odds for second marriages are somewhere in the neighbourhood of 6 out of 10.

That's not to say that second marriages can't be successful. I personally happen to be a big believer in second marriages, which is probably a good thing given I chose to marry someone who had been married before. Personally and professionally, I can tell you successful second marriages take a lot of work. They're very different from first marriages. Second marriages endure lots of different stress factors from first marriages. Unfortunately, lots of couples make the mistake of thinking, 'If we love each other enough, we can get through anything.' While love certainly helps, it's not a substitute for sharing expectations and good communication. Take Victoria and Sebastian, for example.

A couple of years after saying 'I do' they found themselves struggling to keep their marriage together. It was a second marriage for both. Sadly, there were a few complications they hadn't considered before heading to the altar. One, Victoria was a widow and had younger children. Sebastian's son was grown up, finished with university and on his own. When Sebastian married Victoria he saw himself as a parenting authority with her children. Because the children had lost their dad he thought he would fill in as their new father figure. From Sebastian's point of view, fathers made decisions and provided discipline.

Victoria, on the other hand, felt Sebastian had no authority at all. From where she stood she was the children's only parent and Sebastian had no business interfering with how she was raising them. As a result Victoria made decisions regarding the children on her own and never consulted Sebastian on discipline issues. It didn't take long before Sebastian felt very bitter towards both Victoria and her children. Needless to say this had a huge impact on their relationship.

BEFORE YOU SAY 'I DO'

Before you say 'I do', it's probably wise to spend some time with your prospective new spouse discussing your expectations. Be sure to lay the necessary groundwork for your relationship by discussing issues that have the potential to affect the quality of your marriage.

Consider addressing important issues, such as:

- Celebrating holidays
- Discipline

- Schedules
- Relationships with one another's children
- Relationships with ex-spouses
- Finances
- Each other's roles as partners in the marriage and as parents
- Each one's top three values as an individual and as a couple
- The most important factors about family and how to support those values

TIPS FOR A SUCCESSFUL SECOND MARRIAGE

▶ Set aside time to be a couple

Between adjusting schedules, juggling children every other weekend, dealing with ex-spouses and managing financial issues, second marriages can be extremely demanding. Therefore make attending to your relationship as a new couple a priority. While your schedule may be full, stay committed to scheduling time for the two of you on a regular basis. Even if it's a coffee date every week or putting the children to bed early so you can watch a film together, set aside time to honour your relationship.

▶ Limit the energy you give to divorce-related issues

Even under the best of circumstances, managing relationships with ex-spouses takes work. If you have the misfortune of dealing with a contentious ex (on either one or both sides), it can definitely take its toll on a new relationship. When issues arise, make sure you limit the amount of emotional energy you invest. Set up an agreement with your spouse to spend only a specified period of time talking about ex-related issues or divorce-related problems (preferably minutes, not hours). Avoid the pitfall of making the focus of your relationship teaming up against the enemy; it's not a good basis for a relationship. If you catch yourselves spending too much time venting, remind the other of your commitment. When emotions are intense don't over-talk it, instead table the discussion and give yourselves a break from the drama. Once you've had a chance to regroup, you can return to the discussion with a new focus.

▶ Make decisions involving your ex or the other household as a couple

While it may seem obvious, many couples discount the importance of making joint decisions. When issues come up regarding your collective brood or the other household, make an agreement to discuss things with one another before making a decision. Many bonus parents often feel incredibly frustrated when they are left out of the parenting loop. While they may not be biological parents they are still directly affected by interactions with the other household. Although your ex may not always like having to wait for an answer, out of respect for your spouse, touch base before making a commitment to something that will potentially affect his or her life too.

▶ Don't put your spouse in a position in which he or she has to choose between you or the kids

In newly formed families sometimes making decisions about how to handle things can be tough. It's also a time when new spouses can easily feel like the odd man out between children and biological parents. Be mindful that biological parents can often feel caught in a bind between their commitment to their children and the commitment they have to their current spouse. Let's say, for example, in the past your spouse has always gone to his ex's house to spend Christmas morning with his children. He loves watching them open their presents and knows being there is really important to his kids. Suppose you had your heart set on spending your first Christmas together alone over a quiet breakfast at home. What do you do?

If you are the one who's feeling shafted, don't make matters worse by giving your spouse an ultimatum. For the time being, be the bigger person and support your spouse's role as a parent. After things have cooled off, set aside time to discuss the issue and let your spouse know how you feel. Once you reach an understanding, then you can make a plan for how to handle things differently in the future. Remember, finding ways to compromise is an essential component of a successful second marriage.

POINTS FOR MERGING FAMILIES

While it would be brilliant if merging families was a piece of cake, in reality it's a transition that often takes work, dedication and a fair amount of patience. As you move forward into the unchartered waters of blended family life, keep the following points in mind.

▶ Give everyone time to adjust

One of the things that makes blended families unique is that members have a different past and different family histories. Be aware that relationships with one another need time to develop.

BONUS PARENTS AND BONUS CHILDREN

Several years ago, while teaching a parenting class, I was introduced to the term 'bonus'. 'Bonus' by definition means 'an unexpected benefit, something given or received in addition to'.

Since becoming a step-parent I have never felt comfortable using the word 'step' to describe the relationship I have with our children from my husband's first marriage. When I learnt about bonus language I was thrilled to discover a more positive way to describe by-choice family relationships. Once the kids and I talked about it we decided the term 'bonus' felt like a much better fit for our family.

If you're interested in learning more about bonus families, check out bonusfamilies.com.

Don't get caught up in unrealistic expectations of immediately becoming one big happy family. Take a more thoughtful approach by investing time in developing special and unique experiences as a family. One way to do this is by creating memorable ways to spend time together, such as developing new traditions for the Christmas season or special occasions, taking annual family camping trips or exploring ways to merge rituals from each family.

If you are a new bonus parent (that is, a step-parent), put energy into getting to know your bonus children and building your relationships with them. If you are a biological parent, don't pressure your children into immediately embracing the concept of a new family.

▶ Make sure everyone feels connected and respected regardless of where he or she lives most of the time

Even when space is tight, do your best to help the children in your family feel physically connected to your home, whether they live with you full time or not. This is especially important when you are merging children from two different families. Consider decorating your home with photos of children from both families and with photos of everyone together. Also, if you can't provide everyone with his or her own room, make sure each child has a special place to keep personal things. It's also a good idea to set up family rules early on about honouring privacy and respecting one another's belongings. For example, if Mike has an iPod it should not be okay for his bonus sister, Jane, to use it without Mike's permission when he is with his other parent.

> Avoid comparing your new spouse with your former spouse in front of children ('Your mum never cooked as good as Jane,' or 'Ray is so much more fun than your dad'). Not only is it disrespectful to your children but it also undermines the positive image they have of their other parent.

▶ **Honour children's need to have occasional one-on-one time with a biological parent**

Although you may be the greatest blended family on the face of the planet, keep in mind you don't need to spend every waking moment together. One key factor in being a successful second family is honouring the relationships that existed before you became a family (especially children's relationships with biological parents).

If you are a bonus parent, respect the fact that your bonus children will still need one-on-one time with their biological parent. Not only will your bonus children appreciate it, but it may also open some doors to building a more meaningful relationship with them.

At times being a bonus parent can be a challenging and thankless job. However, with patience, time and a good dose of elbow grease, most find it can also be a rich and rewarding experience. When parenting your non-biological children, don't underestimate the value and level of influence you have in their lives. While they may not always be good at showing it, who you are to children and how you are with children do matter.

Guidelines for bonus parents

▶ **Avoid becoming a parenting authority too quickly**

Before becoming a parenting authority with your bonus children, take time to develop your relationship first. In the early stages it's best if biological parents remain the primary disciplinarians, with bonus parents filling a supportive role. Whenever possible, talk in advance with your spouse about how the two of you want to handle parenting matters, such as family rules, respect and establishing values.

▶ **Give bonus children space to get to know you**

Allow children to develop their relationship with you over time. Consider taking an interest in things that are important to them, as a way to get to know them. Remember, children frequently struggle with loyalty issues when a parent remarries. Often children worry that accepting Dad's new spouse means betraying their mum. If you feel children are conflicted, offer them the reassurance that they don't have to pick one over the other. It can also help put children at ease if you can find ways to support their relationship with a biological parent. For example, you might help your bonus kids make something special for Mum on Mother's Day or take them shopping to buy a nice Christmas gift for Dad.

▶ Steer clear of replacing a biological parent

To be frank, bonus parents are not replacement parents, part-time parents or substitute parents. They are additional parenting figures in children's lives. Regardless of how you may feel about your bonus children's other parent, avoid trying to take the place of children's biological parents. Even when a biological parent has behaved badly or has withdrawn from a child's life, children typically still need to positively identify with that parent on some level. Keep in mind that part of your bonus children's self-image is also tied to that other parent. While it may not always be easy, do what you can to be a loving addition to children's lives without taking the place of the other parent.

▶ Don't force bonus kids to call you Mum or Dad

As W.C. Fields would say, 'It ain't what they call you, it's what you answer to.' When making a decision about what kids should call a bonus parent, go with what feels comfortable for children. Don't put pressure on children to call you something that doesn't feel okay for them.

Remember, special relationships are not defined by a name but rather by the respect and love you have for one another. Given time, you may find that the unique relationships you have with one another become special all on their own. In our family, my bonus kids were quite young when I became part of their lives. For them, calling me by my first name, Christina, seemed to feel most comfortable. Since my bonus daughter wasn't particularly good at pronouncing *ch* sounds, she dubbed me 'Pristina'. Over the years, being Pristina has transformed into a term of endearment and continues to represent a special connection between us.

▶ Handle special occasions such as Mother's Day and Father's Day graciously

When parents remarry and bonus parents enter the scene Mother's Day and Father's Day can easily create a very awkward and uncomfortable situation for children. Even if you're very involved in your bonus children's lives, don't guilt-trip them into acknowledging you on Mother's Day or Father's Day. It's more helpful to allow children the opportunity to decide who they would like to recognise on those days.

If your children choose to acknowledge only their biological parents, support that choice. Talk with your spouse ahead of time about the situation. While being excluded may feel a little hurtful, don't take it personally. Sometimes children can feel very conflicted about their relationship with a bonus parent. Your children may be worried that acknowledging both would either anger or hurt their biological parent.

If your child gets a new bonus parent

Having another significant adult become a part of your child's life can stir up lots of different feelings, especially when it's a person you may know very little about and didn't have any say in choosing. While it can be difficult to have someone else involved in your children's lives, remember you will always be the only mum or dad your children will ever have, regardless of who else comes into the picture. Quite honestly, children can never have too many positive, healthy adults loving them. If you are having a hard time, find some way to separate your feelings about the new bonus parent from what your children need. To put things in perspective, ask yourself, when your children are spending time in the other home, what kind of experience do you want them to have? The truth is, most of us would sincerely want our children to be safe and loved instead of feeling like outsiders looking in. The best way to accomplish that is by supporting those connections.

> Supporting your child's relationship with a new bonus parent can be especially difficult when infidelity has occured. Although you may not condone or agree with the circumstances that led to the new relationship, remember that the anger or hurt you feel should not be your children's burden to bear. While you may not be ready to forgive, find some way to make peace with it for your children's sake.

▶ Don't put your children in a loyalty bind

Often when a new bonus parent comes on the scene, children can sense our apprehension or discomfort. It's not uncommon for children to feel worried about how a parent will react if they accept this new person in their lives. Children are usually fiercely loyal to their parents. They may seek your permission to love or care for a bonus parent. Whenever possible, help ease your children's anxiety by reassuring them that you know the relationship they have with you is special. It may also help for children to hear that they don't have to pick one over the other; they can love both of you.

▶ When possible, speak positively about your children's bonus parent

Although you may have told your children you want them to have a good relationship with their bonus parent, usually a one-off conversation isn't enough. Be sure you're sending children a consistent message by speaking positively about their bonus parent. If finding something nice to say is particularly difficult, then consider offering feedback on the positive things they do for your children. For example, if your child tells you about how his bonus dad took him fishing, you might say something like, 'It sounds like you really had a good time with him.'

RESOURCE INDEX FOR PARENTS AND CHILDREN

The following listings offer some general recommendations for resources that may be helpful to you and your children. It is by no means an exhaustive list but rather meant to provide you with a place to start. Suggestions have been categorised for you by topic; however, they are not listed by preference nor meant to be a direct endorsement of the material.

Additional books and resources can be found at local libraries, local bookshops, and through large online bookstores such as:

- amazon.co.uk
- thebookdepository.co.uk
- whsmith.co.uk
- waterstones.co.uk

For an updated list with my newest suggestions on books and resources visit: divorceandchildren.com.

Because the web is ever-changing, only a few select online resources have been listed in this appendix. For a more comprehensive list of regional resources go to:

for England and Wales
resolution.org.uk/parentinglinks

for Scotland
scottish-collaborativelawyers.com

RESOURCES FOR CHILDREN
Books

Be sure to preview any books or videos before giving them to your children. While a resource may come recommended, remember some resources may not be appropriate for *your* children or circumstance. In addition, it's best if you know what your children are reading and watching. Not only will it give you the opportunity to be prepared for possible questions but it can also be a great way to engage your kids in meaningful conversations.

For younger children (ages 3–7)
Two Homes, Claire Masurel
(Walker Books Ltd: new edition, 2002)
This charming story explores how life changes for little Alec when Mum and Dad no longer live together. Despite the fact that he now has two of everything, one thing stays the same – how much Mum and Dad love him.

Two of Everything, Babette Cole
(Red Fox: new edition, 2000)
An entertaining book that approaches the tough topic of divorce with wit, humour and colourful illustrations. Reinforces that children are not responsible for divorce or parents' problems.

Mum and Dad Glue, Kes Gray
(Hodder Children's Books: 2010)
A moving story for young children about a boy who desperately wants to mend his parents' broken relationship. This brilliantly written book reaffirms that while Mum and Dad may no longer love one another they will always love you.

When Katie's Mum and Dad Separated, Sarah Ferguson, Duchess of York
(Lloyds Pharmacy: 2007)
Provides child-friendly advice on coping when parents separate, and gives reassurance for children who think they may be responsible for their parents' separation. Available at lloydspharmacy.com.

The Huge Bag of Worries, Virginia Ironside
(Hodder Children's Books: 2004)
Not specifically related to the topic of divorce, this charming book by Agony Aunt Virginia Ironside offers children insight into how to manage their emotions when facing larger-than-life problems.

Rainy Day, Emma Haughton
(Doubleday Children's Books: 2000)
Using the imagery of a rainy day this heart-warming book reveals a simple yet engaging story of a boy and his father. Together they learn how to handle disappointment and upset when life doesn't turn out the way they hoped.

For older children (ages 8–12)

The Suitcase Kid, Jacqueline Wilson
(Yearling: new edition, 2006)
Follows Andrea West and her faithful companion, Radish (a stuffed rabbit), as they journey though the trials and tribulations of joint custody life. Well written and heartwarming, *The Suitcase Kid* addresses tough issues such as parents who don't get along, differences between homes and stepfamily life.

Mom's House, Dad's House for Kids Feeling at Home in One Home or Two, Isolina Ricci
(Fireside: 2006)
Guidebook designed for children 10 years old and up. Explores the process of separation, divorce and forming stepfamilies. Includes tips, exercises and examples that help children build skills as families change.

Help Hope Happiness (Save the Children) by Libby Rees
(Aultbea Publishing Company: 2005)
In this self-help guide, this young author offers helpful strategies
for dealing with challenges in life. Although it does not specifically
address the topic of divorce, it reassures children they are not alone
and provides suggestions for positive ways to handle your problems.

Clean Break by Jacqueline Wilson
(Yearling: 2008)
Engaging fictional story for pre-teens and teens about a family
learning to cope when Dad leaves. This seasoned author tackles
the tough real life issues while leaving readers with a sense of hope.
(9 and over)

DVD and Workbook Programme

*Lemons 2 Lemonade: How to Handle Life When Things Go Sour
between Mom and Dad* by Christina McGhee and Stephen
Loughhead
(Divorce and Children, LLC: 2nd edition, 2007)
An upbeat and entertaining programme offering a comforting and
hopeful message to kids dealing with the difficulties of divorce.
Creatively answers children's questions and offers the tools to deal
with tough real-life situations. The companion workbook gives
children a way to express the different feelings they have about
how their family has changed. While formatted for an American
audience, the information for children is relatable and offers
parents the opportunity to initiate discussions around challenging
topics. For ages 5–12. Available at divorceandchildren.com/chil-
dren.html (ships from US).

Teens (ages 13–18)

*The Divorce Workbook for Teens: Activities to Help You Move beyond
the Breakup*, Lisa M. Schab
(Instant Help Books: 2008)
Helps teens understand their feelings, cope with parental fighting
and learn to be happy after their parents' divorce. Activities deal

with emotional issues, help develop communication skills and address practical issues such as living in two homes.

The Divorce Helpbook for Teens, Cynthia MacGregor
(Impact Publishers: 2004)
Offers vignettes, strategies and solid advice while providing help to teens struggling to answer tough questions when their parents split up.

Is Anyone's Family as Mad as Mine? A Survival Guide for Teenagers, Kathryn Lamb
(Piccadilly Press Ltd: 2006)
Has nothing to do with divorce and everything to do with helping teens move beyond one-word answers. Written with wit and humour, this book offers case studies of different types of families and loads of scenarios about different ways to respond. Have a teen that doesn't talk? You might want to stick a copy of this under their pillow.

RESOURCES FOR PARENTS
Support services

Divorce and children
divorceandchildren.com
Hosted by divorce coach and parent educator, Christina McGhee. Offers helpful information, practical advice and tips for separated and divorced parents on how to help children successfully manage family change. Services include individual telephone coaching for parents, speaking and professional trainings.

Relate
relate.org.uk and relateforparents.org.uk
Providing a wide variety of services for couples and families throughout England and Wales including relationship counselling

for individuals, couples, families, young people and children. Additionally, Relate hosts a number of informational workshops designed to address many important life issues.

Excellent support library offered with numerous topic-specific books and resources available: relateforparents.org.uk/resources.php

Relationships Scotland

relationships-scotland.org.uk

Offering a network of local services throughout Scotland including family mediation, relationship counselling, child contact centres, groups for adults and children and family support. Workshops for separated and divorced parents may also be available in some areas.

Cafcass

cafcass.gov.uk

Website provides information and resources for children, teens and families. Also offers an outline of the court process when parents cannot agree on arrangements.

Contact Centres

England, Wales and Northern Ireland

National Association of Child Contact Centres – NACCC

naccc.org.uk

The largest network of child contact centres and services for England, Wales and Northern Ireland. They provides services that support safe ongoing contact between children from separated families and their non-resident parent or other family members.

Scotland

Relationships Scotland

relationships-scotland.org.uk/family_support.shtml

Direct link to information about child contact centres throughout Scotland, as well as a brief video about services.

Single Parenting Support

Gingerbread
gingerbread.org.uk
Dedicated to successful single parenting, this site gives guidance and support along with A–Z fact sheets to help you stay informed.

One Parent Families Scotland
gn.apc.org/opfs
National organisation committed to providing support to all families, particularly single parents. Resources and information are designed to help build opportunities for those parenting on their own.

Informational Workshops for Separated and Divorced Parents

Parenting After Parting *sponsored by Resolution*
resolution.org.uk/parentevents
Created by divorce coach and parent educator, Christina McGhee, these interactive and informational workshops focus on helping parents help their children successfully manage the impact of divorce or separation. Courses not only offer parents an opportunity to share ideas with one another but they also empower and provide a sense of hope for families. Designed to address the real-life challenges and tough issues many parents face when parenting out of two homes.

For additional information about other parenting resources go to:

England – resolution.org.uk/parentinglinks
Scotland – relationships-scotland.org.uk

TOOLS FOR COMMUNICATING BETWEEN HOMES

My Time Chart
A weekly planner that helps children keep track of how and when they are spending time with each parent. Laminated and supplied with dry-wipe pens, it is both easy to use and easy to update. (For children aged 4–10.) Available at resolution.org.uk.

Online family calendars
Online family calendars can provide an easy way for separated or divorced parents to communicate and share information between households. Many of these websites also offer other features, such as the ability to request scheduling changes, exchange photos, track expenses or post notes about important events.

Paid services
For parents looking for better ways to communicate and share information:

- Our Family Wizard: ourfamilywizard.com
- Our Great Kids: ourgreatkids.com

For higher conflict situations where time needs to be tracked or documented:

- Kid Mate: kidmate.com
- Parenting Time Calendar: parentingtimecalendar.com

Free tools
If a monthly or annual fee doesn't fit your budget, consider setting up an online calendar through a free service. Email providers such as Yahoo!, AOL, Google and Hotmail offer online calendars that you can customise and share with others.

OPTIONS FOR MINIMISING YOUR INVOLVEMENT IN COURT
Mediation

To locate a qualified family mediator in your area, visit one of the sites listed below:

England and Wales
National Family Mediation, nfm.org.uk

Scotland
Scottish Mediation Network, scottishmediationnetwork.org.uk

Scottish Mediation Register, scottishmediationregister.org.uk

Collaborative law

Resolution
resolution.org.uk
Resolution's family lawyers are committed to the constructive resolution of family disputes. Its members follow a code of practice that promotes a non-confrontational approach to family problems. Resolution encourages solutions that consider the needs of the whole family – and in particular the best interests of children. The site includes a parent advice centre, along with directories and background information for local solicitors.

Scottish Collaborative Family Law Group
scottish-collaborativelawyers.com
Dedicated to helping families find a better way of managing separation. Members of this group are experienced in avoiding lengthy legal battles and instead seek solutions that best suit the individualised needs of families. Links, FAQs and a solicitor database are also provided.

International Academy of Collaborative Professionals
collaborativepractice.com
Aimed at helping parents divorce with dignity; provides an overview of the collaborative process and a free downloadable Collaborative Divorce Knowledge Kit. Offers helpful links, resources, and listings for collaborative lawyers around the world.

Book

A Client's Guide to Collaborative Divorce, Putting Your Family First, Gillian Bishop
Colourful 44-page guide written in a straightforward way that offers parents crucial information and tools to successfully navigate the collaborative process. Includes a sample participation agreement and a self-evaluation questionnaire, along with an overview of court-based/dialogue-based approaches. Available at: flip.co.uk/about/downloads.asp

RESOURCES FOR LIFE AFTER DIVORCE

Books

Step-parenting
How to be a Happy Stepmum, Dr Lisa Doodson (Vermilion: 2010)
Easy-to-read guide that uses real-life experiences to help you cope with the myriad of roles you juggle as a stepmum. Offering sound advice and tips while reassuring you that you're not alone.

The Step-parents' Parachute: The Four Cornerstones of Good Step-parenting, Flora McEvedy (Piatkus Books: 2009)
Providing guidance through the often unchartered waters of step-parenthood, this relatable book helps you define your role, while looking at your own behaviour and addressing the diversity of stepfamily life.

Online

Being a Stepparent
beingastepparent.co.uk
Provides extensive information on many of the everyday situations and experiences that step-parents face. Whether you're dealing with what your stepchildren should call you, sorting financial matters or how to navigate your new relationship with your partner's ex, you'll find helpful guidance, thorough resources and expert advice.

RESOURCES FOR PARENT ALIENATION

Because of the controversy surrounding alienation good resources and support for parents dealing with this issue are often limited. Below are listed some of the more well-established sources of information that exist. Presently the majority of the listings offered below are based in the US.

Books

Divorce Poison: How to Protect Your Family from Badmouthing and Brainwashing, Richard A. Warshak
(Harper Paperbacks: 2nd edition, 2010)
An excellent resource for parents dealing with a vindictive ex-spouse who is engaging in alienating behaviours that are significantly compromising your relationship with your children. Helps parents identify alienation, from subtle to severe, and provides good information on how to respond to the situation.

Divorce Casualties: Understanding Parental Alienation,
Douglas Darnell
(Taylor Trade Publishing: 2nd edition, 2008)
Covers a broad range of topics regarding parent alienation. Designed to help parents identify and appropriately respond to alienation, addresses common tactics used by alienating parents, tools for managing alienation and case examples from parents.

A Family's Heartbreak: A Parent's Introduction to Parental Alienation, Michael Jeffries
(A Family's Heartbreak, LLC: 2009)
First-hand account of an alienated parent's journey. Shares experiences with his son's rejection and deals with the frustrations of an unresponsive legal system.

Breaking the Tie That Binds, Amy Jo Baker
(W.W. Norton & Company: 2007)
Based on research with adult children who were victims of parent alienation. Offers strategies and hope when struggling with the effects of alienation.

DVD

Welcome Back Pluto: Understanding, Preventing and Overcoming Parental Alienation, Richard Warshak: *warshak.com*
Shedding some much-needed light on the complex and often misunderstood topic of parent alienation *Welcome Back Pluto* offers insight regarding the various ways alienation affects parent–child relationships. This programme identifies damaging behaviours from the subtle to the extreme, provides relatable examples, clear explanations and practical suggestions for addressing many difficult alienation-related issues. Appropriate for teens, parents and professionals. (Ships from US.)

RESOURCES FOR DOMESTIC VIOLENCE, ABUSE OR ADDICTION

Domestic violence

Refuge
refuge.org.uk
0808 2000 247 (24-hour helpline)
Offering safe, emergency lodging to those dealing with domestic violence throughout the UK.

Women's Aid

womensaid.org.uk

0808 2000 247 (24-hour helpline)

Key charity supporting over 500 services throughout the UK to women and children dealing with domestic abuse and sexual violence. Also hosts a special site for children and teens called the 'Hide Out' that offers information about abuse and what to do about it.

Scottish Women's Aid

scottishwomensaid.org.uk

0800 027 1234 (24-hour helpline)

Primary organisation in Scotland working to prevent domestic abuse and end violence against women. Connects women with services such as safe accommodation, information and support while lobbying for a more effective way of keeping women and children safe.

Women's Domestic Violence Helpline

wdvh.org.uk

0161 636 7525 (Monday–Friday, 10 a.m–4 p.m.; Tuesday, 10 a.m. –7 p.m.)

Advice, information and telephone counselling.

Male (Men's Advice Line and Enquiries)

mensadviceline.org.uk

0808 801 0327 (Monday–Friday, 10 a.m.–1 p.m.; 2 p.m.–5 p.m.)

Support and advice for male victims of domestic violence, information for their families and for men who want to change their violent and abusive behaviour.

Everyman Project

everymanproject.co.uk

0207 263 8884 (Tuesdays & Wednesdays, 6.30 p.m.–9 p.m.)

Therapy programme designed to help men who have issues with anger or violent and abusive behaviour.

Addiction

Alcoholics Anonymous
alcoholics-anonymous.org.uk
0845 769 7555 (10 a.m.–10 p.m. every day)
Help for people who think they have a problem with alcohol.

Al-Anon/Alateen
al-anonuk.org.uk
020 7403 0888 (10 a.m.–10 p.m. every day)
Provides support to teens, families and friends who have been affected by someone else's alcoholism. Also helps individuals find local meetings.

Narcotics Anonymous
ukna.org
0300 999 1212 (24-hour helpline)
Organisation that offers assistance to recovering addicts. Provides information about local meetings for those who are trying to stay clean.

Families Anonymous
famanon.org.uk
0845 1200 660 (10 a.m.–10 p.m. every day)
National helpline offering free support to anyone affected by the drug abuse of a family member. Nationwide self-help groups are available.

ACKNOWLEDGEMENTS

Over the years my career has developed in ways I never imagined possible and it has been an amazing journey. Of course, it has not been a road I have travelled alone and absolutely none of it would have been possible without the love, support, guidance and inspiration of many to whom I am immensely indebted.

If it takes a village to raise a child, I'm pretty sure the amount of support I have received could have easily filled up a small island somewhere off the coast of Indonesia. Special accolades to islanders: Euan Mackinnon, Resolution editor extraordinaire, for helping me cultivate my transa-Atlantic voice and teaching me which 'American' words to avoid as they would clearly make any self-respecting Brit blush. Kindred spirits, Elizabeth Wallace and Elaine Halligan, who were both kind enough to weigh in on a moment's notice and give me a crash course on accessing help and resources in the UK. My good mate, Sam Whittaker, for buying the first advanced copy of my book and also setting in motion a chain of events that massively changed the scope of my work. Hats off to my long-time friend, respected colleague and co-presenter David Hays, who has graciously tolerated my endless stream of crazy ideas and helped me find ways to bring them to life.

For their collective legal expertise and editing skills, *merci beaucoup* to James Pirrie and Catherine Karlin. I am particularly grateful for their willingness to put up with an onslaught of impossible deadlines, countless revisions of the legal chapter, a multitude of meticulous questions and, at the end of it all, being gracious enough to still take my calls. Working with both of you has been delightful.

An additional note of thanks to the members of the Parenting After Parting Committee and the family law organisation, Resolution for embracing the value of supporting separating families. You have been an outstanding group to work with and the dedication of your membership to transforming the practice of family law has been nothing short of impressive.

Without a doubt the last five years have been completely mind-blowing. I don't think I could have survived without the unrelenting support of the vivacious and talented Catherine Noyes. You are not only one damn good publicist, you have a gusto for life that constantly keeps me inspired. Thank you for always finding ways to help me put my very best self out there while celebrating every single moment of the journey. I feel extremely blessed to have you in my corner as both a dear friend and colleague.

To those bold and beautiful ladies who have taken me from writing novice to published author, thanks to my literary agents, Anna Power and Francesca Barrie with Johnson Alcock. An additional note of immense gratitude is offered to Merel Reinink who first approached me about putting together a book proposal. Even though I was pretty sure I wasn't a writer, thankfully she saw something I didn't. For taking this project from proposal to print, I am very grateful to the folks at Vermillion/Ebury Publishing. Special thanks goes to Editorial Director, Susanna Abbott for skillfully meeting publication deadlines without compromising quality. To Deidre Sanders for graciously supporting this book and for focusing attention, raising awareness and rallying support for separated families through her ongoing work with the Kids In The Middle Campaign.

To the parents and children I have worked with over the years – it has been both a privilege and an honour to join each of you on your individual journeys. Thank you for trusting in me and providing me with the opportunity to receive as much or more than I gave. Particular thanks to each of the families who participated in the *How to Divorce Without Screwing Up Your Children* documentary, your dedication to getting it right for your children was as impressive as the courage it took to share your stories with the world.

A heartfelt thanks to my fabulous family, Jennifer, John, Kati and Carson, Teresa, and my parents Nancy and Gordon Penny and Gene Cole. There are not enough words to described how very blessed I feel for the many ways each of you have added to my life. We're not the most conventional lot but of course, I wouldn't have it any other way. A special note of thanks to my mother, Nancy Penny, who has waited a very long time to see these words in print. Mama, I owe it all to you!

Last but certainly not least, to my incredible husband Scott and our four very cool yet uniquely different children, Ryan, Raegan, Madison and Emmalee. Thank you for putting up with long hours, trips away from home, endless amounts of brainstorming, tweaking and re-tweaking, 'wisdom' talk and my general preoccupation with the written word for the past year. Thank you – your love, dedication and support means everything to me.

resolution
first for family law

Resolution is a family law organisation committed to the constructive resolution of family disputes. Our 5,500 lawyers and other professionals follow a Code of Practice that promotes a non-confrontational approach to family problems. Our members encourage solutions that consider the needs of the whole family – and in particular the best interests of children.

We offer information and advice on all of the many challenges that parents face when separating, including child maintenance, parenting apart and sorting out your finances. You can download fact sheets, request information packs and find out how you can contact a Resolution lawyer near you at our web site www.resolution.org.uk.